FRANCE
PHYSICAL FEATURES

0   50   100   150   200 Miles

0   50 100   200   300 Kilometers

UNITED KINGDOM

NETHERLANDS

GERMANY

52° 4° 2° 0° 2° 52°

Lys

Meuse

BELGIUM

STRAIT OF DOVER

COLLINES DE L'ARTOIS

Escaut

Sambre

ARDENNES

LUXEMBOURG

50° ENGLISH CHANNEL Somme 50°

SEUIL DU VERMANDOIS

Sûre

GULF OF ST-MALO

Seine Oise Aisne

Moselle

Marne

Meuse

Moselle

Brittany

Orne

Risle

Eure

PARIS BASSIN

Aube

SEUIL DE LORRAINE

VOSGES

Rhine

48° Aulne Maine Sarthe Loir Loing Yonne Armançon Seine SEUIL DE LANGRES 48°

Blavet

Vilaine

Rance

Mayenne

Loire

SEUIL DE L'AUXOIS

Burgundy

TROUE DE BELFORT

MORVAN

Doubs

JURA

SWITZERLAND

Loire

Maine

Sèvre Nantaise

SEUIL DU POITOU

Indre

Creuse

Cher

Vienne

Limousin

Arroux

Saône

Ain

L. of Geneva

Rhône

Vendée

Sèvre Niortaise

SEUIL DU CHAROLAIS

46° BAY Charente MASSIF Allier 46°

OF

Isle

Vézère

CENTRAL

SEUIL DE JAREZ

Loire

Rhône

Ardèche

Isère

Drôme

ALPS

ITALY

BISCAY Garonne Dordogne Lot

44° BASSIN AQUITAIN Aveyron Tarn Gard Durance Var 44°

Adour Baïse Agout Hérault Argens MONACO

Gave de Pau Garonne SEUIL DU LAURAGUAIS Ariège

SPAIN PYRENEES Aude Têt

ANDORRA

SEA

42° 42°

MEDITERRANEAN

Heights in meters

> 1000

500-1000

200-500

100-200

0-100

CORSICA 10°

6°

42°

BAY OF BISCAY

Maine

Vilaine

Rhône

RHODANIEN

SILLON

The Americans
and the French

The American Foreign Policy Library

CRANE BRINTON, EDITOR

The United States and Britain REVISED EDITION Crane Brinton
The United States and the Caribbean REVISED EDITION Dexter Perkins
The United States and South America: The Northern Republics Arthur P. Whitaker
The United States and China NEW EDITION—COMPLETELY REVISED AND ENLARGED John King Fairbank
The United States and Scandinavia Franklin D. Scott
The United States and Japan THIRD EDITION Edwin O. Reischauer
The United States and France Donald C. McKay
The United States and Mexico REVISED EDITION, ENLARGED Howard F. Cline
The United States and India and Pakistan REVISED AND ENLARGED W. Norman Brown
The United States and Italy H. Stuart Hughes
The United States and Argentina Arthur P. Whitaker
The Balkans in Our Time Robert Lee Wolff
The United States and the Southwest Pacific C. Hartley Grattan
The United States and Israel Nadav Safran
The United States and North Africa: Morocco, Algeria, and Tunisia Charles F. Gallagher
The United States and the Arab World William R. Polk
The United States and Canada Gerald M. Craig
The Americans and the French Crane Brinton

The Americans and the French

By CRANE BRINTON

Harvard University Press

CAMBRIDGE, MASSACHUSETTS

1968

Preface

The American Foreign Policy Library was founded in 1945 at the initiative and under the editorship of the late Sumner Welles and the late Donald C. McKay. Their experience of World War II had convinced the editors that the new problems of international politics stemming from the Allied victory required from the American public a wider and more thorough knowledge of our historical and current relations with important regions of the world. For each volume of the Library they aimed at a standard which would combine the authority of the expert in the field with the simplicity and clarity of good popularization.

Donald C. McKay's *The United States and France,* based on a thorough knowledge of French history and first-hand acquaintance with the land and the people, was published in 1951. The book admirably fitted the standards and the purposes of the Library at the time. But an essential element in the plan of the series was a periodic revision of each volume, something very important for books which are essentially handbooks for current use. Notably in the case of France and Franco-American relations the situation was greatly altered in the two decades after Professor McKay's book was conceived and written. In the late 1940's General de Gaulle could seem a figure of the past, futile in the politics of the Fourth Republic, already embalmed in history; and the great *miracle économique* that has in many ways transformed France materially

—more important, has altered the spirit of that land of classic *mesure*—could hardly have been foreseen two decades ago.

There is no doubt that Professor McKay would have successfully revised and added to his book in a second edition. Unhappily, he died in 1959 without having begun the task. As his successor in the editorship I was confronted with the pressing need, if the purposes of the Library were to be fulfilled, of providing a treatment of France and Franco-American relations taking account of changed conditions. It seemed to me awkward and even misleading to attempt to add to Professor McKay's book a new chapter dealing with the last two decades and unfair to his reputation to attempt to alter his text. In the circumstances it seemed wisest to publish an altogether new book, altering somewhat the title so as to protect the identity of Professor McKay's book, which will remain an important part of the literature of the subject.

I long shared with my colleague McKay the field of modern French history at Harvard and served with him in the Research and Analysis Branch of the Office of Strategic Services. I had written for him one of the first books in the American Foreign Policy Library, *The United States and Britain,* which also very much needs to be brought up to date, but not having kept up closely with Anglo-American affairs in the last two decades, I have thought it best to commission a new book on the subject from an author who will come more freshly and more intimately to it than I possibly could. With France and French affairs, however, I have been continuously concerned, and have traveled frequently in that country from 1944 to the present.

I do not think I need here add appreciably to my *envoi* in the last few paragraphs of Chapter Nine of the present book. I deeply regret the present evil state of relations between the Americans and French, and hope that this book may throw some light on the surely not altogether irremovable factors that have brought about that state.

My debts to individual French men and women are too numerous to mention without making unfair distinctions. They go back nearly half a century to my first struggles with manuscript materials on the great French Revolution. In the United States I wish especially to thank Professor Edward S. Mason of Harvard, who has, if not precisely certified my economics, at least cleared them as passing; and Dr. Jacques Kornberg, who did a very thorough job indeed on the statistical appendix of this book. And I want most particularly to express my gratitude to Thomas J. Wilson in this year of his retirement. As Director of Harvard University Press and as my friend, he has provided encouragement and support not only for this volume but for the American Foreign Policy Library as a whole.

CRANE BRINTON

Cambridge, Massachusetts
October 1967

Contents

One   *The Hexagon*   1

Two   *Frenchmen: The National Character*   28

Three   *France and the United States: To the Second
          World War*   50

Four   *France and the United States: The Second
          World War and Its Aftermath*   76

Five   *The New France: The Material Basis*   103

Six   *The New France: The Fifth Republic*   133

Seven   *The New France: The Cultural Revolution*   173

Eight   *The United States and France: The 1960's*   215

Nine   *The United States and France: The Possible
          Future*   241

        Appendix: Facts about France   261

        Reading Suggestions   281

        Index   297

The Americans

and the French

Chapter One

The Hexagon

1. This is a book about France and the relations between France and the United States. In one narrow but impeccably factual sense "France" denotes some 212,000 specific square miles of this earth inhabited by some 50,000,000 individual Frenchmen; and "United States" denotes some 3,600,000 square miles inhabited by some 195,000,000 individual Americans. In a wider sense, what these two terms mean to the multitudes who use them defies the cataloguing mind.

Some day far off, when science fiction has come true and man has transcended the existing limits of his reasoning powers —and those of his machines—present efforts to describe, to comprehend, to make real these millions of individual human beings and their trillions of interrelations among themselves and with their physical environment may well seem ludicrously inadequate. In the meantime I shall have to go ahead and *generalize*, perhaps with some help from the struggling social sciences, but without their rigor and their "sterile" vocabulary, indeed with tools fashioned for the most part in the pursuits of literature and philosophy, and not radically changed since the ancient Greeks. I shall have to write that "France" thought, believed, behaved in this way, the "United States" in that way. I shall have to use, with due caution and qualifications, those indispensable and misleading stereotypes about national character—French logic, French parsimony, French *amour,* American pragmatism and distrust of ideas, American youthful energy, and many more. The reader will have to keep constantly in mind the fact that the great decisions in Franco-American relations are made in each country by a few men —that, indeed, since de Gaulle's accession to a "strong" presidency in 1958 they are finally made in each country by one man; yet we must keep quite as firmly in mind the fact that the decisions the policymakers arrive at are influenced by what they believe their millions of fellow-countrymen want, or at least will accept.

This task of generalization is surely simplest for those hundred and fifty million acres labeled "France" on the map. Since 1766, when the acquisition of Lorraine rounded out its territories to the northeast, this France has had roughly the shape of a hexagon. So completely are we now trained to the convenient unreality of the map that Frenchmen commonly refer, sometimes in tones of endearment, to *"l'hexagone."* It would, however, be impossible even for a space traveler given a rare day of complete clarity to see the whole hexagon as such. For although the three sides on the sea—the Channel, the Atlantic, and the Mediterranean—and a fourth side along the lofty and straight line of the Pyrenees on the south would be clear enough, the eastern side with the Alps, the Jura, and the Rhine would be much less distinct, and the line between France and Belgium-Luxembourg-Germany on the sixth or northeast side would be as invisible from any height as the line between North and South Dakota, a fact of very great importance in all of French history.

Not even the physical geography of the hexagon is simple and uniform. The French in their unregenerate days a few decades ago, when they traveled very little outside their own country compared with the Germans and the British, not to speak of the Americans, used to defend themselves by saying, "Why should we leave France? We have everything here." Although the extraordinary variety of the French scene—its physical geography modified by man into human geography— is a stereotype of all writing about France, it is almost irreproachable and unavoidable. France is not quite twice the size of Nevada, a state that looks to a traveler relatively uniform. In the small area of France almost all the kinds of natural scenery found in the United States (excluding Hawaii and Alaska) can be approximated. The level wheatlands away from the villages of La Beauce look like wheatlands in our prairie states. The Vosges are our Appalachian mountains, the Alps and Pyrenees snow mountains not wholly unlike those of our West. The rocky coasts of Brittany are not unlike parts of the New England coast, the dunes west of Bordeaux not unlike those of the Carolina banks or southern Oregon. Californian moviemakers can easily shoot a scene from the French Riviera right at home in California. There is nothing in France quite like our Southwest, though parts of Provence, back a bit from the coast, have barren limestone mountains that are like true semiarid country.

Of the mountain chains that rim the hexagon the Pyrenees on the south and the Alps on the southeast are lofty, youthful mountains, and true "natural boundaries" insofar as such boundaries can be said to exist for the political creations of mobile and restless men. Mt. Blanc in the Alps of Savoy, nearly 16,000 feet high, is the highest in Europe, unless the Caucasus are considered a European chain. The Pyrenees are somewhat lower, with a few peaks slightly over 11,000 feet. But even where they come down to the Mediterranean and the Atlantic, the Pyrenees are not easy mountains to cross, and except at or near their eastern and western ends they have never been crossed by railways or indeed by a really major highway. France has not often been successfully invaded by land from the south. The Alps have been somewhat less of a barrier, no doubt largely because history long ago made Rome and Italy what they have been: Rome, a great expanding military power, and later Italy, a rich land full of prestige and worth invading. From Caesar and Hannibal to both Napoleons soldiers have crossed the Alps between France and Italy often enough, and so too have traders and travelers. In modern times three railways—one, using the Simplon tunnel passing through a part of Switzerland—and five major highways, to which a sixth, tunneling over seven miles under Mt. Blanc, has recently been added, make passage between the two countries relatively easy.

A third much lower range on the southeast, the Jura, has for the last four or five centuries been a political boundary between France and some kind of Swiss state or states. The Jura is a series of neatly folded mountains, much of it limestone, good pasture and timber country. It has not, however, been an ethnic or linguistic boundary in medieval and modern times. Its people are almost wholly French-speaking, ethnically at least as mixed as most West and Central European stocks, "Burgundians" not very different, for the physical anthropologist, from their German-speaking "Allemanic" neighbors. Further to the north lie the Vosges, again relatively low mountains much like some parts of our Appalachians. On the south, between the Vosges and the Jura is the *troué de Belfort*, practically a plain, some twenty miles wide, much too wide for easy defense. On the north too the Vosges drop off into hilly country, which historically at least has never been a barrier to armies French or German. The French do not, however, regard the Vosges as part of their cherished "natural" boundaries on the east; for them the Rhine serves that purpose, though in spite of some two centuries of attempts to extend that river line to the sea, they have had to settle for about one hundred miles of the Rhine between Alsace and Baden.

The land rises a bit as the French political boundary moves into the northeast line of the hexagon. These hills are the Ardennes, a not very fertile plateau deeply cut by rivers, of which the principal is the Meuse. This is by no means comfortable fighting country, but like all the rest of this disputed area where the French and Germans have long mingled it has been the scene of major military action. Here the Germans broke through in 1940, and here the Americans held the last desperate offensive of the German army in the Battle of the Bulge five years later. The last seventy miles or so of the Franco-Belgian border are gently rolling or level country, perhaps to an even greater extent than the Ardennes a fighting cockpit with no natural barrier. The linguistic line all the way from Switzerland to the sea is most irregular, but apparently has not significantly varied since the middle ages. There are French- (or Walloon-) speaking peoples in Belgium, and German-speaking peoples in France, but since the return of Alsace-Lorraine to France in 1919, no significant numbers of French-speaking peoples in Germany.

Somewhat to the south of the geometric center of the hexagon is the Massif Central, old and complex mountains, in part made up of long-extinct volcanoes (sheep graze in their craters today) on the whole rough, infertile, though with some good valley lands, and not particularly rich in minerals. The old province name of Auvergne is sometimes used nowadays for the whole region, which is actually much more extensive and includes parts of several old provinces. It is in fact a varied region. To the south of Auvergne are high limestone plateaus known as *causses* with shallow soils that do not hold water. Toward its southwest lie the Cévennes, relatively low but still very wild mountains, the *désert* in which the French Protestants, after the revocation of the Edict of Nantes in 1685, kept their faith alive through a century of persecution. (*Désert* in French is not the English word "desert," but merely land "deserted" by human beings.) In the north of Auvergne are the extinct volcanoes, the *puys*, capped by the Puy de Dôme, about 4,500 feet high. Here in an area rich in mineral springs are some of the great French spas, Vichy, Royat, La Bourboule.

Finally, in the northwest of the hexagon there are the almost leveled roots of very old mountains, granitic or metamorphic, with mostly poor or indifferent soils. The actual peninsular part of Brittany is such a region, called Armorique by French geographers from the old Celtic name for the coastal part of the region. The central hills of the peninsula are only a few hundred feet high, but the rocky, much indented coasts are scenically most impressive. In Normandy, too, there is a hilly broken region, which with the development of modern tourism has been given the touristic and highly inaccurate name of *la Suisse normande*. Here was fought in a region hitherto without such glories some of the most important actions of the Allied invasion of 1944. The rest of France, something more than half, is level, rolling, or mildly hilly country, *la belle France* of tidy farmland, rich but not extravagant, given to *mesure* and the other classic graces, the France of the poets and the painters. The symbol of this France has come to be the middle Loire valley, Touraine and its adjoining provinces, the "Château Country" of the modern tourist agencies. Here the land is not quite flat, as it is in the wheat-growing Beauce just to the north, but gently rolling, well-watered, with vineyards, orchards, and gardens, long rows of poplars, the *peuplier d'Italie* now at least as French as Italian. All are tied together by the Loire, an often intemperate river, not really navigable, given to floods and quicksands, not a suitable river for this Vergilian France, though there are those who hold the Loire not a bad symbol of the France of *frondes*, revolutions, and falling cabinets.

This France of plains, hills, and river valleys is, however, by no means all of one piece. Its most important section is the *bassin de Paris,* the old Île de France at its center, but spreading out into Normandy, parts of Picardy, and most of Champagne. The geography textbooks all compare this region to a series of concentric saucers, with Paris itself—indeed the Île de la Cité, the island center of Gallic Lutetia—at the center of the smallest saucer, and with Montmartre and the hills of the Paris suburbs the rim of the smallest saucer. As the saucers get bigger, they are not perfect shapes, especially to the south and southwest. But to the northeast and east—toward the Germanies—they conform quite well to the metaphor. It is the rims of these saucers, from the Meuse right to the city itself, that have made the true strategic walls of Paris. For centuries the critical battles have been fought here in defense of the city and the nation. The first World War—from the Marne through the Chemin des Dames, Ste Menehould, Verdun, the Argonne and further north—was decided in these fields. The region as a whole is fertile, its poorer soils supporting important forests. Much of Normandy, Picardy, and Champagne is underlain by chalk, but has good, reliable rainfall and has long been important grain country, and in recent times has a great acreage devoted to sugar and fodder beets.

Two great river valleys, that of the Garonne in the southwest and that of the Rhône in the southeast, both with good farmlands, are quite different. The Garonne has a wide-spreading basin, with many major tributary rivers, Dordogne, Lot, Tarn, Ariège, Gers, of varied soils, and at its mouth, the estuary called the Gironde, a center of some of the greatest vintage wines. The very swift Rhône and its quiet northern prolongation, the Saône, make a comparatively narrow valley, especially narrow in its middle reaches, between the Alps and the Massif Central. Around Dijon to the north, however, is the great wine region of Burgundy, and to the south is the rich fruit and vegetable growing section of Provence. The Rhône, instead of an estuary like the other major French rivers—Loire, Garonne, Seine—(they are not great, of course, on an Amazon-Mississippi-Volga scale) has a delta, still very wild in its lower reaches, but tamed in the last few years into profitable rice fields in its upper part.

Nature itself has made even these classic farmlands of France far from uniform. Indeed there are, thanks in part to the disturbances in relief made by the glaciers of the Ice Age spreading out from the Alps and Massif Central, patches of swampy, sandy, or sour soils scattered throughout most of France. The Dombes, northeast of Lyon, is a strange region of exceedingly shallow ponds and glacial soils. The Sologne is a poor swampy plain almost in Touraine itself. Southwest of Bordeaux is the Landes, moorlands that nowadays support little but pines and are subject to horrid forest fires. Also subject to such fires are the pine forests of the Mediterranean littoral behind the narrow thread of the Riviera resorts.

France belongs in the temperate zone, but, once more, for so relatively small a territory, it has considerable variation in climate. The northwestern regions along the Atlantic and the Channel benefit from the North Atlantic Drift Current and usually have damp, mild winters and moderate summers. Toward the east a continental climate gradually takes over, with hot summers and cold, often snowy, winters. The Mediterranean coast can be hot indeed in summer, as can even such Atlantic coastal towns as Bordeaux and Bayonne. Yet in winter the lower Rhône valley is subject to a fierce north wind, the mistral, uncomfortable but rarely freezing. The Riviera, at least in its middle and eastern ends, is protected from the mistral. Here citrus fruit can be nursed through occasional frosts, though commercially the chief crop is, or used to be before the present French industrial revolution took to synthetic chemicals for the purpose, orange blossoms for use in "natural" perfumes.

But by and large—and this is a fact that has its parallels in many other phases of human relations—French travelers who complain of the heat or cold of Washington or Chicago conveniently forget that in much of France they can encounter similar extremes. The French went in for central heating some time ago, well before the British, who needed it more; in their present industrial revolution they are beginning to indulge in *climatisation*—air-conditioning.

2. The basic reason for so small a country as France to present such varied aspects lies not so much in physical as in human geography. Such geography, to which French scholars have long contributed, always has had an important historical dimension. Over the centuries there has emerged one of the most important generalizations that must be understood if the France we have to deal with today is to be understood. The very concept of the hexagon, geometric, symmetrical, neatly centered, uniform, suggesting permanence, is a fine symbol for the centripetal drive of centuries of French history. But this drive has always been against strong centrifugal resistances, deeply embedded in whatever makes France, and never wholly conquered or suppressed, even today. These divisive tendencies have never been based solely on territorial divisions, certainly not in modern times, yet they have often had such bases, as with the Albigensian heretics of the middle ages in Languedoc, the Protestants of the sixteenth and seventeenth centuries, also strongest in the South, the Catholic and royalist resistance to the great French Revolution in the Vendée and in Brittany. Anglo-Saxon opinion generally, and certainly common American opinion today, exaggerates the extent to which France is a divided country, always on the verge of political disorder and instability. Yet there is surely an element of truth at the bottom of all this hostile exaggeration. To borrow from

the more literary and impressionistic side of that incomplete science, psychology, it may well be true that those who cry loudest for order, discipline, controls are the ones whose natural intemperance and wildness most need such controls. France today is certainly a firmly centralized state and society; French culture in its dominant facets over the centuries has sought to make effective such ideals as classic law and order, *mesure*, symmetry, discipline, *le génie Latin*. Yet something very deeply embedded in the French people drives them to resist the rules, the disciplines, the obedience they have been taught for so long, resisting usually in the name of *la France éternelle*. Charles de Gaulle, nourished in this classic, this Latin, tradition, turned heroically against his lawful hierarchical superiors in his Promethean gesture of June 18, 1940.

Professional caution and decency hardly permit the unverifiable suggestion that there may be touches of reality in ethnic labels so often abused, that the French are by blood or at least by genes not Latins, but Celts, not classicists but romantics. It is safer simply to note that, like all the great European nations, France has been welded together into a nation-state from many once-independent political entities over a long period, roughly one thousand years since the accession of Hugh Capet as king of "France" (in 962 not much more than the Île de France from Paris to Orléans). So many factors, indeed so many of what in ignorance are called accidents, went into that process of unification that it cannot really be understood. Sufficient to note that it was not an easy process, that its theater, France, unlike England, was not an island but a most exposed part of the European continent, unprotected by those famous "natural boundaries," which moreover were attained only toward the end of the process, and therefore, to the difficulties of overcoming local resistance was added the necessity of warding off foreign enemies. Most important, this long process of building national unity was one that left marks, indeed wounds, as the past perversely continues to survive.

Though we Americans are in a sense fond of history—museum history (colonial Williamsburg), memorial history (centenaries of all sorts), prideful history (the shot heard round the world)—we tend to forget or suppress history as a part of the human condition, history as a living problem, indeed a burden. Many of us do not always realize that our own Civil War is, once again, as contemporary for us as the great French Revolution is, or was until yesterday, for the French. The French, indeed, call their history since 1789 *histoire contemporaine* and though there are signs that the Revolution of 1789–1794 has not been fought quite so vigorously in the last few decades, it is still not as much part of a frozen past as our now well-glossed-over American Revolution.

One clear, simple indication of the thousand-year struggle to make that symbolic hexagon can be found in the history of an extraordinary variety of local subdivisions—political, administrative, religious, economic "jurisdictions." Some of these, cities, towns, and villages, go back to the Gauls and earlier; in the South, many of them are of Roman and, as in the case of Marseilles, of Greek origin. But for present purposes the base line may be the feudal fragmentation of about A.D. 1000 when the Capetian rulers of the Île de France, helped no doubt by the central position in the Seine basin of their capital, Paris, and by the prestige of that name "Francia" and its relation to Frankish glories—*gesta Dei per Francos,* God's deeds by means of the Franks—began the creation of the France we know. Of that feudal fragmentation I need only note that, in spite of certain theories of a hierarchical structure leading up to a king (indeed at first to an emperor of more than just France) what we would now call political reality lay in dozens of independent units like Normandy, Brittany, Champagne, and the Île de France itself. Many of these units, especially to the east and south, were even by feudal law not then a part of France.

The historical details of the unification of France are not pertinent here. This unification was until 1789 achieved under the auspices, indeed usually under the active leadership, of the Capetian monarchs, members of a long-lived house, fertile in male heirs, and perhaps on the whole—though it numbered many incompetent and unlucky kings—above hereditary royal average in political intelligence. A united France was achieved in many ways, by marriage, by war, by diplomacy, by bloody repression, by conciliation and concession. It was greatly complicated by the tie—can it be called accidental or at least artificial?—between France and the British Isles established when William the Bastard, Duke of Normandy and a vassal of the King of France, became king of England in 1066. Later it was further complicated by some unwise alienation of parts of the realm as feudal *appanages* to take care of younger sons, whose successors often tried to set up independent states. Above all, this long process was most uneven, marked by periods of rebellion, civil war, foreign war, sometimes to the point where it seemed that France would break up as Germany and Italy had. Probably the worst of these low points, and certainly in its resolution the most dramatic and important, brought to the rescue St. Joan of Arc (burned at the stake in 1431). With our advantage of hindsight we can say that Louis XI (1461–1483) with his conquest of Burgundy pretty well finished the job of unification in the territorial sense, but much remained to be done. Indeed, as Tocqueville pointed out, the French Revolution itself really put the finishing touches on the centralizing work of the Capetians.

The Revolution provided a neat symbol of this centralizing process by creating—quite literally, inventing—the governmental units which, with certain exceptions to be noted below, now stand directly underneath the nation-state itself. These are the *départements,* of which there are ninety-five in metropolitan France (which includes Corsica), and four overseas, Guadaloupe, Martinique, French Guiana, and Réunion. The National Assembly that set up these departments in 1791 meant their capitals to be readily accessible to all their citizens. Each department is headed by a prefect appointed by the central government and removable by it; but each also has an elected general council responsible to the voters. The departments have little, if any, hold on the emotions, or even the sentiments, of their inhabitants. They are named from natural features, rivers, mountains, estuaries—Gironde, Côtes du Nord, Yvelines, Vosges, Marne, Pas de Calais—and were deliberately designed to take the place of old provincial units—Brittany, Languedoc, Roussillon, and the like—which had some hold on the emotions of their inhabitants, some echoes of the old centrifugal successes. They have certainly proved successful from that point of view. No one is ever moved to want to die for, or even to play football for, the Deux-Sèvres, the Eure-et-Loir, the Bouches-du-Rhône. There is one faint trace of human sentiment attached even to these rationalist products of the eighteenth-century Enlightenment. The Seine-Inférieure (Rouen, Le Havre) had its name changed recently to Seine-Maritime, the Loire Inférieure (Nantes) to Loire-Atlantique, the Charente Inférieure to Charente-Maritime. *Inférieur* in French, like "lower" in English, refers to much more than physical space, indeed, is a word that in any human relation offends the perfect democrat; and France is, in spite of what some Americans seem to think, a most democratic land.

At the other extreme of subdivisional size, the National Assembly in 1791 gave juridical existence as municipalities equipped with mayors and councils, to some forty-odd thousand communes. But these were and are far from artificial, though they had never before been so neatly organized for administrative purposes. They are the cities, towns, and villages of old France, many of them in origin very old indeed, some of them quite new. The cities, of course, like all modern Western cities now are composed mostly of streets and buildings no older than those of Philadelphia—or even Chicago.

Toward these places their natives feel a kind of normal human emotion not worlds apart from what Americans feel toward the "home town." Perhaps it is a deeper feeling than in the United States, for the Frenchman is more likely to have stayed in or near the place where he was born. He is not nowadays, however, quite as likely to have so remained, for, as we shall see, villages are steadily losing population to the cities. A vast majority of the eight million inhabitants of Greater Paris simply cannot have been born there. The same is true of many other cities, especially of fast-growing ones like Nice and Toulouse.

It is hardly necessary to add that French towns and cities have their boosters and their chambers of commerce, and they watch their statistics of population. Terrasson in the department of Dordogne, thanks to some hard-won new industries, some seduced from nearby, bigger Brive in the Corrèze, grew from 3,700 inhabitants in 1962 to 6,000 in 1966 and is aiming next at 10,000. It is having trouble annexing its neighboring dormitory village, Cublac, for Cublac is in the Corrèze.*

Between the department and the commune the neat system of French local government has two minor subdivisions, the *arrondissement* headed by a subprefect, originally designed so that its capital (*chef-lieu*) should be no more than a day's ride from any part of it, and the still smaller canton, largely a unit for the lower courts of justice. All these subdivisions from department to canton are wastefully numerous in this motorized age; but France is a democracy, and reforms eliminating such unnecessary jurisdictions would mean loss of jobs and patronage for thousands. We Americans should have no difficulty understanding, and perhaps even sympathizing with, the French in this matter. After all, there are those Georgia counties—and not only those.

* "Terrasson a réussi sa révolution économique," *Périgord Magazine,* October 1966. This is a local promotional publication.

The French have found a solution for this problem, not a heroic one, but one with some thousand years of precedents. From the accession of Charlemagne on, obsolete or otherwise inconvenient jurisdictions were rarely eliminated; instead, new ones were added, and the old ones with their dignified appointments remained, gradually losing their meaning but not—or not wholly—their emoluments in cash or prestige. An experiment in larger local governing units initiated under Vichy has been continued by subsequent regimes. These new "economic regions" group about six departments under regional prefects promptly christened by the journalists "superprefects," perhaps not quite so powerful as that Latin preposition implies, but still very important in the new French "mixed" economy. Some of these new "regions" have been given names of old provinces which the revolutionists of 1789 sought to suppress, Picardy, Burgundy, Languedoc; others, Center, Rhône-Alpes, Midi-Pyrénées, are mere geographic names. One significantly couples a very old province, coated with a thick patina of history and sentiment and a synthetic, modern, tourist trade name, Provence-Côte d'Azur. Finally, in 1966 a true metropolitan district was set up for Paris, the old department of Seine restricted to Paris city limits, the adjoining Seine-et-Oise eliminated, and the new departments of Val d'Oise, Hauts de Seine, Seine St. Denis, Val de Marne, Essonne, and Yvelines set up from the old Seine, and Seine-et-Oise. The authorities of the central Parisian area were given a good deal of power, but few if any jobs were lost.

The needs of the modern social-service state in France as elsewhere have produced a vast complex of special agencies that do not fit exactly into any neat jurisdictional ladder. From the very start of the modern system in revolutionary and Napoleonic times much had to be done outside the straitjacket of the departments. Napoleon's national educational system, capped by universities, was organized in "academies" grouping departments into regions; and even in this system, there were at the highest level "special schools" not strictly universities. Among these are the Ecole Normale Supérieure, nothing remotely like the old American normal school, but a very advanced graduate school, entrance to which is highly competitive; and the Ecole Polytechnique, a very advanced institute of technology, entrance to which is also open only to those who survive an intense competition. The army too is organized outside the departmental system and has its own regional areas.

Once more, the customary foreign judgment, in particular, English and American judgment on French government, that it is fully, inhumanly, and yet somehow inefficiently centralized is, to say the least, exaggerated, and certainly for the France of the 1960's not quite up to date. The familiar story of one of Napoleon's ministers of education who takes out his watch, notes it is 11:00 A.M. and remarks casually and proudly, "It's 11 o'clock and in all the lycées [high schools, roughly] of France the senior class is reciting the first ecologue of Vergil," a story probably not quite accurate in 1810, is certainly not accurate today. For one thing, since the end of World War II marked the end of the anticlerical attempt to make all French education "public" there have been church schools, and other free schools of the kind we call "private"—or if we are good democratic Americans—"independent" schools.

Certainly our American federal system makes some difference between the spirit of our government and that of France. The complete chaos of American higher education—or its useful variety, if that's the way you feel about it—is unimaginable in France. Our fifty different ways of regulating the sale of alcoholic drinks, our fifty different divorce laws, astonish Frenchmen, who tend to exaggerate our federal freedoms as much as we exaggerate their bureaucratically centralized constraints. After all, in both countries local pressures of the kind we call the "pork barrel" are always at work, though usually through quite different channels. No French government could wholly neglect public works in one region at the expense of another.

Save for a few political thinkers, the French themselves have never been quite as worried as their Anglo-Saxon critics over the straitjacket of centralization. The royalists, led by Charles Maurras, used to attack the Third Republic in the name of regional freedoms, decentralization, the fruitful local variations of old. But this was largely a stick with which to beat their republican enemies. Certainly that incorrigible admirer of imperial Rome, Charles Maurras, was no democrat and did not believe in anything so Anglo-Saxon as *le self-gouvernement*. There are still Frenchmen who, like many Americans, feel distrust of the welfare state. But they are not presently a determining political force. It is true that in general the French, unlike the English, do not exactly love their police; the popular name for them, *les flics*, like the American "cops," is mildly, but not ferociously pejorative.

Finally, in part as a long legacy from the past, there are certain territorial focuses of French particularism that have no legal place on the map today, nor in any little box in those nice bureaucratic tables of organization—the formalized peck order or hierarchy—we are all familiar with today. But the *pays* and often the province (though, as I have noted, they are no longer legal, functioning subdivisions of the French State), have a place in the hearts and heads, too, of millions of Frenchmen. The feelings that bind a Frenchman to Brittany or Anjou no longer have the kind of strength that bound Robert E. Lee to Virginia, though long ago by the solidest test of such sentiments—the propriety of dying and killing for the fatherland—it was fitting to fight for Burgundy, Brittany or Normandy as *patries*. Of course, it is no longer fitting to fight for Virginia either. French local patriotism is perhaps rather stronger than the run of American feeling toward a state, though perhaps not much stronger than the feelings of beleaguered Mississippians or old-fashioned Vermonters.

Furthermore, the provinces, just because of their past (remember, they no longer exist as actual legal units) have proved very useful for the numerous central and local agencies that promote the tourist industry. The charm and romance of the regions are advanced with all the techniques of modern promotion and directed as much to Frenchmen as to foreigners. Such promotion seems to intellectuals in particular synthetic and vulgar, and they turn against it. France being the land it is, some of this scorn for local feeling rubs off on other than intellectual groups. At any rate, the French are most unlikely to produce such a song as "When It's Apple-Blossom Time in Normandy" of the American popular song trade.

The *pays*, on the other hand, though also no longer on the legal map of France is surrounded with little of the tourist publicity the provinces get and is the focus of much more disinterested sentiments. There are often many *pays* in a single large province like Burgundy. The word comes from the Latin *pagus*, an indication of the fact that the *pays* is the oldest traceable unit of French land, older than the conquest of Gaul by Caesar. The *pays* often have Gallic names and were no doubt basically old tribal divisions, sometimes pre-Celtic. They are now marked off by all sorts of visible signs, land use, sheer look of the land after centuries of farming and building, a well-known product—Brie cheese, for instance, from la Brie in the Île de France—sometimes merely as the old trading and farming area of an important town; for example, the Beauvaisis is the *petit pays* around the cathedral town of Beauvais. The *pays* have no exact boundaries, partly because of fragmentation in the medieval centuries. There is much overlapping among these subdivisions, which are often loosely called "regions."

But they are real enough and often the object of careful, loving historical and geographic study. Some representative writings about *pays* are noted in the reading suggestions; all are dealt with in the seventy-odd volumes of Ardouin-Dumazet.*

3.　In support of my thesis that the human and geographic
　　unity of the hexagon is not a fixed and unchanging mono-lith, but rather a never wholly completed fusion of disparate elements, human and geographic, I must devote a few more pages to the subject. "France, one and indivisible" is a slogan, a needed slogan, for France has always been divided and only slowly, painfully united. Apart from, and no doubt more important than, the kind of geographic variety the tourist sees, there are social and economic differences. The most conspicuous, clear to any tourist, are the ethnic groups around the edges of the hexagon, groups that in much of our modern world would be known as "minorities." And there are in France a few Bretons, perhaps a very few Flemings, Alsatians, and Basques who feel oppressed, who want to have national freedom or at least home rule.

Not even in Brittany, however, where several hundred thousands have Breton, a Celtic tongue, as their natural speech (French is only learned in school, often not very well) is there a genuine separatist movement. The Germans, who occupied all of Brittany during the second World War, tried very hard indeed to nurse such a movement, but they got nowhere. Breton nationalism is surely no stronger than Welsh or Scottish nationalism and no menace to present-day French unity. The Alsatians, who speak a German dialect and among their middle and upper classes often speak standard German, a very few Flemish-speaking people in the north and Italian-speaking people in the region of Nice, and some hundred thousand

* See Appendix I, section 1, "The Land and the People."

Basques at the western end of the Pyrenees, who speak an agglutinative tongue not clearly related to any other known tongue, make up the rest of non-French-speaking Frenchmen. Until the Revolution of 1789 and the beginnings of the mass-based state, the upper classes of these groups learned French, and the rest had no need to learn it, for they had no direct share in the French community. The Revolution with its democratic thrust brought on attempts at imposing all things French, including language. Indeed, even before the Revolution, some regions, like the Franche-Comté (the Free County of Burgundy), which had been left to itself by its distant Spanish rulers, resisted annexation by France. There has, therefore, been some forced assimilation. But the French will insist that even in Teutonic Alsace there has not been a true "minority" problem for decades and that however much some French nationalists have talked about making these people into full French-speaking, French-thinking, French-feeling Frenchmen, the practice of French governments toward them has never been like that of many central European ruling groups toward their minorities. And the fact seems to be that the governments are right.

If you wish to confirm this, go, for example, to the French *pays Basque*, look and listen, and then cross over into Franco's Basque provinces and do the same. In Spain no Basque signs and precious little Basque spoken, at least in the hearing of tourists. In France, Basque signs everywhere and Basque spoken freely. Briefly, in the middle years of the third Republic in France, there was an attempt, partly anticlerical in inspiration, to make the French Basques, mostly good Catholics, into conventional French *bons républicains*. This has now been given up, and it seems as though most Basques are, in the Fifth Republic, good Frenchmen, good republicans, and good Basques. You will indeed see painted slogans in the Basque country, such as "4 + 3 = 1," a cryptic slogan of Basque nationalists who want the unification of the four Spanish Basque provinces and the three French ones in one presumably independent or at least autonomous state. But these and the various, though not much varied, Communist graffiti common all over France are not in themselves very menacing symptoms of coming revolutions. These daubed signs on walls and posts have not yet been followed up by the customary methods of serious and desperate minorities: plastic bombs, riots, assassinations. It looks as though French national unity is as secure as any in our contemporary world.

In sum, the French ethnic minorities enjoy fairly complete freedom to preserve their own language, their own culture, subject to no more than the nongovernmental pressures within any modern society, including our own, toward cultural uniformity. Those pressures are strong and have perhaps insured that even Provençal, in spite of its distinguished revival in the last century, will not survive as a language of high culture. But it will be a long time before all traces of local differences in France are flattened out into the deadening sameness that worries so many intellectuals today. The unmistakable accent of Marseilles shows no more signs of disappearing than does the equally unmistakable metropolitan accent we somewhat too narrowly associate with Brooklyn. Local differences are no longer a threat to French unity. But they sometimes have been such in the past, and the absorption of their speakers—if you prefer, their conversion—into loyal French citizens has not always been easy and has left a clear mark on French awareness of the need for unity.

Again, though there is in France no such really dangerous socioeconomic territorial gap between regional haves and have-nots as that in Italy between the prosperous North and the poverty-stricken South, there is in France a milder gap of a not wholly dissimilar nature. This is a gap, still in evidence, between a "progressive," partly urban and industrial, relatively rich northeast and southeast, and a conservative, rural, relatively backward northwest and southwest. Actually there is no such neat division as these terms would suggest. The dividing line is sometimes drawn as a diagonal north-south line from the mouth of the Seine to the mouths of the Rhône, with the regions on the eastern side of this line advanced, those on the western retarded. But there are pockets in each half which do not conform to the generalization. Today, at least, Nantes-St. Nazaire is a true industrial area, and so too are cities like Limoges and Toulouse near the line, but still on its western side. On the other side, there are poor regions like much of the southern French Alps (except where they reach the sea on the Riviera) and much of rural Burgundy apart from the great wine region of the Côte d'Or. The Center, save for a few industrial cities like Clermont-Ferrand, is poor country, its southern departments—Lozère, Cantal, parts of others—the most deprived of all. Politically the West, especially in the northern and central parts, has been the stronghold of the Right, of the Church, of the small farmer and the small businessman. Yet three departments of the central part of western France have long been Leftist and anticlerical. Only in a municipal by-election in 1966 was this solid radical block of Corrèze, Haute Vienne, and Guéret broken. In sum, French political divisions cannot be mapped neatly or indeed classified by any simple socioeconomic categories. This applies even to the Communists, who are by no means, as I shall note later, wholly recruited from a proletariat and a perverted class of intellectuals.

French religious divisions too have a rough geographic basis, not quite identical with that between the economically and politically conservative and the progressive regions. Nor is the important division that between Catholic and Protestant. There are over a million Protestants in France, influential in business, administration, and cultural life beyond their numerical proportion in the population. Among the Jews there is at least an equal proportion of influential people as among Protestants. Anti-Semitism, which reached its peak in the early twentieth century after the Dreyfus case, ceased to be respectable even among the upper classes after the fall of the Vichy government and the disclosure of the horrors of Nazi concentration camps. Those who know France best hold that anti-Semitism was never strong among the mass of the French people. The really deep religious division in France is between Catholics and those who commonly claim to be above "religion" and for whom there is no good single label—anticlericals, secularists, freethinkers, agnostics, positivists, Marxist materialists, all basically "rationalists" hostile to revealed religion. In France such non- or anti-Christians certainly number in the millions, though no satisfactory official census can be taken of them. To their number, for political matters, can be added a certain number of very indifferent and nonpracticing Catholics. The Catholics are strongest in the North and West, their opponents in the South and in the great cities. The stereotype of the reference books labeling France a "Catholic country," however, is not quite accurate in the sense that such a statement is substantially accurate for the Republic of Ireland, or even Italy, Spain, and Portugal, or the province of Quebec.

Finally, no one can write about French geographic divisions without mentioning the familiar contrast of Paris and the provinces. Here too the stereotypes, French as well as foreign, need some qualification. Paris and the provinces (some Parisians and the majority of provincials) have on at least two occasions been in physical conflict. The first fighting came during the great French Revolution, when the radical Jacobins in command of Paris succeeded in repressing a "federalist" revolt of their rivals, the Girondins, from Lyons, Bordeaux, Caen, and other provincial towns. One result of this struggle of the 1790's is that the term "federalism" has never had for the French the agreeable overtones it has for us Americans; it is usually a term of unfavorable connotations. Then in 1871, with Paris under the control of the radical *Communards,* who wanted to fight the already lost war with Prussia to the bitter end, a French army, widely supported in French public opinion, repressed the Paris Communard revolt in a violent struggle. Paris has historically stood for the centripetal forces of France, the provinces often for the centrifugal forces. But as I have insisted, this opposition of Parisian center and provincial peripheries is a relation, a dialogue, a continuing one in which neither side has been wholly crushed or eliminated, and which has been partly responsible for the reputation for instability France has had in the last few centuries.

So then Paris is France and is not France. It has long been the place to which the ambitious in politics, in art and letters, in science and learning are almost inevitably drawn. There are always exceptions, such as the *félibriges,* the poets of Provençal culture, led by Mistral, who defiantly remained in their province. There are even occasional scientists and scholars who manage to live contentedly at provincial universities, though a surprising number manage partial commuting even to Strasbourg from a Parisian residence. Paris in the last few decades has, like London, become a regional center of major modern industry. But there are great provincial cities—Lyons, Marseilles, Rennes, Strasbourg, Lille, Bordeaux, Toulouse, and others—with an active cultural life, much local pride, and important commercial and industrial undertakings. There is, in terms of human sentiments among the Parisian common people, a not disastrously deep sense of superiority to dull, stodgy provincials, and among many provincials a not very bitter feeling that Parisians are frivolous, sinful, and not really very happy human beings. Like so much else I shall have to deal with in this book, such feelings in some form are common in the Western hemisphere. New York is no longer thought of in Iowa as quite the sink of iniquity it was believed to be a generation or two ago, but not even our American mass media in a mass society have quite wiped out such sentiments. Paris, like London, has in its own land no strong rival as a symbol of national cultural achievement in enterprise, science, politics, the arts. Berlin, New York, Rome, and Madrid have no such monopoly as cultural symbols in their lands. But the antagonisms this Parisian monopoly arouses are not, in a world of conflict like our own, of great depth. Paris is hardly a deadly drain on the talents of the rest of the country. Indeed, economic decentralization, though not to the degree the critics of the present French government want, has made great progress since World War II. Cultural decentralization has made less progress, though it is more than French intellectuals will usually admit.

France is still, for the most part—save conspicuously for the roadside litter left by motorists *en pique-nique*—a tidy country, still *la belle France*, a well-groomed lady, never ostentatiously made up, never flaunting her beauty. Democracy, industrialism, mass culture have left their mark on the France the traveler sees. Public municipal housekeeping—removal of the incredible trash our packaged age produces, maintenance of parks, lawns, and the rest of what the British call "amenities"—are not quite up to the best of Dutch or Scandinavian standards, but usually far ahead of American practice in such matters. Americans landing at a New York pier on a trip back from anywhere in western Europe, including France, are or should be shocked by the filth of New York streets along the North River. Yet much of the ugliness of our age has begun to creep into France. There are the ribbon-slums produced by the motor road, the old slums of the central cities, the newer ones in the industrial suburbs, especially noticeable around Paris in its "Red Belt," where poverty, aided by folk-habit, still does breed Communism. One can even see now and then in open country the beginnings of that final—one hopes—and ugliest blights of the motor age, the "auto graveyard." Especially in the countryside, village and town dumps are not well concealed.

As yet no French intellectual has felt moved to write a French *God's Own Junkyard*—and the range and depth of the complaints of French intellectuals and their opportunities to express them in print are at least as great as those of our own intellectuals. Moreover, the many planning agencies of the new France are fully aware of the need for both urban and rural conservation and improvement. An old quarter of Paris, the Marais, a center of fashion in the seventeenth century, since degenerated into a slum, is in the process of renewal, not by complete destruction of the old, as in central Boston, southwest Washington, and many other American cities undergoing renewal, but by careful planning to preserve and refurbish what is good in the old. New French housing, until the 1950's architecturally undistinguished and not very abundant, has recently come nearer to meeting the demands of a growing population. The French have even begun, in frank recognition of our American initiation of the policy, to set aside areas of natural beauty as national parks. They are meeting the same sort of difficulties from owners of grazing rights, timberlands, summer and winter resorts that we have met.

It is the classic *look* of France that men and nature have collaborated to achieve, Vergilian for the most part, but sometimes, in the Alps, the Cévennes, the moorlands, the deserted *causses* of the Massif Central, Byronic, even Ossianic, that has helped to create that perhaps diminishing breed, the Francophile, the foreigner who falls in love with France—and sometimes, though not always—with the French. The French people as individuals, as mere human beings, confront their would-be lovers with existential depths, with surprises and resistances which their land, tamed physically and metaphysically as Mother Earth has been nowadays, does not contain. The phrase, *la belle France* has fully entered the vocabulary of American travel publicity, but not *les beaux* or *les bons Français*. Some American travelers, put upon, they think, by taxi-drivers, waiters, porters, guides, and the like intent on cheating them, have been known to wish they could have France without the French. I must attempt to plumb further some of the difficulties that have long plagued Franco-American relations, by no means only at the level of formal diplomacy.

Chapter Two

Frenchmen:

The National Character

1.   Everyone knows those smooth coins of intellectual com-
      merce, the stereotypes of national character, the volatile,
gesticulating Frenchman, the thrifty Scot, the proud Spaniard
obsessed with the point of honor, the practical, energetic, somewhat naïve American, the phlegmatic Dutchman, the lyrical
Italian. There is usually some element of truth in such stereotypes, however distasteful they are to the sophisticated mind.
At any rate, the little trick of countervailing intellectuals,
asserting in the manner of Oscar Wilde at his worst the exact
opposite of the stereotype—the spendthrift Scot, the apologetic
Spaniard, the other-worldly, impractical American, the steady
phlegmatic Frenchman is intellectually no better—perhaps
worse, if you hold that intellectuals ought to be responsible
people.

Although the problem of national character, in fact, the
problem of generalization about any large group of human
beings, has interested many practitioners of the still struggling
social sciences and is indeed at the moment fashionable, none
of the devices or metaphors commonly used in these sciences

really helps much—not the "model," not the "paradigm," not the "image," certainly not the "theory" or the "uniformity." Quantification, even quite simple statistics, is of little use. Polling techniques carefully used can be helpful, especially in attempting to analyze American opinion of France and of specific acts of the French government, and of course French opinion of the United States and of our governmental policies. But the subtler problems of what makes a Frenchman French and not just another specimen of homo sapiens escapes such methods. I must, however, insist that his Frenchness is real, if not exactly quantifiable. Americans, in particular, nowadays mostly unphilosophical nominalists pushed thereto by economic success and addiction to what they think is scientific method, need constant reminders that the immeasurable, better, the nonmeasurable, is not necessarily the unreal. Frenchmen, though not precisely romanticists by temperament and outlook, usually do not need such reminders of the inadequacy of the methods of quantification.

Of course a lot of nonsense—nonsense not only when measured against the standards of science, but nonsense by the simpler standards of mere good sense—has been written about the French. The more imaginative devotees of Freud have found evidence in French economic caution, frugality, addiction to small-scale enterprise that the French suffer from arrested development at, or regression to, the anal-erotic stage. Even so clever, experienced, and often sensible a commentator on Europe as Salvador de Madariaga sometimes oversteps the line between insight and fantasy. He holds, for instance, that there is something significantly French in the prevalence of the vowel "e" in their language. He writes, "for *e* is the middle vowel equally distant from the full-blown vowels a, o, u (oo) and from the unrestrained i (ee). . . . The *eu* form [as in *peu*] suggests measure and moderation." Madariaga also finds the

rationalist, simplifying character of the French in their reduction of Latin words to their schematic abbreviated outline, as in
âme from Latin *anima* and *août* from Latin *Augustus.**

Yet Madariaga's book is an interesting and valuable one in
spite of its excesses of insight and a useful example of the
necessarily "literary" approach to the description of the national
character. This literature is enormous, varied, and should be
approached with caution and moderation—French moderation,
perhaps, if that quality really is a part of their national character. You will hardly find a consensus in this literature, and
certainly not if you include the writings of non-Frenchmen
about France. A Henry James, a Matthew Arnold, a Sieburg,
a Curtius, even a Denis Brogan, inevitably tell almost as much
about their own personal and national characters as about that
of the French. The literature is as voluminous as that on the
human geography and look of France, and at its best no doubt
represents a loftier effort of the human mind. It does not, however, provide materials that will satisfy the ardent semanticist
searching for specific referents.

2.   The literature on the French national character, whether
        written by foreigners or by Frenchmen, does display in
the last century and a half or so a coherence that seems to
produce a rough consensus. The main features, the "notes" it
finds in the French national character, can be summarized,
even though in this process the work of subtle and distinguished minds gets reduced to commonplaces, stereotypes. This
reduction, however, may have real value, because it seems
likely that the stereotypes circulating among the masses are in
fact a still further simplification of the stereotypes circulating
among the ruling classes and the intellectual classes.

* Salvador de Madariaga, *Englishmen, Frenchmen, Spaniards* (London: Oxford University Press, 1931), pp. 194–195 ff.

The Frenchman, by common consent, including his own, is a devotee of logic, reason, order, clarity. Salvador de Madariaga who makes his Englishman a man of action and his Spaniard a man of passion, makes his Frenchman a man of thought and summarizes neatly: "The Frenchman is a chess-player. Life is for him a series of manoeuvres and General Staff work."* And the German Ernst Robert Curtius, though he notes that "the idea that the French mind is purely rationalistic" is "an idea which everyone who penetrates into the genuine and deep nature of France at once perceives to be false," nonetheless also insists, quite properly, that the clichés, based on a kind of vulgarized Cartesianism, have firmly established the legend of "that sane human reason which every French peasant possesses."** Hundreds of similar instances could be cited without exhausting the resources of an ordinary American public library. That the French are logical, too logical, is something almost all of us Anglo-Saxons can agree on.

Just what this French "reason"—perhaps it should have a capital, Reason—is and whether it is a good thing or a bad thing for the French and for those affected by what the French say and do are by no means a matter of consensus. Eighteenth-century educated opinion, holding the Enlightenment to be essentially a French product, felt this French devotion to Reason and the French language, that marvelous instrument for logical thought (*ce qui n'est pas clair n'est pas français*), to be a very good thing indeed. The romantics of the early nineteenth century, on the other hand, especially if they were English, German, or American, found French addiction to logical reasoning a limitation, a crippling of the full emotional and imaginative human being. Their favorite epithet of condemnation was "shallow." Coleridge went so far as to maintain

---

* Madariaga, *Englishmen, Frenchmen, Spaniards,* p. 33.
** Ernst Robert Curtius, *The Civilization of France,* trans. from the German (New York: Macmillan, 1962), p. 94.

that, though Englishmen and Germans could have genius, the best the French could do, because of their addiction to mere logical reasoning, was to have talent. The French had no culture-heroes, no giants of literature, no Shakespeare, no Dante, no Cervantes, no Camoens, no Goethe, not even an Emerson.

Because I am here attempting only to summarize a set of generalizations about the French, I will not comment on the validity of these statements. I wish to note, however, that most of these commentators were pretty clear about what they meant by reason and logic. They meant the way the human mind works when confronted with problems that can be solved as the mathematician, the bookkeeper, the engineer solve their problems, by methods close to common sense, methods in no way transcending ordinary human experience of this world. Coleridge once more makes the thing clear. Expounding on the Kantian distinction between *Vernunft*, true Reason sounding the depths and the heights, and *Verstand*, just vulgar understanding of the kind a businessman uses, he pointed out that the French usually could not rise above *Verstand*. Later Englishmen were sometimes kinder in their judgments on this matter, though it is hard to find an Englishman who praises unreservedly anything he regards as French. Matthew Arnold found the French more cultivated, less barbarous, than the English, more aware of the basic decencies or disciplines essential to civilization, but still not very profound, not very imaginative—the French have no Shakespeare.

A second note of French culture, related to or derived from French addiction to reason, is their fondness for classic form, the golden mean, that *mesure* which is so much more than our "measure." The link between the two notes is usually established through French inheritance from the Greeks and the Romans. France, the argument goes, is the true heir of the classical culture of the Mediterranean world, the culture of Aristotle, Praxiteles, Sophocles, Thucydides, and their Latin successors. France incorporates *le génie Latin,* civilized, symmetrical, urbane, disciplined, reasonable, aware of human limitations, full of Roman *pietas* and *decor.* Here is a fitting comment from a foreigner: "Securely self-enclosed stands this monument of Latin France, raised in the course of centuries. It is unmetaphysical, conceived not as a tower of Babel but as the most perfect possible dwelling-place for the most perfect possible people. Reason has built and reason sustains it, teaches it proportion, harmony, clarity and reasonableness. . . . The French spirit is clear, cheerful and free from extremes, like the French climate."*

Against all this and much more of the same, meant to be favorable to France, there stands in the minds of those who write like this an image of the anti-France. Such are Nordic barbarism, Nordic romanticism, obscuring mists, soulful bleatings, Nordic, or better and more specifically, Anglo-Saxon and Teutonic inability to accept human limitations, the disciplined decencies. Yet just as some Americans have seemed tempted by the unAmerican, so some Frenchmen apparently have been tempted by the unFrench. Even such, however, the Mme. de Stael of *On Germany,* the eclectic philosopher Victor Cousin, the late Romain Rolland and other admirers of German culture end up by making France the happy synthesis of North and South, palm and pine, classic and romantic. The belief in the *génie Latin* has been a powerful complex of beliefs, an article of faith buttressing the central faith in *France, mère des arts, des armes et des lois.*

A third note follows at least as logically from the basic assumption of French rationality as classical Latinity. This is French devotion to the small-scale enterprise, to the immediate family, to the small farm, to the tool (as against the machine), that is, to the human, the confinable, the real, the "rational" as

---

* Paul Cohen-Portheim, *The Spirit of France* (New York: E. P. Dutton, 1933), p. 29.

that word was understood before economists and technologists gave it inhuman meaning. Donald McKay, with characteristic American attention to the economic aspect, has put this note of French life clearly: "Caution seeps into almost every corner of French life. It is evident in the market place, where the average businessman is very reluctant to take risks even in the interests of greater profit: he prefers to operate in his cautious and traditional manner for a more modest—and, he believes, a more assured—income. In a world in which the characteristic business is family-owned, the fact that financial operations are closely scrutinized by those immediately interested has contributed further to this attitude of caution. This outlook has tended to inhibit the rapid industrialization of France in an age when she was competing with other countries of more adventurous business spirit."*

With equal clarity and sharpness he puts another phase of this same French caution, the French preference for age and experience over youth and experimentation: "Again, the French have generally distrusted youth and preferred the experience of age for places of responsibility. The bitter German gibe of the thirties ran that France was governed by men of seventy-five because those of eighty were dead. And the French, despite the magnificent triumphs of their countrymen in the field of pure science, have been slow indeed to apply their own findings—and even more those from abroad—in practical fields. It has *not* been in France that the discoveries of Pasteur have made their greatest impact."**

Hardly any other French trait, save perhaps addiction to logic, has been brought forward more often in the past at the level of sophisticated criticism of things French than this one of caution, conservatism, reluctance to venture into the unknown,

* Donald McKay, *The United States and France* (Cambridge, Mass.: Harvard University Press, 1951), p. 39.
** McKay, *The United States and France*, pp. 39–40.

the untried, with its corollary of the rule of the aged. Here is the comment of the German Ernst Robert Curtius: "This element in French civilization also accounts for the fact that in France mature age is preferred to youth. France does not possess, like Hellas or Germany, an ideal picture of youth. It is 'unyouthful,' in the manner of ancient Rome. *'La France méprise la jeunesse,'* writes Jean Cocteau, *'sauf quand elle s'immole pour sauvegarder la vieillesse. Mourir est un acte de vieux. Aussi chez nous la mort seule donne du poids aux jeunes. Un jeune qui rentre de la guerre a vite perdu son prestige. Il redevient suspect.'* Even the language has no special word for youth; it has to do the best it can with the somewhat unsatisfactory expression: *jeune homme.* The word adolescent is often used in a joking sense (*'se dit surtout des garçons, et alors souvent en plaisantant.' Littré*); this comes out still more strongly in the word *jouvenceau.* When Taine wrote his beautiful essay about the youths of Plato he had to use the circumlocution *Les jeunes gens de Platon*—which to us seems to convey a loss of something specific. Thus also there is no word which quite corresponds to the German *mädchen* or the English 'girl.' *Fille,* if it is not more precisely defined, may mean daughter, or unmarried woman, or prostitute. A girl must be described as a *jeune fille.*"*

I come now to the fourth note—the firmest, most real and earthy France of legend, a France her lovers would maintain is no legend, not even a stereotype. This is the France of *douceur de vivre,* of the good life, of Sieburg's *Gott in Frankreich,* a France symbolized by, though not confined to, those two great skills and pleasures, those of the table and those of the bed. Contrary to common American belief, it is not unlikely that, forced to choose, many Frenchmen would put the pleasures of eating and drinking somewhat ahead of the pleasures of *amour,* if only because they are more easily extendable and

* Curtius, *The Civilization of France,* p. 225.

permanent. At least one restaurant in France, where as everywhere advertising is a fairly trustworthy reflection of the national character, has the slogan, "Pleasure in food and drink: the first to arise, the last to fade away."

On this note it is hardly necessary to dwell. There is surely a consensus among all but acute Francophobes, followers of food fads, puritanical lacerators of the flesh, and those with defective taste buds—all told in this world, no doubt, a really alarming number—that French cooking has no rival in the world, except perhaps the Chinese. And because Marxist insistence on the material satisfaction it seeks for all men is, nevertheless pretty puritanical about what it holds are decent satisfactions, Communist China will soon cease to be a rival, if it has not already done so. Note, however, that a large-scale, efficient (that is, rapid and inexpensive) and, just possibly, fully safe, sanitary, and figure-flattering cuisine is completely impossible. It is highly inefficient to have bakers prepare fresh bread for every meal, at a minimum twice a day—still today an almost universal French custom. It is, from the point of view of time, trouble, and money saved, much better to go to a supermarket, buy half a dozen big loaves of sanitarily wrapped bread, put them in the refrigerator—or even in the freezer—to last for a week or so. But no week-old bread can taste like fresh bread: this, in our age of the relative, may stand as an impeccable absolute. So far, the French cuisine has stood up against the temptations of freezers and convenience, though there are Frenchmen who complain that it is showing signs of yielding. There are indeed supermarkets with packaged and even precooked food in France today.

L'amour of course, is a much more complicated business. This French word, acclimated in American, means exclusively in our language, *but not in French,* what Americans otherwise call "sex." In French, it means "love" in all the vast range of meanings that word can have. Whether or not the French make love more often and more skillfully than other peoples is an unanswerable question. It is not even certain that they talk more openly about it than do other peoples, including ourselves. They do indeed write a lot about love and lovemaking; no literature has a more impressive list of brilliant psychological studies of the relations between men and women. Again, there seems to be no way of measuring the degree to which French literature in comparison with other modern literatures is especially concerned with the physical aspects of such relations. At any rate, it is a fair guess that, in this mid-twentieth century, French preoccupation with sex in the mass media is no greater than such preoccupation in our American mass media; and certainly the freedom to print clinical details and to use the frankest terms is today rather less in France than in the United States, not wholly, because, as the Leftist critics of the French regime would like to make out, Madame de Gaulle is a prude.

The concern with love and lovemaking is simply another, and perhaps more striking, example of a "note" of national character raised—or lowered—to a stereotype, one that Frenchmen themselves often feel a kind of compulsion to display. Madariaga finds another linguistic evidence of French emphasis on these matters. In the great majority of cases, he notes, the Latin ending "or" becomes in French "eur," with that pursed, somewhat reluctant vowel sound "eu": *honor* becomes *honneur*, *furor*, *fureur*. But love, *amor*, immoderate, powerful, unconfined, produces the full-blown, emphatic sound of "oo": *amour*.* Just as there are Scots who so cherish their national reputation for parsimony and thrift that they bring it forward conspicuously in words and occasionally in deeds even though as individual Scots they are by nature extravagant, so there are Frenchmen of chaste behavior and no very obvious sexual drive who nonetheless feel that in company they have to come forward with an off-color story, a witty display of Gallic saltiness.

* Madariaga, *Englishmen, Frenchmen, Spaniards*, p. 195.

At just this point another endowment of which the French are proud, *esprit,* comes to join with their concern for *amour* to produce the witty twist of the improper which they call *l'esprit gaulois.* The untranslatable *esprit* comes closest here to the English "wit," but the French word has complex overtones of intelligence and good judgment; the dictionaries and the admirable idealistic periodical, *Esprit,* to the contrary notwithstanding, the French word in most uses has lost almost all its older Latin senses of soul, spirit, *Geist.* The aphorism in, for instance, the work of La Rochefoucauld, is a genre in which the French are very good indeed. A good aphorism embodies in its *esprit* precisely this mixture of epigrammatic wit, detachment (which often looks to the pure in heart like cynicism), realistic concern with the facts of life, lively and unsparing intelligence.

In the distress of our best friends we always find something that does not displease us.

We should not be offended that other people conceal the truth from us, seeing how often we conceal it from ourselves.

The more one loves one's mistress the closer one is to hating her.*

There is something in this kind of aphorism that jars the Anglo-Saxon, unless indeed he is an out-and-out Francophile. Many Frenchmen too are jarred by such aphorisms. This is one of those difficult and unfortunately common junctures when the stereotype will no longer serve, where one has to try to go further into the way things really are. Perhaps another of La Rochefoucauld's maxims will provide a start: "We cannot look squarely at death or the sun" (no. 26). This should seem cynical only to the most complete sentimentalist or the most determined true believer. It is not even witty. For the most part, and no doubt fortunately, human beings do not look squarely at death, or the sun, or themselves—or at France or

* François La Rochefoucauld, *Maxims,* trans. Louis Kronenberger (New York: Random House, 1959), nos. 533, 516, 111.

the United States. Most never really look at all, at least not as the artist and the scientist look. Yet there is space between those two aphoristic poles, the folk wisdom of "seeing is believing" and the no doubt intellectually snobbish "believing is seeing." The whole body of French literature surely has more writing that comes closer to the pole of realism than to the pole of fantasy and illusion. La Rochefoucauld seems more French than Bernardin de St. Pierre. And because some of the uncommon always rubs off on or sinks into the common, the ordinary Frenchman has at least his moments of appreciation for the "reality-principle."

Yet Bernardin de St. Pierre was French. So were many other, different illusionists and faith healers. Cagliostro, Mesmer, and other charlatans of the soul were welcomed in the midst of the French Enlightenment by the very enlightened, like La Fayette. The almost forgotten Emile Coué was one of the most successful faith healers of our own century, which has abounded in them. And if the opposite of realism is taken to be not philosophical idealism, but sentimentalism, there is so much French sentimentality that one is tempted to deny the stereotype of devotion to realism. Greuze, Diderot of the *comédie larmoyante,* Dumas *fils* (and *père,* too, in a different way), Murger, the composers who put much of this into music—Massenet, Charpentier, and the like—the list is long. The French are particularly touched by the spectacle of the wronged in love, the innocent perpetrator of the crime of passion, the victim of *Vénus tout entière à sa proie attachée.* This theme in the hands of Racine becomes indeed the highest art, the profoundest psychology. There are, however, extremely few Racines, even in France. The theme can and easily does become as tawdry as the theme of *ridi, Pagliacci.* Yet even "laugh, clown, laugh" can in French be given a characteristic witty variant, almost but not quite stripped of sentimentality. Figaro remarks that **"je me presse de rire de tout, de peur**

d'être obligé d'en pleurer"—I hasten to laugh at everything for
fear of having to weep over it.

Still traceable in a lineage of ideas descended from the prime
note of intellectuality, devotion to *la raison raisonnante,* there
comes another note familiar in all writing about France—a
discordant one in this harmony. The French—Walter Bagehot
puts it clearly—are too intellectual, too bright, too addicted to
searching for logical explanations—to be capable of political
stability. They lack that good English stupidity which brought
Victorian England to the top. This reputation for political
instability and its attendant train of doubts about the reliability
and usefulness of France as an ally is in some ways the most
important of all our stereotypes for the history, particularly the
recent history, of official American governmental relations with
France. Later I shall attempt to judge how far French reality
corresponds with French reputation in this matter. For the
present it is enough to note that such is their reputation, at least
among de Gaulle's "Anglo-Saxons."

The reputation rests, to be sure, on an array of facts that
can be put in nice statistical order. Since 1789, (not counting a
few transitory ones like the Hundred Days of Napoleon's return
from Elba in 1815) France has had at least thirteen regimes:
constitutional monarchy of 1789, republic of 1792, republic of
the Directory, republic of the Consulate, republic of the
Empire (it was *formally* a republic "entrusted to an emperor"),
Bourbon Restoration, bourgeois monarchy of Louis Philippe,
Second Republic, Second Empire, Third Republic, the Vichy
state of Pétain, the Fourth Republic, the Fifth Republic. A
favorite statistical reproach of instability is the life span of
ministries under various regimes. Those of the Third and
Fourth Republics, the most conspicuously unstable of all, aver-
aged less than a year, with a record of three years for the
longest-lived. Back of all this is the French system of splinter
parties, five or six major ones, up to a dozen or more counting

all the groups organized as such, plus, of course, the notorious fact that by no means every deputy would feel that fine Anglo-Saxon compulsion called party loyalty, certainly not if tempted by the offer of a ministry. All governments, save during periods of one-man rule, as under Napoleon I, Napoleon III, and de Gaulle, were coalition governments, difficult, as are all coalitions, to hold together.

The Frenchman, then, is an individualist above all in politics. He is going to think for himself, feel for himself, be himself. But one can be oneself only as measured against others—and against the common thing. The Frenchman is therefore a quarrelsome individual and a poor citizen. Donald McKay puts it this way: "The Frenchman is an individualist. He wants to stand on his own feet. He is psychologically of the stuff from which democrats are made. Intellectually, he holds his own views with great tenacity, and compromises only with real hesitation and suspicion—hence political parties are formed with difficulty (since they necessarily include more than one Frenchman) and, once formed, they almost invariably start on a process of fragmentation."*

Why are the French that way? The answer is made somewhat difficult by the fact that political instability, the multi-party system, frequent changes of government, even of regime, have in the twentieth century been common among peoples not usually supposed to share much of the French national character. Indeed one need go no further than their Nordic neighbors. Germany has had four regimes in the twentieth century, Wilhelmine Empire, Weimar Republic, Nazi "Third Reich," Federal Republic (West Germany), not to speak of a fifth, not wholly German in origin, the present Democratic Republic (East Germany). The Wilhelmine empire, which had something very close to parliamentary government because cabinets depended by no means solely on the Emperor, also

* McKay, *The United States and France*, p. 40.

had the multiparty system. The word *Putsch* is as good German as *coup d'état* is French, though the German word suggests a futility the French does not. One can always argue that the Germans—and the Italians, the Belgians, the Greeks, the Spanish (before Franco), and a good many other peoples of the free world who do not enjoy two-party politics—share whatever elements in the French national character explain French political instability. One can also argue more plausibly from the same set of facts that political instability is not a simple result of a simple national character of any kind.

Certainly this attribution to the French of political instability —political indecency is not too strong a term to describe the feelings of many Anglo-Saxons in this matter—is not a part of the French self-image. Their writers have with fair regularity complained of the lack of national unity in that beleaguered land, but they rarely attribute their political quarrels to any inbred French character, not even to their logicality. Nor are such interested students of things French as the Germans likely to emphasize any profound depths of political ineptitude among their neighbors. Rather it is British and American opinion that sees fit to put the emphasis on French political unreliability.

There are many other notes that have been sounded over France, so many and so varied that, sounded together, they would make an incredible cacophony. There is French considerateness and politeness, forever there, forever denied by outsiders cursed at by taxi drivers, cheated by hotelkeepers, uninvited to the homes of Frenchmen to whom they bear fine letters of introduction. There is French quietness, simple French pleasures, the *pêche à la ligne,* fishpole propped up on the banks of the fishless pond, unperturbed and unexpectant fisherman reclining nearby with his white bread and red wine. There are those un-American characters, the *petits rentiers,* the little bureaucrats, the little businessmen, not really lazy, indeed often bustling, at least always talking, but so unenterprising, so unworthy of that fine French word, entrepreneur, which our economists have been forced to borrow because of the unfortunate pre-emption of its etymological English equivalent, undertaker.

There are always the sheer insults, often spread by men of good will and, as between any two given national groups, usually reversible. The old-fashioned contraceptive device known to the English as a "French safe" was known to the French as a *lettre anglaise.* And here is the high-minded Emerson, repeating though perhaps not wholly vouching for a very old ethnic insult: "They tell you daily in London the story of the Frenchman and Englishman who quarrelled. Both were unwilling to fight, but their companions put them up to it; at last it was agreed that they should fight alone, in the dark, and with pistols: the candles were put out, and the Englishman, to make sure not to hit any body, fired up the chimney,—and brought down the Frenchman."*

The French are devoted to such noble ideas as *droit, justice, humanité, solidarité,* to their own fine motto *Liberté, Egalité, Fraternité;* and yet these same French lack civic spirit and responsibility. There is the Frenchman as soldier, with those qualities of dash and daring which the Italians summed up as *la furia francese.* These qualities of impatient daring and skills have been brought up to explain the extraordinary successes of the French in Alpine skiing of recent years, just as something of the sort was used to explain their domination of world tennis in the 1920's; yet in track they have never had great success in the dashes, but have had in the longer runs that require precisely the patience and staying powers they are supposed to lack, qualities also necessary to their favorite sport, the long-distance bicycle road race. There is the French ability, shown

* R. W. Emerson, *English Traits,* ed. H. M. Jones (The John Harvard Library; Cambridge, Mass.: Harvard University Press, 1966), pp. 96–97.

so often in the last thousand years, to come out of those troughs
of defeat and despair into which they have so often fallen.
There is French ingenuity and ability to extemporize, their
"*système D*" (*débrouillard*, literally, "un-fogging," getting out
of the mist—always this note of clarity).* There is French
nationalism, French love of *la patrie;* there is *la Marseillaise.*
But here, as the final note, more consideration must be given to
the matter of French nationalism.

People, in the West, where the modern nation-state arose,
and nowadays, increasingly, people all over the world, share
what an anti-nationalist English Edwardian essayist, Arthur
Clutton-Brock, called the "pooled self-esteem" of nationalism.
Yet, somehow, perhaps not altogether undeservedly, the French
are held both by foreigners and by themselves to cherish a
particularly intense, emotional, yet disciplined love of country.
They have in Joan of Arc a superb patron saint, doubly sancti-
fied by State and by Church. *La Patrie, elle la crée avant même
que le mot soit inventé* (she created the fatherland even before the word was invented) said Raymond Poincaré of her.
The Revolution and Napoleon finished the job of making
France a nation of patriots, all taught from infancy their duties
and privileges as Frenchmen. The frequent stereotyped comment is true enough; with some shocking exceptions like
Charles Maurras, in whose mind all foreigners and many
French citizens—Jews, Freemasons, radicals, immigrants of all
sorts—were métèques ("half-breeds" gives the right connota-
tion in English), forever incapable of being French—save for
a few such racists, nationalism in France has never been exclusive, never racist. The French have always been willing to
make converts to Frenchness, even of Negroes, Malagasy, and
Indo-Chinese of the old Empire.

There is a naive, touching belief, not wholly dead even today,

---

* *Système D* and *débrouillard* nowadays often have a definitely pejorative sense, *too* clever, "slick."

a product of the eighteenth-century Enlightenment and of French revolutionary expansion, that all men are potential Frenchmen and really want to be Frenchmen. This French belief, however, belonged to a minority of hopeful intellectuals and reached the commoners in no great strength. Or rather, it reached them as a diluted belief in the ultimate emancipation of the human race through the triumph of reason. It was never quite the equivalent of the current innocent American conviction that everyone in the world really wants to be an American because Americans have it best. Still, American and French nationalism have in common this universalist, proselytizing touch, a touch that makes even more real for theirs than for other nationalisms Arnold Toynbee's remark, "nationalism is the real if unavowed religion of the West." The Nazi kingdom of heaven on earth was shut to all but members of the Master Race; less exacting nationalisms, British, Spanish, many others, still maintained a peck order. But not so, at least in theory, for the French. Their Empire would, like the Republic, one day not too far off achieve *Liberté, Egalité, Fraternité* for all humanity.

3. Here then is a portrait of the Frenchman: rationalist, devoted to the golden mean and the *génie Latin,* prudent, conservative, given to the small-scale enterprise, distrustful of and incompetent at large-scale production, avoiding the depths and the mysteries, indeed, without a culture hero like Shakespeare or Dante, with only St. Joan and Napoleon as inadequate, really rather superficial equivalents. This Frenchman is a realist, perhaps even a cynic, a hedonist, yet temperately so except perhaps in eating and lovemaking, capable of one kind of depth, that of sentimentality, politically unstable, hard to govern, apt to resist authority, yet in many ways devoted to *le droit,* an individualist, yet molded by history and

society into a vigorous and cohesive patriotism, polite, yet capable of inconsiderate rudeness and indifference, devoted to humanitarian ideals, but not in practice a good humanitarian.

This synthetic portrait—and synthetic is the right word—could be almost infinitely varied, for the literature on the French national character is enormous and inconsistent. Above all, if one were to focus on folk-beliefs and folk-feelings of Americans about the French, it would be necessary to note even more scornful and contemptuous judgments, along with a few even more complimentary ones. For the present, this not very prophetic passage from Sieburg should suffice. He is speaking of the French *rentiers,* early retired and enjoying unfruitful leisure: "The enterprising genius who tried to awake new demands in these people would simply be wasting his time. They are content to cultivate, satisfy sometimes even to refine, those they have had for centuries, and the result is what we call tradition. . . . The general atmosphere may still be summed up by saying that the Frenchman would rather sit by his own fireside than at the whirring loom of time."*

Since Sieburg wrote even the French *rentier* has deserted his seat by the fireside. He is not so much seated at Goethe's whirring loom of time as busily helping by investment and by working to harness that loom to atomic power, tidal power, even, at Font Romeu in the Pyrenees, to the direct rays of the sun. It looks from here as though France were now in the midst of still another revolution, this time one that involves an extraordinary alteration of many old habits, traditions, and folkways, not merely a political change of regime, nor even a socio-economic change, like that of 1789, which as Tocqueville saw was essentially an extension of the work of the ancien régime.

* Friedrich Sieburg, *Who Are These French?* a translation of his *Wie Gott in Frankreich* (New York: Macmillan, 1938), pp. 110–111.

The revolution that began in the last years of the 1940's and is still going on may well be a more thoroughgoing, almost unprecedented break with the French past. In this chapter I have sought to assemble from that past an admittedly impressionistic and cursory set of views on what history has made of France, on the French national character. Although these views are inevitably incomplete and, more important, stereotyped, they are nonetheless not wholly unreal, untrue—or they were not so when the wise observers here cited wrote them. Some of them are still true and will long be so; others will be transmuted into something quite new.

Stereotypes change, no doubt rather more slowly than does the complex reality they imperfectly but usefully condense into human terms, but they do change. Before Bastille Day it was the French, under an orderly succession of kings all named Louis, who had a reputation for political stability. In the western world of the eighteenth century it was the British, who after all had not long before cut off one king's head and driven another into exile, who had a deserved reputation for political intractability. Two Stuart rebellions, riots over excise taxes, over "Wilkes and Liberty," culminating in the Lord George Gordon anti-Catholic riots of 1780, when London was for three days in the hands of a mob, certainly did nothing to alter that reputation. The nineteenth century changed all that. Nowadays even during a strike, which is the strongest kind of social protest the British will permit themselves, the strikers have been known to play soccer with a team of the police.

One reason for our American difficulties about France would appear to be that we have not yet revised our image of it. We feel vaguely that something is happening in France, perhaps something new. Yet our commentators still treat de Gaulle, for instance, as if he were a reactionary, an old and innocent patriot of the last century. They think de Gaulle's *grandeur* (a word that, in fact, he uses very sparingly in his many public pronouncements) a silly piece of nostalgia for a past, for an Age of Louis XIV or of Napoleon, never to be recovered on this earth. There *is* nostalgia in de Gaulle's *grandeur,* and there is something of the eternal French feeling for *la patrie.* But there is something new, as new as de Gaulle's revolutionary— and unheeded—prewar appeal for a new army, a new tactics, a new strategy based on modern technology.

Here Curtius sums up what I have been seeking to establish about the old France in this chapter.

In literature—French as well as foreign—and in educated public opinion, we find a great number of more or less pregnant conceptions of the essence of the French nature, a formidable series of definitions of the French character, of the French spirit, and of the French, pure and simple. In France itself, writers, critics, psychologists and scholars have tried again and again to create a definition of this kind. Writers and others construct an "ideal Frenchman," or a "normal Frenchman," or a "consistent Frenchman." This Frenchman is just as abstract, just as unreal, as the man who figured so prominently in the philosophy of the eighteenth century. To reduce the French spirit to a definition is a more or less (mostly less) amusing literary pastime; and when it has been done, little has been achieved for real knowledge. Indeed, this theorizing is not merely futile, it can have a very harmful and illusory effect. When it is used as a standard it makes it impossible to gain any spontaneous apprehension of French life. Someone meets a French writer or artist who does not fit into this theory, and at once he draws the conclusion that this person is "un-French"—instead of saying the opposite: "This Frenchman forces me to correct and broaden my conception of the French character."*

Next, however, must come a brief survey, a kind of clinical case history, of relations between the United States and France

---

* Curtius, *Civilization of France,* p. 212. Curtius is one of the wisest and yet most sympathetic writers on what I have above dared to call the "old France." Of course, this France will long endure, quite possibly converting, and certainly modifying, the "new France" that is rising in our time. (See Chapter Five.)

over the last few centuries. These relations, in part diplomatic, are most simply and patently relations between rather limited groups of individuals, rulers, members of the political establishment, professional diplomatists—in short, relations between the "government" of France and the "government" of the United States. But even these relations are not independent of what millions of ordinary private citizens in both countries think and feel about France, the United States, and Franco-American relations. The informal relations among ordinary Frenchmen and Americans are usually vicarious ones of reading of many sorts, watching television, and listening to the radio. They are based at least partially on the stereotypes dealt with in this chapter. Not even the pollster, aided by computers and flossy mathematics, can measure precisely what these relations are, what they mean, how they affect what really happens in international affairs. But they exist, and one is forced to believe that they are important. The stereotypes of national character are the essential coins of cultural interchange, coins often worn smooth, often clipped, adulterated, counterfeit, rarely fresh-minted, but clearly indispensable for the interchange.

Chapter Three

France and the United States:

To the Second World War

1. Relations between Frenchmen and Americans, informal
   for the most part, had been going on for a century or so
before there was a United States capable of formal diplomatic
relations with France. Even the fighting in our various French
and Indian wars was informal. For New Englanders and New
Yorkers the existence of a French menace on their northern
borders was for years a very real thing, more real than any
acute danger from a foreign power was to seem to Americans
until the Russians acquired their own atomic bomb only recently. The menace was compounded by the fact that France
was a Catholic power, in no mere rhetorical sense the hereditary enemy of the overwhelmingly Protestant British colonists.

The alliance with France signed in February 1778 by the
American rebel government meant therefore a break with past
experience. In terms of eighteenth-century international politics—and not only those of the eighteenth century—the French
alliance was perfectly natural. Rebels usually find it useful to
appeal for aid to the most conspicuous and conveniently available government hostile to the government against which they
are rebelling. The Franklins, the Jeffersons, the Adamses, and

the other leaders who made the alliance, many of them good children of the eighteenth-century Enlightenment, were not afraid of France as an agent of popery; some of them, notably Jefferson and even in some ways Adams, admired France as a nation in the forefront of the Enlightenment. The actual alliance had been preceded by almost two years of not so secret aid in arms and ammunition from the French government, operating under cover of such private agents as the dramatist and man of affairs Beaumarchais. The alliance was normal, well prepared for, hoped for, and expected by those who were making the American Revolution.

It was, however, for a great many ordinary Americans an alliance against the grain of history. The rhetoric and myths that culminated in the "Lafayette we are here" of 1917 began at once, but so too did the doubts and difficulties, the dislikes, sometimes the hatreds that have marked Franco-American relations ever since. This was the honeymoon period for both French and Americans, among the articulate many of the governed as among the governors. Underlying Yankee feelings come out in John Adams' verdict from France in 1778: "Luxury, dissipation, and effeminacy are pretty nearly of the same degree of excess here, and in every other part of Europe." Yet Adams goes on to say of France—and this in a letter to his wife and perhaps therefore relatively unposed—that "the great cardinal virtue of temperance, however, I believe flourishes here more than in any other part of Europe" and to make other kindly remarks.*

The basic distrust of France is demonstrated most clearly by the worries among the very highest-placed of American revolutionaries, including Washington himself, about French designs

---

* Quoted in H. M. Jones, *America and French Culture, 1750–1884* (Chapel Hill: University of North Carolina Press, 1927), p. 246. Adams adds a very typical touch. "I have found nothing to disgust me, or in any manner disturb me, in the French nation, any evils here arise altogether from Americans."

in Canada. It is generally accepted that Lafayette was sent
south to Virginia, where he achieved his greatest military successes, rather than north to Canada on a suggested second
attempt to acquire for the new United States the "fourteenth
colony," partly because it was feared that what he and the
French really planned was the recovery of New France. The
fear was wholly natural, and perhaps not wholly unjustified.
Nothing ever came of the suggested invasion of Canada except
a few miles of unfinished road in the Vermont wilderness designed to outflank the British in the Champlain-Richelieu
valley.

Still, the alliance was a success. The United States were
freed, and by 1789 it became possible though not yet necessary
to say that the United States *was* freed. The French got their
partial revenge on Britain, but very little else except a big
increase in their national debt, an increase which threatened
bankruptcy and made inevitable the first step in the great
French Revolution, the calling of the old medieval parliamentary body, the Estates General, for the first time since 1614.
The alliance remained technically in force even after the conclusion of peace with Britain in 1783, but it was not to survive
the decade of the 1790's. A world war broke out in Europe in
1792, destined to last, with only one brief interval of general
peace and under various alignments of powers, until 1815.
France fought as she had ever since Louis XIV on two fronts,
against a European land coalition and against the sea power of
Britain. The wars of the Revolution and Napoleon were in
American eyes essentially Franco-British duels, in which the
sympathies of many, perhaps most, Americans were divided
between the pro-French antifederalists and the pro-British
federalists. Yet what really emerged from the partisan domestic
struggles, particularly acute in the 1790's, was in fact that great
American national policy, then as firmly rooted among the
people as among its leaders: isolationism. In its developed

form, the policy was firmly announced to the world in 1823 as the Monroe Doctrine, which sought to isolate the whole New World from the specific European state-system of international politics. American isolationism was always a strictly political and military doctrine, embodied in the folk-mind in Washington's Farewell Address and summarized in that mind by the famous phrase warning against "entangling alliances." In spite of the often acutely self-conscious nationalism of the times, there was never cultural, economic, or social isolationism.*

The formal alliance with France went under in the bitter partisan struggle between Hamiltonians and Jeffersonians, or to use respectable party names not stained with un-American hints of the cult of personality, between the federalists and the antifederalists. The leaders of the new French Republic, brought up in admiration for and almost complete misunderstanding of the only slightly older American republic, were quite incapable of the kind of diplomacy that might at least have kept the United States benevolently neutral in the war that began in 1792. They assumed that some kind of intrigue had put Washington and the federalists in power, that the American people were wholeheartedly with the French, and that all that was needed was for French diplomacy to encourage the American people to assert through their legislators their sovereign will to help republican France against monarchical Britain, thus continuing the good work begun in 1776. These Frenchmen in power at the time, especially the faction known as the Girondins, seem actually to have been, for Frenchmen, pretty innocent diplomatists; they certainly were inexperienced in international politics. Yet they may not really have believed that nations are capable of such collective emotions as gratitude or sympathy; they may merely have been moved by whatever it is—surely nothing so simple as greed or

---

* With respect to France, this fact comes out very clearly in Jones's admirable monograph *American and French Culture, 1750–1848.*

desire for power—that moves political leaders of expanding powers to keep on expanding.

What really happened is for once clear enough, and so far not very much subject to the zest of historians for historical revisions. The French minister to the United States—we had not yet attained the dignity and wickedness of ambassadorship —"Citizen" Genet, sent out in 1793, was wined and dined, made speeches, was warmly welcomed by the antifederalists and by their press, and in general conducted himself in a way wholly novel for a diplomatist in the aristocratic eighteenth century, though by no means unknown in our own truly democratic age. He actually commissioned American privateers to prey on British commerce. In many speeches and responses to the eternal toasts of those days he appealed openly to the American public to repudiate Washington's administration. He offended powerful business interests, but even more important, he offended the sensitive national awareness of our importance and our weakness. Washington asked for and secured his recall. The Girondins fell from power, and their successors, involved in the manifold crises of the Reign of Terror, had other things to worry about.

Yet the lull was brief, for the central, unavoidable difficulty was one that sooner or later was to bring us into every general European or world war, the fact that we have from the start, even as a nation of two and a half million, been a major trading nation. We have always insisted on freedom of the seas for our commerce; and because that commerce has always been of importance to Britain—by 1917 of life-and-death importance— and therefore in the interest of Britain's enemies to choke off, one or more belligerents are sure to attack that commerce, no matter what international law on the subject may be. In the great world war of 1792–1815 both major belligerents, Britain and France, felt free to attack our ships, the more since this was the period of apogee for that convenient form of semilegitimate piracy known as privateering. In colonial times American privateers often had made a very good thing of the enterprise, which was the foundation of many still important and respectable Yankee family fortunes. Some privateers continued to do well even in the revolutionary and Napoleonic periods. But because both sides also attacked our shipping officially and formally with their own navies, the British often impressing our seamen, our losses were heavy.

John Adams, succeeding to the presidency in 1797, succeeded to the problem of freedom of the seas. His troubles with France were complicated by the fact that to the rulers of the France of the Directory the recently concluded treaty between the United States and Great Britain (Jay's Treaty) seemed to show that the new federal republic was pursuing a pro-British policy. During the resulting negotiations between the United States and France the French Foreign Minister, Talleyrand, and some other insiders attempted to secure bribes from the American commissioners. This "XYZ affair" (from the anonymity of the French demanders) was fully exploited in the United States under the stirring slogan "Millions for defense but not one cent for tribute." An undeclared naval war between the two republics, not on a very large scale, followed directly on this dispute. These sea fights, formally ended by a treaty in 1800 which abrogated the alliance of 1778, were to be the last organized fighting between French and Americans until our Moroccan landings in 1942, but they were by no means the last of the disputes between the two governments.

The Louisiana Purchase of 1803, for the Americans surely one of the most important of all our governmental dealings with France, was for Napoleon himself and for French opinion generally of little importance. In the midst of the great opportunities that faced the *Grande Nation* in Europe, the plans for a renewed New France in North America could be cheerfully discarded. In the long list of diplomatic transactions between the two powers, the Louisiana Purchase is curiously unimportant as a bearer of love or hatred, gratitude or regret. Not so for the other aspects of Franco-American relations during the administrations of Jefferson and Madison. A candid historian must admit that in the prolonged crisis over freedom of the seas during this Napoleonic World War it is a toss-up as to which was morally more shocking, the French or the British violations of international law as Americans understood that law. Both sides attacked and seized or sunk American ships. Both sides erected elaborate and naturally conflicting rules of blockade. Both sides were responsible for deaths of American citizens. The British, however, under the—with them—popular slogan "Once an Englishman always an Englishman," impressed into their service American seamen; as the increasingly stronger naval power Britain simply had more chances to outrage us and to do us greater quantitative damage; and perhaps, because even presidents, secretaries of state, diplomatists, and other experts, as we should now realize, are aware of and even share the emotions of their followers, the fact that the dominant American party in power in those years, the National Republicans, was, if not pro-French, at least definitely anti-British, helped swing the balance. At any rate in 1812 we went to war with the British, separately, by no means allied with France. We came in too late and were too powerless to be of even indirect assistance to the French in their final stands from Leipzig to Waterloo.

In the next great event in our history as a world power, France played a relatively unimportant part, but still a part, in triggering the events that led to the unilateral declaration in international politics known as the Monroe Doctrine. Spain, restored after 1814 to independence by Napoleon's defeat, showed signs of wanting to get back her American colonies, which had taken advantage of the European situation to revolt. Moreover, under the Austrian Metternich, it seemed as though all Europe was making a united effort in the name of Legitimacy to restore everything as it had been in 1789. The Congress of Verona in 1822 gave France, anxious to retrieve a little *gloire* after Waterloo, a mandate to march into Spain, where monarchical legitimacy was menaced by a new revolution. The march was easily successful, and it was widely believed that with French backing the Spanish government was about to make a major military effort to restore its rule in the Americas. Actually the French were by no means anxious to get into more trouble in the New World, especially as territory in North Africa was so much nearer and so much easier to acquire. The Monroe Doctrine was later to be invoked against the French in 1844 in a minor way over the debts of the republic of Texas and after our Civil War in one of the most acute of Franco-American crises, but at the moment of its enunciation it called forth no more than a few French editorial comments on our brashness.

The July Revolution of 1830, though it did not make France a republic and hence was not altogether praiseworthy in American eyes, did put the citizen-king Louis Philippe on a constitutional throne, not as king of France, but as king of the French. On the whole we thought this a step forward, and it looked as though our relations with France would once more be relatively friendly. But the thirties were to witness one of the most acerbic of our quarrels, a quarrel not softened on our side by the participation of two distinguished and undiplomatic personalities, Andrew Jackson as chief executive and James Fenimore Cooper as a major journalist. But the tone of even the Whig journals was firm, and that of many of the Democratic ones sometimes insulting. The *Democratic Review* in 1837 announced that "we consider the appearance of Louis Philippe as a mere interlude in the history of France, resembling some of Shakespeare's clowns, introduced to relieve the gravity of the drama; a mere pause in the Revolution."*

* Quoted in E. B. White, *American Opinion of France: From Lafayette to Poincare* (New York: Knopf, 1927), p. 109.

The cause of this outpouring of rhetoric was the dispute, then a quarter of a century old, over indemnities claimed by Americans for damages suffered from the French during the long world war ended in 1815. The new regime in France agreed by formal treaty to pay five million dollars in satisfaction of spoliation claims. But France now had, it seemed, separation of powers. The Chamber of Deputies simply refused to appropriate money to carry out the Crown's treaty. Americans, who should at least have understood French difficulties with the separation of executive and legislative powers, grew indignant, and the French replied with more indignation. Yet neither side wanted war over what the Richmond *Whig* called "so silly a cause," and both were content to accept British mediation. The French paid up, but the spilled rhetoric remained.

The Revolution of 1848 in France was naturally welcomed in this country, and the accession of Napoleon III as naturally condemned. The alliance in the Crimean War and later of the two great European overseas powers, Great Britain and France, seemed to some Americans another threat to the Monroe Doctrine, the more serious because an important element in the Democratic party with eyes on Cuba, Santo Domingo, and other Caribbean Islands feared another unilateral declaration, this time by Britain and France, against American expansion in our own hemisphere. But at the level of formal diplomacy nothing serious arose until, taking advantage of our Civil War and making use of the customary claim on foreign debts unpaid, Napoleon III sent French troops to Mexico. The trouble began with a joint occupation of Vera Cruz in 1861 by Britain, France, and Spain, strictly to insure collection of debts. When it became evident that the French were planning to use their army to set up what we should now call a satellite state in Mexico under an Austrian prince, Maximilian, as Emperor, Britain and Spain withdrew. French troops got to Mexico City just before Gettysburg, and Maximilian was declared Emperor.

But there was vigorous Mexican resistance, and after Appomattox the United States government formally went to work to enforce the Monroe Doctrine by diplomatic means. Napoleon, faced with new troubles in Europe, withdrew his troops from Mexico in March 1867. Maximilian, without French support, capitulated to the Mexicans under Juarez and was executed in June of the same year.

The very existence of a monarchy on our borders was in the 1860's at least as shocking to American opinion as the existence of a Communist Cuba a century later. An occasional voice in the North (and more in the South during the actual fighting of the Civil War) was raised in favor of letting Maximilian establish himself if that were possible. But for the most part Americans even in the South were at least unsympathetic to his cause, and once the war was over, government and people were solidly against so un-American an institution as an Empire of Mexico. Our quarrel with France was indeed settled, without even an ultimatum, let alone a formal break in diplomatic relations. In the final two years of complicated negotiations we displayed the kind of firmness and patience in diplomacy with which we are not usually credited. The whole affair, however, was once more a serious traumatic break in the formal relations between the two countries, one that may—such transmissions are not really understood—have had a cumulative effect still at work.

Yet from 1867 at least until the 1920's there were in the mutual dealings of the two governments no major crises or ensuing bitterness of the kind that arose in the XYZ affair, the Napoleonic Wars and the consequent spoliation claims, and Napoleon III's intervention in Mexico. The Third Republic was not precisely our kind of republic, but it was at least no wicked monarchy. The rapid growth of the new French Empire overseas was chiefly in Africa and Southeast Asia and, in the late nineteenth and early twentieth century, did not seem to

concern us greatly. There were some minor points of irritation.
We ourselves in those days, though many Americans nowadays
seem unaware of the fact, had imperial ambitions. The French,
established in Tahiti by the 1840's, had to be warned off the
Hawaiian Islands. In Africa, the Negro republic of Liberia,
founded under private American auspices as a refuge for freed
slaves, lay between the French Ivory Coast and British Sierra
Leone. In the partition of Africa, both France and Britain took
advantage of the uncertain frontiers of Liberia to seize land,
and it was rumored that France was planning to establish a
protectorate there. We ourselves could not under our traditional policy establish a formal protectorate, but we could and
did announce "the moral right and duty of the United States
to assist in all proper ways in the maintenance of its [Liberia's]
integrity."* The United States in the administrations of Roosevelt and Taft could and did go further. We sent a commission
to Liberia which recommended what to most Europeans—and
to many Americans—looked like at least the establishment of
an American "sphere of influence" there. Americans assumed
Liberian debts, reorganized the Liberian army, and insured
that on the map of Africa Liberia should be colored with
neither the red that custom dictated for lands of the British
Empire nor one of the varied shades of blue or purple usually
employed for those of the French Empire.

The long preliminary discussions that culminated in Lesseps'
attempt to build a Panama canal stirred up some American
opposition and some firm statements from American political
figures that the United States would have to control any canal
built to join the Atlantic and Pacific. But the Panama Canal
Company was after all a private enterprise, Lesseps worked
hard and successfully to win over important American business
interests, and the American press for the most part refused to

* Cleveland in his annual message to Congress for 1886, quoted in
White, *American Opinion of France*, p. 215.

get excited over the plan. From the first, Americans were skeptical of the chances that the plan would succeed, and its failure amid serious financial scandals in the French government aroused only mild expressions of satisfaction here. In terms of diplomatic relations, neither the French failure nor the eventual American success in building the canal was accompanied by anything like a crisis.

Nor did our final participation in the world war that began in 1914 bring any great immediate troubles. The detailed history of those years will of course show many minor sources of trouble, but on the whole our activity as the not yet so christened "arsenal of democracy," in both financing and actual delivery of munitions and food to the Allies, went as smoothly as such things go in this world. Our actual military participation, if only because our forces fully engaged were relatively small, led to no such strategic and tactical difficulties as those we encountered in the world war of 1939–1945. Pershing simply was in no position to challenge Foch on the broadest questions of policy.

The end of the war, however, brought a continued series of crises in Franco-American relations. Indeed since 1919 we have never really had good formal relations with French governments, certainly not as good as those with, say, Britain, but not even as good as with the Germany of the Weimar Republic, the present West German Federal Republic, or Japan since 1946. There has been, save for the anomalous situation in North Africa in 1942, no actual fighting between Americans and French, but there has been a series of nagging difficulties, much mutual distrust, and, to put it mildly, a steady drifting apart.

Early in 1919, after the brief euphoria of Wilson's reception in France, the disagreements and mutual misunderstandings began to pile up. New historians, Marxist or simply sociologically disposed and inclined to minimize the importance of individuals, should be reminded that some of the trouble can be laid to the clashing personalities of Wilson and Clemenceau, just as, a generation later, some, in fact much, of the trouble can be laid to the equally clashing personalities of Roosevelt and de Gaulle. Keynes, Nicolson, and others have brilliantly, perhaps too brilliantly, analyzed the American Presbyterian Messiah, Wilson, never quite reconciled to his crucifixion, and the French veteran of years of parliamentary infighting, Clemenceau, a skeptic about the possibility of improving the behavior of human beings, even including Frenchmen, but a firm and passionate believer in salvation for an immanent and transcendental France. Still, it is very doubtful that anyone could have solved to the satisfaction of both French and American governments the problems not so solved at Versailles. The United States was in no state of mind to assume responsibilities in Europe. France was in no state of mind to put the trust in her ally Britain and her old enemy Germany that would have been necessary to organize Europe with the minimum of success achieved a hundred years earlier at Vienna or even, *for Western Europe,* thirty years later with the Marshall Plan and its sequels.

A brief catalog of the mutual griefs of the two powers will suffice. Both suffered from the loss of illusions at the peace conference: the French had expected from us an alliance and a guarantee of protection from Germany; we, or at any rate Wilson, had expected from France willing collaboration in a League of Nations and a democratic world made not merely safe but happy. Because American expectations were perhaps even more unreasonable than those of the French, our disillusion was no doubt even deeper than theirs. The impossible reparations demanded of Germany and the linked Allied war debts to the United States, although their importance to the economies of Western lands in the 1920's has been exaggerated, had, when translated by journalists and politicians into the terms of deeper human emotions, an importance that can hardly be

exaggerated. Still, things might have gone better. The prosperity of the Coolidge era was general to the West; Locarno,
the continued scaling-down of reparations, and many other
adjustments, even with Communist Russia, in the 1920's held
promise of a return to something like the comparative serenity
of the nineteenth century. The Great Depression brought a
renewal of difficulties. French repudiation of their war debt
to us is still racked up against them in Congress today. In the
gradual rise of what became the Axis of Germany, Italy, and
Japan, in the conflict of totalitarian and democratic societies,
in France the threat of a civil conflict, in all the troubles of that
Time of Troubles, the 1930's, the United States nursed, but not
in silence, her own economic wounds. Our government under
Roosevelt was of course on the side of democracy and against
totalitarianism—but not vigorously so, notably not at first with
regard to Franco and Mussolini. At any rate, if we did not
appease, we did nothing except talk, or as our French critics
liked to say, preach. And, given the normal conservatism of our
professional diplomatists and the strength of conservatism in
our mass media, we were not very helpful to Blum and the
Popular Front in France in their last-minute effort to stand up
against the Axis on all fronts.

The coming of war did not surprise our government, nor the
American public. Pro-German feelings, strong in 1914, were
almost nonexistent in the United States in 1939. We were
already prepared to become the "arsenal of democracy." But
we were not prepared for the fall of France. That event
shocked us and set the stage for a new set of attitudes and
relations between the two countries, still essentially at work in
American and French minds today.

2.   Relations between those who rule in the United States
and those who rule in France are but part of the necessary
background of present difficulties between the two countries.
Also important are the relationships between "public opinion"

in two old modern democracies and the specific foreign policies of the two governments. These are difficult problems to answer, and ones that the social sciences have by no means solved. It is no doubt true that in such democracies the government can not only lead but to a degree mold, public opinion. It is also true that in the great serious matters of religion, morals, broad political attitudes, and the like, what is here loosely but firmly called public opinion usually changes, unlike mere fashions, with almost glacial slowness. Yet finally, it is also true that under conditions by no means well understood major policies, and public opinion about them, can even in a modern democracy change with startling speed. Less than a decade after the Japanese were dirty yellow bastards they have become in American opinion admirable if somewhat puzzling allies, almost as good as we are at our proper business, which, as Calvin Coolidge is supposed to have said, is business.

At any rate, it is inconceivable that "public opinion" in these matters should be either a wholly independent variable, or a variable wholly dependent on whatever a given government desires. An American opinion generally favorable to things French, a French opinion generally favorable to things American, would surely have some ameliorating effect on our formal governmental relations, especially at the present critical juncture in our affairs. No such condition exists today, and indeed has not often existed, in spite of all the toasts to Franco-American friendship from Lafayette to . . . well, someone must drink them even today on those twin holy days, the Fourth and the Fourteenth of July.

Of course public opinion is never a monolith, never unanimous. Although no really exact, statistically based model can be constructed in order to understand how Americans feel about France and Frenchness and, conversely, how the French feel about us, one can risk the figure of speech of a spectrum from the ultraviolet of American Francophilia to the infrared of American Francophobia and conversely for the French. Yet the colors involved are not political colors, especially not the red, and the center of the spectrum is big out of all proportion. Perhaps the conventional distribution curve used for the distribution of grades in a student population would be better. Moreover, the strength, numerical and emotional, of groups with specific attitudes toward France or the United States has varied considerably over the years.

There has certainly been for nearly two centuries in this country a hard core of lovers of France. The lovers of a foreign land and culture in any modern society are always a minority, never recruited to any great extent from the masses, strongest among intellectuals and artists, *rentiers* and country gentlemen, but not unrepresented among the merely wealthy and successful businessmen and managers. Politicians and government officials are usually trained to master their affection, if any, for foreigners, but such affection exists not infrequently among them. American Francophiles have probably never been so numerous or so influential among our ruling classes as American Anglophiles. The tweed-clad outnumber the winetasters; the English-speaking Union is stronger than the *Alliance Française*. Both sets of xenophiles have often had to put up with some patronizing, and even rebuffs, from the objects of their affections. But like all true lovers, they keep their affections undiminished. American lovers of France have traditionally found in the France they loved quailties simplified as stereotypes in the previous chapter—*mesure, clarté, esprit,* unembittered realism about human nature, fondness for good food and wines, good conversation, good lovemaking. Writers and artists, long loving, strong, and numerous among American Francophiles, have fallen off greatly from their peak in the 1920's. Paris seems to many of them no longer a refuge from American or any other vulgarity and has given way to Rome, in its turn nowadays yielding to the horrid pressures of our

Western mass culture, leaving them at the moment nowhere really satisfactory to go to. There are still American lovers of France, even among artists and intellectuals, but they are clearly less numerous today than in the past.

If ideas had logical consequences in human heads—and other parts of our anatomy—the fact that politically and to a degree intellectually we and the French are the eldest heirs of the eighteenth-century Enlightenment, that even in behavior we translate into action more of the "principles of 1776 and 1789" then do British or Germans, would lead to more mutual sympathy. There is of course some reality behind those toasts to Franco-American friendship on the ground of our common pioneering in the cause of democracy. Another group of Americans, although their feelings are less intense and whole-hearted than those of Francophiles motivated largely by social or artistic aims, although they do not really earn the suffix -phile, is the so-called non-Communist Left, secularists, free-thinkers, who find much of French culture good and who over the decades have at least been mildly pro-French. Such American "liberals" are troubled, however, by French lapses from Enlightened grace, by both Napoleons, by de Gaulle, by the long existence of French royalism and French clericalism; they are shocked by French failure to establish a nice Anglo-Saxon two-party system; finally, as good democrats, they are not to the same degree as the true Francophiles in revolt against vulgar American opinion of the French, which has long been generally unfavorable, especially as regards French morals and French politics. This last factor blinds many such American liberal democrats, unless they have somehow got to know France well, from recognizing the importance, indeed the existence, in modern French life of ethical aims and moral behavior much like their own.

Francophobia, at least in its extreme form, has, on the other hand, never been in this country anything like as strong as

Anglophobia. Obviously France since the final loss of Canada in 1763 has never been a serious direct menace to us. There was no hangover of hatreds such as followed the ejection of our British rulers. No ethnic group of importance in this country added to such native Francophobia as did exist in the way the Irish, and later the Germans, added to our native Anglophobia. At times of crisis in Franco-American diplomatic relations in the 1790's and 1830's orators and journalists sometimes used the violent language of a true phobia, but on the whole American feelings toward France have been dislikes rather than hatreds and melt into the general set of attitudes of Americans toward France and things French.

There is such a set of attitudes, as there is an "American" set of attitudes toward Progress, Science, Education, Beauty, or any other concern of men. These attitudes toward France, held by millions, are more subject to fashion, more at the mercy of specific circumstances, less intensely and firmly held than those here noted as forms of philia or phobia. But they exist as realities for all but the most determined nominalist or reductionist; they have a kind of consistency in spite of variations in time and place, and they are, one must believe, important in actual international politics.

First of all, there is a basic ambivalence in the attitude of most Americans toward France. In many fields, French prestige is high. In spite of sustained, well-financed, and by no means unsuccessful efforts to promote American *haute couture,* in spite of recent denigrations of Paris as a center of creative art, in spite of the widespread reaction of some American intellectuals against French culture, ordinary Americans continue to set a snob value, which is also a money value, on French clothes for women, on French paintings, on French wines and cheeses, and on much else of French origin. A surprising number of the specific details in Howard Mumford Jones's *America and French Culture, 1750–1848,* published in 1927, still seem current. Even such favorable judgments, however, contain a touch of ambivalence. French achievements are seen as not really very masculine, not really achievements in fields that count in this world, for example, heavy industry, war, and sport. I have already briefly noted that there is a similar ambivalence in American recognition of the way in which the French have been and are democrats—wavering ones, not really decent ones.

The attitudes unfavorable to France tip the balance quite firmly against that country in American opinion—stereotyped, uncritical, ignorant, perverse if you wish to put it that way, but still there, still important. An attitude most central and most long-lived has certainly survived among many Americans, not merely among Radical Right circles, however dead it may be among liberal intellectuals. At the time of the Franco-Prussian War in 1870, James Russell Lowell wrote to Charles Eliot Norton: "If the Prussians don't win, then the laws of the great game have changed, for a moral enthusiasm always makes battalions heavier than a courage that rises like an exhalation from heated blood. Moreover, as against the Gaul, I believe in the Teuton. And just now I wish to believe in him, for he represents civilization. Anything that knocks the nonsense out of Johnny Crapaud will be a blessing to the world."* Now this will sound out of date indeed to many readers, and it is true that in the form of the antithesis Gaul–Teuton the sentiment would not now be put in quite the same way. We might even agree among ourselves that the melting pot has really melted, that only the John Birchers, American Nazis, and such like members of a lunatic fringe still hold to any version of Nordic superiority. Yet the new amalgam still carries over by a kind of transference the old contempt for lesser breeds without the law, the old sense of superiority exhibited by the shocking and only partly humorous British "niggers begin at Calais." Amer-

* Quoted in White, *American Opinion of France*, p. 178.

icans *not* of White Anglo-Saxon Protestant background (understand also Germans, Scandinavians, Scots) are still perfectly capable of holding that the French are somehow of inferior human stock.

It is true that such assertions are controversial, and an attribution of racism as a causal factor in American unfavorable estimate of France today may be wrong-headed. Even more risky, especially in the contemporary mood of positivist if not reductionist social science, is the assertion that somehow we have inherited the English smug contempt for the French that goes back at least to Crécy and Poitiers and gets well expressed in the ethnophaulism—which we certainly have inherited—"frogs." But without postulating a Jungian "collective unconscious," so scandalously unreal to a social scientist, it may be asserted that there *is* a cultural inheritance, that ideas do breed, if not precisely through chromosomes, and that WASPS have for a very long time set the tone of American attitudes toward the world. And White Anglo-Saxon Protestants have hated, sometimes feared, and always looked down upon the French, even indeed before there were Protestants by that name and before there were any nonwhites in their experience. But if both these factors in American attitudes toward France are rejected as vague and unreal, two others at least seem hardly to be contested.

There is first the reputation, already noted, that the French have for political instability, unreliability, for a kind of political indecency. The frequent cabinet changes during the Third and Fourth Republics were a scandal to almost all American publicists, few of whom ever mentioned the continuity and stability of the French Civil Service. When, as under the Second Empire and the Fifth Republic, there was governmental stability at the top as well as just under the top, American publicists were equally scandalized by French addiction to extremes of authoritarian rule: the French just did not have the ability to compromise necessary for a proper democracy. In the old racist days of the first Roosevelt the reason for this weakness was often given as the Latin (sometimes the Celtic) basis of the French stock. Nowadays the tendency is to take up Bagehot's theme: the French think and talk logic too much, take "ideas" in politics too seriously, repeat in effect the dogmatic and unrealistic outburst of Robespierre in 1793 against the argument that the slaves in the French West Indies were not ready for full democratic freedom: "Let the colonies perish rather than a principle."

A second reproach against the French is moral rather than political: they just do not measure up to our best American standards of behavior. A central theme here—the Freudian might regard this fact as revealing with regard to Americans as with the French—is French obsession with sex, in literature and in life, their Folies Bergères and furtive sellers of pornography, their bedroom farces, and much else. But, though Americans making this judgment of the French seem to hold the un-Christian view that indulgence in sexual pleasure outside the marriage bond is the greatest of the sins, they discern other if less serious moral failings among the French, for example, addiction to boasting, dishonesty in commercial dealings (especially in dealings with American tourists), susceptibility to bribery, and general untrustworthiness, symbolized in Lowell's insulting "Johnny the Toad."

All these are the kind of generalizations no sensible person would accept. Certainly American Francophiles do not share any such attitudes. Nor, one hopes, would responsible persons in government, business, science, literature, and art who have dealings with the French. The avant garde and perhaps even the main body of creative intellectuals and artists in this country at the moment no longer hold France, as they used to only a generation ago, to be their second, perhaps their first, *patrie*. But these intellectuals do not make the censorious moral judgments about the French that the mythical average American—though he is hardly more mythical than that still real person, George Babbitt—makes. The Frenchman thus seen by ordinary Americans may be a man of straw; but, if so, he is a big sturdy fellow, alive in his own way.

3. The ethical principles of objectivity, detachment, fairness toward the other, the outsider, are difficult indeed to achieve in our world, where the nation-state is the culminating center for the emotions the anthropologist sums up in his term "in-group." In this respect, it is hard to disagree with the thesis of Reinhold Niebuhr, well expressed in the title of his book, *Moral Man and Immoral Society*. Americans who reproach the French with sexual immorality, especially in these days, clearly take to heart neither the Christian "He that is without sin among you, let him cast the first stone" nor its rationalist Enlightened equivalent,

> O wad some Pow'r the giftie gie us
> To see oursels as others see us!

But, the French are equally unfair when they reproach Americans with crass materialism, commercial dishonesty, hypocritical idealism, contempt for the beautiful and the good, all sorts of vulgarities. There are Americanophiles among the French, though they have never been numerous in our time. In the eighteenth century it was a French fashion to admire America and Americans as something nearer to what Nature intended than anything that could grow up in the Old World. Franklin, the rage of Parisian salons during his stay in France, was erroneously held to be a child of Nature instead of what he was, a very well self-taught child of the European Age of Reason. This attitude did not survive far into the nineteenth century and among French intellectuals has long since disappeared completely. Those who really like and admire us tend to come from among the more enterprising businessmen, from engineers, scientists, and the like, who admire in us precisely our material achievements, our pragmatic attitudes, our energies, our optimism, so disliked by the intellectuals. But lovers cannot be catalogued by class or vocation. You can find Frenchmen even among politicians, journalists, scholars, and other intellectuals who can be said at least to like us and to admire some things American. And, just as with American toasts to the memory of Lafayette and Washington, to the closeness in no mere calendar sense of Independence Day and Bastille Day, to all the rest of the official apparatus of that friendship which has been said to rest on so much mutual misunderstanding, it should be noted that for the French all this is not just pretense, that such traditional sentiments remain as a kind of backlog to our relations that we do not have even in our relations with Great Britain.

As for French Americanophobes, they are certainly verbally strong and relatively numerous, surely a majority today among those who write, teach, devote themselves to scholarship, music, or the fine arts, in short, to use a Russian word said to be necessarily obsolete in its Marxist homeland, the intelligentsia. With these as with less gifted human beings, fashions if not clichés rule, and fashion is now on the side of Communism and against us, at least among writers, artists, and musicians. What a Sartre, a Simone de Beauvoir, a Genet think about us is not, as a matter of fact, very different from what many of our own alienated intellectuals think about the ways of the rest of us. It is true that few American writers quite dare to exhibit as much ignorance about ourselves as do these French. Not even a Nelson Algren or his like could have written as Sartre wrote in his *The Respectful Whore,* a play in which the racial problem in the American South is certainly not treated with French *mesure* or French realism. But there is no need to attempt a catalog of what French intellectuals object to in us. A good and almost too typical sample should suffice: "This country [the United States], once so passionate about individualism and still scornfully calling the Chinese 'a nation of ants,' had itself become a nation of sheep; repressing originality, both in itself and in others, rejecting criticism, measuring value by success, it left open no road to freedom except that of anarchic revolt; this explains the corruption of its youth, their refuge in drug-taking and their imbecile outbreaks of violence. Of course, there were still men in America who were using their eyes to see with. . . . There were a few literary magazines, a few almost secret political newsletters that still dared oppose public opinion. But most of the left-wing newspapers had disappeared. *The Nation* and *New Republic* preserved only the narrowest margin of intellectual independence. The *New Yorker* had become as much a part of the Establishment as *Partisan Review*."*

Ordinary, average, typical French attitudes among *le peuple* toward the United States have generally been, and still are, more favorable than the corresponding American attitudes toward France. They are not without some ambivalence. M. Dupont, the French Mr. Smith, has not in our century thought of Americans as simple children of Nature, or even as frontiersmen fighting Red Indians and shooting buffalo in Buffalo. The recent vogue of Westerns in French television, done *à la française* with French actors, is accepted by the audience as make-believe, much as with us and our own Westerns. It is true that in the French versions the Indians are the good guys who come out temporarily at least on top of their white aggressors, but this should surprise no one. The older belief in Americans as somehow simple, unsophisticated, at bottom kindly, survives hostile propaganda. Frenchmen who

* Simone de Beauvoir, *Force of Circumstance* (New York: Putnam's, 1965), pp. 372–373.

have dealt in two wars with doughboys and G.I.'s are likely to carry as an abiding impression their kindness to children, their obvious desire to be liked and admired. Because in two wars the run of American soldiers also showed that they did not think much of the French (except the children) and thought much better of their German enemies, it is surprising that so much good will toward Americans survives in France. Ordinary Frenchmen are as aware as are their intellectuals of the United States' material achievements, size and strength. Long before Disney, the French image of the United States was that of a huge Disneyland. But what the intellectuals disliked the others tended to like, sometimes to like very much—and want for themselves.

There are unfavorable aspects in this common French attitude toward Americans. The lack of sophistication that they admire in our fondness for children they held responsible after the First World War for our awkwardness, blunders, and final partial withdrawal from international politics. We lack, they think, the patience and skills necessary for effective diplomacy; now that we are very much in the center of international politics, they still think of us as lacking the necessary old-world skills and patience, though unlike their intellectuals, they do not think of us as crude, wicked aggressors. Hollywood, our other mass media, and their own have combined to make the French see us as addicted to crime and violence, fond of and rich enough to indulge in the grosser pleasures of the flesh, but not very subtle or graceful in such indulgences. Many in conservative circles are as alarmed as many Americans are by the conventional picture of our juvenile delinquency, crime waves, divorce rate, Negro ghettos, alcoholism, and drug addiction, but chiefly because they fear that France is on the same road. Naturally they are not altogether without a certain satisfaction at our plight as they see it.

Yet in broad lines, general French opinion is not unfavorable toward us, while general American opinion is in the balance unfavorable toward the French. In spite of the presence in France during two wars of millions of Americans, in spite of tourist travel and student interchanges, increasing nowadays in both directions, neither people can be said to know and understand the other, and both must get along with the kind of concepts of the other dealt with in this chapter. But such is the common condition of relations between national or ethnic groups. Even in the best of such relations, where travel and communication is easiest, as between the United States and Canada, or England and Ireland, mutual understanding and friendship is sometimes far from easy. Americans and French, though they do not share a common language, have much of importance in common. Their relations are clearly closer, for instance, than those between Americans and Chinese or—though this will no doubt be contested—those between North Americans and Latin Americans. Yet the last few decades have seen a worsening of Franco-American relations, not merely between the governments of the two countries, but between the two peoples. In these decades the two peoples have come to be more alike in many ways of living—"modernization" will do as a summary term for these ways—but their stance in international relations has continued to differ more and more widely.

Chapter Four

France and the United States:

The Second World War

and Its Aftermath

1. When the Second World War—or if you are a punctilious historian, the Fifth or Sixth World War—broke out in 1939 there were almost no Americans siding with the Germans and very few echoes of the old isolationist position, "let them all stew in their own juice." The American press and American opinion generally was not only favorable to the Franco-British side, but quite confident that in spite of the scandalous Molotov-Ribbentrop agreement removing Communist Russia from the list of his enemies, Hitler would be beaten without a war as prolonged and as bloody as the last one had been. The fall of France in June 1940 came then as a shock to Americans in the government and in the street, and it proved to be the beginning of the grave deterioration of Franco-American relations in our time.

Save for the small minority of true Francophiles, there was little sympathy, and much blame, for France in this country. The blame often no doubt hid disappointment and sorrow, but it was the blame that stood out. France had reaped the whirlwind, having in fact sown something rather less substantial than the wind. Her political squabbles, her economic backwardness, her inept military preparations, concealed in part by the prestige of her past and by her own pretentious claims, had led to a defeat perhaps to be regretted but certainly not inexplicable, not undeserved. It was now clear that France had not for a generation at least actually been a great power. She could now be counted out, no longer one of a Big Three, or Big Four, or Big Anything. Not all American opinion was quite so severe as this, but substantially such was its upshot. At best, France, once a first-class power, was now a second-class or even "small" power. The armistice with Germany, the occupation of more than half of France, and the founding of the Vichy state in the poorer half confirmed this diagnosis. France was out of the war for the duration and could at best look forward to liberation by foreign power in a distant future. The successful stand of the British in 1940–1941 cheered Americans, who were increasingly hostile to the Axis powers, but the British effort was very commonly held up as an example of national strength and courage that made French lack of national will to fight and all-around degeneration all the more obvious.

With this background, the call to arms by General de Gaulle in London and the small beginnings of the French resistance movement in the Free French (later the Fighting French) made little impression in the United States. De Gaulle was not known at all in this country—he was indeed barely a general at all, a very recent brigadier—and his claim to represent, to embody, the real France could impress only a lover of France who knew French history. For them, de Gaulle's assertions that "I am France" sounded more like Louis XIV than like Joan of Arc. In France itself, when de Gaulle made his appeal from London, in June 1940, only a tiny minority sided with his cause. On the other hand, just how many Frenchmen that summer really felt that *nous, Philippe Pétain* (such was his royal style) embodied the true France can never be known. A minority certainly adhered to Pétain and Vichy to the very end. The

safest conclusion is that in 1940 an overwhelming majority of
Frenchmen—quite incomprehensible, in fact ridiculous as most
Americans no doubt still find their attitude—were sure that if
the French had to accept defeat by Hitler so would the British.
The armistice had been inevitable. It was as simple as that.

This example of national self-esteem was in some sense to
those who knew the French a heartening example of their
normality, for the French were by no means in the depths of
despair that summer. They knew they had not had the protection of a great sea moat like the English, and they knew that
they had often been defeated and occupied in the past. They
admired and rejoiced in British resistance as it developed in
1940–1941. De Gaulle's own firm belief that in the true world
war that was bound to develop Germany could not possibly
win began slowly to take hold as first Russia and then the
United States were drawn in. By the summer of 1944 the Gaullist claim to *be* France, absurd or at least metaphysical, Rous-
seauist, in June 1940, was substantially and realistically correct.
The failure of American policymakers to recognize, admit, and
act on this fact is one of the deepest roots of our present difficulties with France. It was in many ways a perfectly natural
failure and one hard to avoid because the growth of French
Resistance at home, in the empire, and in the Free French
movement itself was obscured by various internal conflicts, by
the inertia common to our State Department as to most ministries of foreign relations, and by the unwillingness of many of
our military leaders to admit the importance of irregular troops
and indeed of civilian psychology in general. As a matter of
fact in this last respect the "London French," using for the first
time on a wide scale the new weapon of radio broadcast, had
had remarkable success in molding opinion in the homeland.
American reporters who followed the troops into Normandy in
1944 were told in many a town how by 1943 everybody listened
to the evening French broadcast from the London BBC, *les*

Français parlent aux Français. But the fact remains that important American policymakers were as unprepared for de Gaulle's success in 1944 as they had been for the military failure of the last government of the Third Republic in 1940.

The informed, politically interested part of the American public, though at first it paid little attention to de Gaulle, slowly came to the side of the Free French. So too had many, perhaps most, American Francophiles, as well as engaged liberals and moderates for whom the Nazis had to be beaten at all costs. With our entrance into the war after Pearl Harbor and with increasing evidence of Vichy collaboration with the Germans, an unfortunate gap opened between informed American opinion and the actual practice of our government. We continued what W. L. Langer has called "our Vichy gamble," at first a good gamble, if not exactly a policy consonant with the highest democratic principles, well beyond the point at which a good gambler would have seen that the odds were hopelessly against him. Our ungracious acceptance of the realities of the situation in France came too late and too slowly. Such acceptance can hardly be regarded as complete even with the final defeat of Germany, because the French were not represented at the Potsdam meeting of Russians, British, and Americans in July 1945. The wounds inflicted on the French in these years were, it is true, psychological traumas, not material losses—save of course for the grave losses of life and personal property incurred by Frenchmen during the campaign of 1944–1945—losses which the French, accustomed to such, took well enough. Moreover, these psychological injuries were very largely confined to the politically engaged portion of the French public, particularly to the leaders of the national Resistance movement, most particularly in fact to the extraordinary man who had initiated that movement, de Gaulle himself, who has never wholly recovered from them. The average Frenchman at the time of the Liberation and to a large extent

even later was almost unaware of the depth and extent of
these troubles, these injuries, these insults to French national
pride as they appeared to de Gaulle and his colleagues. Press
and radio soon made much of them in liberated France, but,
no doubt fortunately, the great public was not inclined to
blame the Americans unduly. For the French were grateful,
again in spite of its cost to them, for liberation and were
shortly also to be moved to gratitude by the splendid gesture
of the Marshall Plan. Still, the gap in both countries between
what the governing few and the governed many knew and felt
about what was actually happening in Franco-American official
relations was surely greater than is usual in free societies. This
gap had and still has the consequences that ignorance and misunderstanding are bound to have in such societies.

2.   For the Free French the very fact that the United States
almost at once recognized the government of Marshal
Pétain as de jure the government of France and sent an ambas-
sador to Vichy, in contrast to the British government, which
refused to recognize Vichy, was a grievance. We were not yet
at war, and any other action on our part certainly would have
been unusual in international politics and international law,
though as far as the latter goes, not more so than our many
later unneutral acts in favor of Britain while we were still
technically at peace with Germany and Japan. But intelligence
sources, especially in the Department of State, decided very
soon that the Gaullists in London were for the most part,
especially in their leadership, far-Rightist nationalists, in no
sense representative of the democratic France we ought to
support. Vichy, though our experts could hardly have held that
its government was based on the "principles of 1776 and 1789"
either, they chose to regard as much closer to the free world
than it was. These judgments were not at the time they were

made wholly wrongheaded. Many of those surrounding de Gaulle were patriotic, conservative army officers, some with royalist and clerical sympathies, to whom the Pétain armistice with Germany had been treason, and de Gaulle's disobedience loyalty. And Vichy did enjoy in those days acceptance by, if not enthusiastic support from, the majority of Frenchmen. From the first, however, the London Free French represented almost the full spectrum of French political groups, save for the Communists, tied until June 1941 by the Molotov-Ribbentrop agreement. As a matter of fact, few even of the conservatives among them were fascist totalitarians. Yet we persisted in maintaining relations with Vichy for a whole year after we had entered the war and did not break with elements loyal to Pétain until long after we had made the landings in North Africa.

As early as the meeting between Pétain and Hitler in October 1940, it was clear that under the influence of Laval, the Prime Minister, the Vichy government was moving toward actual collaboration with Germany. The widely circulated news photograph of Pétain actually shaking hands with Hitler makes a good mark for the beginning of the never-to-be-arrested decline of the Marshal's popularity in France. The entrance of Russia into the war transferred to the Resistance the loyalties of the not inconsiderable group of French Communists. By the time of Pearl Harbor, an accurate intelligence service would have cast grave doubts on the extent to which Vichy had support from the mass of Frenchmen.

We did give some indirect material aid to the Free French through our aid to their British sponsors. But openly and outwardly we did not even attempt to employ the mildly Machiavellian practice of recognizing de facto the Free French as well as the Vichy government. Instead, we chose or at any rate allowed ourselves to be driven or maneuvered into not merely the negative of nonrecognition, but into the positive of hostile disapproval. The list of incidents, slights, exclusions, and other difficulties between our government and that of the French Resistance is long indeed. Here only a representative few need be cited.

One of the earliest, in a sense most trivial, but in another sense most revealing and therefore important, centered on the two rocky islets of St. Pierre and Miquelon (population 5,000), which are all that is left of the French empire in North America. Even before Pearl Harbor, the British and the Canadians were greatly worried over the possibility that the Vichy government, which with our consent and indeed protection clung to the two islands and to the rest of the French possessions in the Americas (Martinique, Guadeloupe, French Guiana), might allow the Germans to control a radio station in St. Pierre, just off the Newfoundland coast. From such a station weather and shipping information could be sent to lurking German submarines at a time when they were a very serious menace. After Pearl Harbor, our government became more directly concerned over this danger and, at least in de Gaulle's opinion, was prepared to join with the Canadians in taking control of the islands. Such infringement of French "sovereignty" was more than de Gaulle could bear, though he might have accepted joint control with his Free French. In those days, however, we never negotiated with the Free French.

President Roosevelt and Secretary of State Hull held firmly to the belief that de Gaulle had promised not to attempt to interfere with Vichy control of the islands. De Gaulle in his memoirs maintains that he consented through his representative Admiral Muselier to refrain from taking the islands, but only on condition that we leave them absolutely alone in the hands of Vichy. Learning of the intended Allied seizure of the islands, he says, he regarded his promise as no longer binding. Muselier under his orders occupied the islands without difficulty in December

1941, to the enthusiastic approval of the inhabitants. Secretary of State Hull, still pursuing with Roosevelt's approval the policy of supporting Vichy, was furious and in announcing official American condemnation of Muselier's act used the words "the so-called Free French." Now "so-called" has a French translation —*"les prétendus Français libres"*—with overtones even more scornful than those of the English expression. Moreover, Hull concluded his statement with the threat, never carried out, to restore by force if necessary the *status quo ante* in the islands, which, after a cooling-off period in Washington, were nevertheless allowed to continue for the rest of the war in Gaullist hands. A trivial incident, indeed, but one which had a lasting effect on the relations between de Gaulle and Roosevelt. As for the American President, the incident confirmed his opinion of the untrustworthiness and excessive touchiness of the Free French leader. He certainly had no intention, virtuous anti-imperialist though he was, of taking the little "colonial" possession away from the French, and he clearly thought de Gaulle's concern over French theoretical sovereignty was a sign of absurd sensitiveness. But sovereignty can be a purely theoretical concern only to the political philosopher and the secure sovereign. We Americans have always been, except during the Civil War, secure in territorial sovereignty. Poor de Gaulle was no political philosopher, but a man of action and a most insecure sovereign. He never forgave that insulting "so-called."

De Gaulle's extreme sensitiveness to the many slights he and his colleagues received in these years was certainly, in by now a cant term, "overcompensation." But the Free French had much to compensate for. The British government, worried lest the French fleet fall into German hands, ordered French ships sunk at Mers el Keber in Algeria. From the beginning, the Free French had had a series of misadventures in attempts to collaborate with the British in wresting bits of the old French Empire from the control of Vichy. Of these the most serious was the failure of a joint Franco-British attempt to take Dakar, the major city of French West Africa, in late September 1940. In British circles the failure was commonly laid to the inability of those unreliable Latins, the Free French, to keep their mouths shut, so that Vichy and Dakar were warned of the whole plan and were well prepared to meet the attack.

Another series of Anglo-French troubles arose as the cause of the Allies began to prosper. In spite of Entente cordiale and Allied victory in World War I, the two major overseas imperial powers of the old days had never quite given up their rivalry, especially in the Near or Middle East. At any rate, de Gaulle was convinced that the British were trying to get Syria and Lebanon, French mandates under the League of Nations, away from France. Unreconstructed British "imperialists" no doubt would have been glad to see a whole Arab world under British suzerainty, but probably the main difficulty here lay in the increasing importance of the United States to the British. The United States under Roosevelt was firmly anti-imperialist; indeed Roosevelt seems to have held that the French must never be allowed to reassume control over any major sections of their old Empire. The British, caught in the middle in disputes of this sort, naturally did their best to mediate—they too had an Empire that conservatives like Churchill at least were determined not to lose—but in a crisis they had to side with the Americans and had to be anti-imperialists, at least with regards to French imperialism.

The central fact about de Gaulle and his Free French followers in the early, critical, and formative years in London (1940–1942) is that they were far from being "free." In terms of their leaders' standing they were distinctly below the other exiled governments in London, for these had once been established governments in their homelands and were often represented in Britain by their lawful sovereigns. Even with those few colonies that rallied from the start, like the French Congo

under its able Negro governor, Felix Eboué, the Free French
had next to no material resources of their own, much less than
the Dutch, for instance, with all Indonesia still under their
control. The situation is neatly pointed up by a story reputedly
from Dutch sources about a ceremonial gathering of all these
exiled governments in London early in the war. A military band
duly played in succession the national anthems of the assem-
bled exiles. In the midst a witty Dutchman turned and whis-
pered to a neighbor, "Ah! the Beggar's Opera."

So too with other no doubt often apocryphal but usually
profoundly true anecdotes (some by now exceedingly commonplace) that center on the troubles with de Gaulle. Faced
with the difficulties of his relations with de Gaulle, who early
adopted for his real France—morally if not legally real—the
double-barred Cross of Lorraine, symbol of Joan of Arc and
much else, Churchill, as everyone knows, remarked that the
hardest cross he had to bear was the Cross of Lorraine. Roosevelt had great fun over the change of sex involved in the role
that he maintained de Gaulle attributed to himself—that of a
reincarnation of St. Joan of Arc. Not apocryphal at all, but
fully documented by an official American publication of the
State Department, is Roosevelt's jesting reference to de Gaulle
as the "bride" upon whom he and Churchill sought at Casa-
blanca in 1943 to impose as "groom" the unimpressive but at
least non-Gaullist General Giraud, whom they had picked to
lead the growing French army in ways more in conformity with
Allied desires.

But the whole North African situation exacerbated Franco-
American relations further. Underneath, native unrest was
stirring in the three North African "possessions" that were the
showpieces of the French Empire. After the failure of the
British and Gaullists at Dakar, however, official Vichy control
in North as well as West Africa was not seriously challenged.
American intelligence reports which insisted that there was

very little support for the Gaullists among the French in North Africa were undoubtedly correct. Moreover, American secret services, not yet united in a Central Intelligence Agency, had contacts not only with Giraud but with other non- or anti-de Gaullists which gave grounds for the belief that we could rely on such support in North Africa without the need of a break, or at least with only a token break, with Vichy. Apart from a small British land force and support from the British navy, the North African landings were to be an American operation; there was no chance that de Gaulle would be allowed to take part in it. There was some sharp resistance from Vichy army units, especially in Morocco, but the landings were successful without serious losses on either side. In France, however, the Vichy government felt obliged to break with ours; attempts to organize in North Africa a French force independent of de Gaulle broke down at once; long weeks of attempts to build up a French civil and military authority from which de Gaulle would be excluded, or included in a subordinate role, also failed. The bitterly Anglophobe head of the French navy, Admiral Darlan, who happened to be in Algiers at the time of the landings, was our next choice after Giraud, a man who lacked any political gifts. Darlan did help bring about order in North Africa, but it is extremely unlikely that he could have achieved what the American government wanted him to do, eliminate de Gaulle as the leader of French Resistance. At any rate Darlan was assassinated by the apparently independent initiative of a young Frenchman within a month, and the various elements that could have tried to prevent a Gaullist take-over were left without a leader.

For the Gaullists did take over completely. By the end of May 1943 de Gaulle himself had left London for Algiers, where on territory legally French the erstwhile exiled Free or Fighting French set up a government, by no means absolutist, headed by de Gaulle. A Comité Nationale de Libération, in our initial-ridden age known as the CNL, already formed in London, was added to and continued to serve as an executive ministry. From various sources—London, North Africa, and, thanks to the increasingly good communications with metropolitan France and often with the connivance of outwardly loyal Vichy authorities, from metropolitan France itself—an informal "Consultative Assembly" was set up. It was actually quite representative of the spectrum of French politics in the old Third Republic. Finally, the various French Resistance movements at home were brought together in a union effective for immediate purposes, in part by their own, in part by Gaullist efforts. An elaborate and successful system of communication by radio, small boat, and airplanes was established between the Algiers government and the "Resistance" in metropolitan France.

From now on there was an increasingly strong French government under de Gaulle in Algiers, working through the Resistance in France itself, and there was an increasingly ineffective Vichy French government under Pétain. The North African landings had provoked the Germans to abandon the not very real distinction made in June 1940 between occupied France (the North, West, and Atlantic Coast) and unoccupied France (Center, East, and Mediterranean Coast) and to take over the whole country. De Gaulle himself in his memoirs writes that the establishment of a free French government on French soil in Algeria marks the point at which it was clear to the world that France was still a great power. But, although in practice Americans both civilian and military from then on worked with the Algiers government, although there was what might be called a grudging and not very trusting American de facto recognition of de Gaulle's government, although metropolitan French and French colonial troops in important numbers fought well in the campaigns of North Africa, Sicily, and mainland Italy, there was still no de jure Allied acceptance of de Gaulle as the head of a French government.

As a final blow, the French of the Comité National de Libération were entirely excluded from the planning and execution of Operation Overlord, the Normandy landings of June 1944. Everybody everywhere knew that something like Overlord was preparing, but not even the German secret services succeeded in finding out where and when. De Gaulle was finally flown in from Algiers to England just before D-day, June 6, 1944, and informed by Churchill in an interview that the Allies were going into France with only token French participation—and certainly without de Gaulle's participation. In a very typical phrase Churchill's description of the scene in his war memoirs closes: "The General was bristling."

In the good folk-sense of the word, the General had a right to bristle. From the French point of view, the situation was worse than mere exclusion. In 1944 even subordinate American officials concerned with planning for Allied dispositions in France once the landings were successful knew that our military planners intended, indeed probably would be obliged to, "occupy" France. The policies tested in the occupation of enemy Italy by AMGOT (Allied Military Government in Occupied Territory) would simply be applied in France behind our advancing armies. Once the *whole* territory of France was freed, the French people would decide for themselves in a fully democratic plebiscite how they wished to be governed. It was hoped and, in many influential American circles, believed that they would not choose to be governed by Gaullists. Until that plebiscite could be taken, British and American military government personnel would, with the aid of wholly *subordinate* French helpers, maintain order in France. Behind this policy, which had the support of Roosevelt himself, for which indeed he was in the end probably chiefly responsible, there lay a deep and widespread American fear, shared to a certain extent by the British, that to entrust the government of France to the Algiers-based Gaullist government in collaboration with the French Resistance groups at home was to invite shocking disorders behind our lines, the impossibility of supplying our armies, civil war among the French, and—culminating horror —the establishment of a Communist government in France. In light of what actually happened this view does not seem very realistic, but at the time it was very honestly held. It was a view supported by the original American intelligence emphasizing the totalitarian character (Rightist or Leftist hardly mattered) of the Free French movement, by the four-year record of diffi- culties with de Gaulle, and to a very important extent by that underlying, indeed *racist*, distrust of the French as politically and morally inferior, liable to revolutionary action, which has long existed among Anglo-Saxon peoples.

The Comité Nationale de Libération and its co-workers in Algiers, London, and metropolitan France had long suspected and, as D-day drew near, were well aware of Allied intentions of applying AMGOT in liberated France. To de Gaulle himself the thought that his France was to be treated as an occupied enemy country was intolerable. The synthetic word AMGOT itself sounded ominous to all good Frenchmen. Because the French too have their peck order of nationalities, in which the Italians stand—or stood in those days—much below them, the very equation of France and Italy under AMGOT was an offense to them. Complete Gaullist exclusion from the military and political plans of the Allies in June 1944 was at the time the culmination of their long series of grievances and, as even so objective and recent (1959) a book as Robert Aron's *Histoire de la libération de la France* shows, has remained a nagging and unpleasant memory.

What would have happened had Allied plans for military occupation of France been fully carried out is one of the unprofitable ifs of history. They were never so carried out, not even in the bridgehead in Normandy. The supposedly inept and divided French, as anyone who understood their history would have predicted, had over the years built up a political organization—in American political parlance, if one wishes to be a bit unkind, a "machine"—that managed to take over from Vichy officials, often at lower levels with the help of Vichy officials, the essential posts of local government, from prefect and mayor to minor clerical workers, before the advancing Allied armies arrived and well before the trained Allied Civil Affairs officers, inevitably placed in rear echelons, could get there. These Civil Affairs officers were often very useful as technically trained experts in varied municipal services— electricity, water supply, sewage—that had to be restored as soon as possible, and they usually were welcomed by the French authorities. But they never "governed" France; *they* were the ones who were subordinates.

The term "Gaullist machine," often on the lips of disgruntled Americans in France at the time, is to a certain degree apt. Effective political action, especially in a situation like that of France in 1944, potentially and in part actually revolutionary, requires a well-organized minority group not overly scrupulous about its methods. But the wholly unfavorable sense that many Americans give the term is not fair as applied to the Gaullist liberation of France. In the first place, the machine was not a perfect, well-oiled one, but rather an improvised one that often broke down, that had to be constantly kept going by trial and error, hit or miss, methods worthy of pragmatic Americans. Much more important, the Gaullists, contrary to much American opinion at the time, really had the overwhelming backing of the French people. Once more, if briefly, there was in France an *union sacrée* as in 1914. It was not a perfect union, and it was in some senses an uninformed union, because the average Frenchman, under Vichy censorship, knew very little about what had been going on in the outside world, and what he had learned from outside sources such as the French-language broadcasts of the BBC was one-sided. Still it was a real union, which included the Communists, who had proved very active and effective in the varied operations of the resistance movements in metropolitan France, from propaganda and sabotage to actual guerilla fighting in the so-called *maquis*. This word, from the Italian *macchia,* was originally applied to the thick Mediterranean undergrowth, like the chaparral of California, and was a favorite refuge for outlaws; by extension it was applied to those resistance fighters who took refuge in the rough, thinly inhabited districts still to be found in parts of France. The Communist guerillas, organized as the Francs-tireurs et Partisans (F.T.P.) were among the most effective of such irregular troops, which by June 1944 had been reasonably well organized nationally as the Forces Française de l'Intérieure (F.F.I.). It was this force, to some extent under the direction of Communist political leaders, which the British and Americans feared would try to take over France and thereby start a disastrous civil war. De Gaulle himself shared some of these fears and as a result accepted the cooperation of leading Communists in his provisional government after the Liberation, hoping thus to tame them. He was wholly successful and, for once, for a quite simple reason. The Russians in the summer and fall of 1944 were understandably, in view of what they had been through, convinced that nothing must stand in the way of a united Allied effort to beat the Germans. The French Communists were told from Moscow headquarters through the old French Communist leader Thorez, who had deserted to Russia at the beginning of the war and who was permitted by de Gaulle to come back to France under amnesty, that they must cooperate fully in the war effort, foreswearing any attempt at revolutionary seizure of power in France. They obeyed.

The Liberation of France then was nothing like the civil war the Allies had feared. There were of course many instances of violence to collaborators, many old grudges more than paid back, much indeed to be regretted by any decent person. But as such great political changes go, this one was surprisingly orderly, with relatively little even of lynching and judicial murder. Laval and a few others were condemned to death and executed. The most ferocious Gaullist dared not treat the old Marshal, hero of Verdun, in this way. De Gaulle himself fervently hoped Pétain would stay in Switzerland, where he had taken refuge. But Pétain, by this time ninety and senile, insisted on returning to liberated France. He had to be tried for treason and condemned, but de Gaulle commuted the inevitable death sentence to imprisonment under not too trying conditions. Pétain died peacefully in 1951.

A good many French women who had practiced what was ironically called "horizontal collaboration" with the Germans had their hair cut off and were given the modern equivalent of pillory. And of course many of the more compromised male collaborators managed to escape to Spain and a few other countries safe for them. A rough figure of twenty thousand actual deaths for "collaborators" in the whole process of liberation seems generally accepted nowadays; it happens also to be the rough figure accepted for the victims of the great Reign of Terror of 1792–1794.

On the other side of the balance, the Liberation was a very good thing for French collective self-esteem. For the French people generally—and even to an extent for de Gaulle himself —these months did something to compensate for the defeats of 1940 and the subsequent tribulations of German occupation, the milking of the French economy for German benefit, and above all the impressment of Frenchmen for forced labor in the Reich. General Eisenhower, against some opposition among both military and civilian aides, decided to allow the French Second Armored Division under General Leclerc, which had fought its way up from Lake Chad and North Africa, to have the honor of liberating Paris. As Allied forces drew near, Resistance groups in the city rose, dramatically threw up some old-fashioned barricades reminiscent of 1830, 1848, and 1870—they were not very effective against German tanks—and, luck and the German commander von Choltitz aiding, helped save the city from the complete destruction Hitler had ordered.* The dramatic Liberation of Paris was thus one of the few successful gestures of reconciliation our high authorities made. De Gaulle himself, the Resistance chiefs, Leclerc and his division, an assortment of Allied military, many of them with no authority to be there, and a great array of journalists, headed conspicuously by Ernest Hemingway, poured into Paris in those last days of August. Even a fortnight later, an observer strolling the liberated boulevards had the impression, rare for anyone looking at urban crowds, of people completely rejoicing, happy, and smiling.

The good will toward Americans evident in those days still persists in many Frenchmen. On our side it was some months before fears of a Communist take-over or some other disastrous French breakdown were quieted. The Allied decision to go through with the planned Operation Anvil, on the Mediterranean coast of France, a landing with important French participation, probably hastened the clearing of French territory of German armies and was another factor in restoring confidence to the French. Highest Allied authority was still unconvinced, and the series of concessions which culminated in the final acceptance of France as a fourth member—a poor fourth but still a member—of the major Allied powers seemed to de Gaulle and his colleagues to have been wrung from reluctant and distrustful men, to have been granted grudgingly and much too late. Still, the concessions were made. De Gaulle,

* The very successful book, *Is Paris Burning?* (New York: Simon & Shuster, 1965), and the motion picture made from it both exaggerate, no doubt for American consumption, the danger of a Communist take-over in August 1944.

whose recalcitrances have never yet been carried beyond a certain point, had unofficially accepted an unofficial invitation to visit Washington, where he went soon after his "bristling" performance the day before D-day. The fruit of this, his most successful interview with Roosevelt, was the formal recognition of the French Committee of National Liberation as the de facto (not yet de jure) civil authority in France.

By the end of July 1944 the whole AMGOT plan for France was in fact scrapped. Though not represented at Potsdam in July 1945, France had played a full part in the San Francisco Conference the previous spring, emerging with a permanent seat—and veto—on the Security Council of the Organization of United Nations. At home the country was brought with surprising efficiency to something like normal conditions of transport, communications, public services of all sorts, a start had been made in cleaning up the rubble of war, and a new constitution, substantially like the old, had been drawn up for the Fourth Republic. This Fourth Republic was destined to be extraordinarily like the Third in its politics, but by the early 1950's very unlike it in economics and, astonishingly, in birth rate. Formal acceptance of France in the occupation of Germany, the award of a French sector in Berlin, in general the full formal restoration of France in international politics followed on the removal from the scene of Roosevelt by death and of Churchill by the defeat of the Conservatives by the Labour Party in a general election in 1945.

There remains the problem of what these long wars did to France and to Franco-American relations. In battle deaths this second war of the century was for France not nearly so disastrous as the first, with perhaps not much more than one tenth as many deaths in the armed services. Civilian casualties from air attacks, trivial in the first war, were considerable for France in the second, but much less than those among British, Germans, Russians, and Japanese. Moreover, this time there was no such epidemic as the influenza epidemic of 1918, which accounted for some twenty million deaths throughout the world. The largest single figure of losses for France was probably the two hundred thousand young men conscripted by the Germans for their labor force who never returned to France. The *material* damage from the second war in France all told was greater than that from the first, but it occurred in no such long, continuous, narrow strip of complete destruction as that left by the trench warfare of 1914–1918. Damage was greatest in Normandy and the West generally, regions that had not suffered materially in 1914–1918. Many factors, however, contributed to bringing the war home to all parts of the country. Modern air warfare strikes everywhere at railway centers, major cities, industrial complexes, communications and power networks; the Germans deliberately destroyed places suspected of harboring active guerilla groups; German garrisons stubbornly held out in many towns such as Royan and Brest, which therefore had to be attacked by the F.F.I.; Operation Anvil in the Rhône valley and the Alps, though rapidly successful, brought the war to regions long spared from battle. By deliberate Allied policy, Paris, though an important center of German military administration, was not subjected to air attack and came out of the war almost undamaged.

It will not do to minimize the horrors of the six years of war for French men and women. These years all told must be reckoned among the worst in French history, which has seen many of them, from the Frankish and Viking invasions through the long defeats of the Hundred Years War, the wars of religion in the sixteenth century, the disasters of the last years of Louis XIV, to the humiliations of the Franco-Prussian War. This time at least France had rallied, and though her armed forces were not numerous, they had conducted themselves well on sea, land, and air. At Bir Hacheim in the Libyan desert in 1942, a French detachment had fought heroically and effectively, contributing largely to the stopping of German General Rommel short of his Egyptian goal; in the Italian campaign hardened French troops played an important part; at the conclusion of the war in Alsace and in southern Germany the French were holding up their end in the final destruction of the Wehrmacht. It is easy, and ungenerous, to point out that all this cannot be compared in importance with Guadalcanal, Iwo Jima, and the break-through at Avranches, to say nothing of the Battle of Britain or Stalingrad. It is also easy to point out that de Gaulle's rhetoric, in its very French way as good and as effective as Churchill's, has perhaps somewhat inflated these achievements. A great many Americans have said and written something like this, though much less delicately. The saying and writing have hardly improved Franco-American relations.

It should be quite clear even from this rapid survey of these war years that at the topmost level relations between Americans and French were very bad indeed and, until after Roosevelt's death, did not improve greatly. It is unprofitable to speculate on whether, if two entirely different persons had been in the place of Roosevelt and de Gaulle, things would have gone better. This is surely the place to echo George Meredith's "no villain need be" and perhaps also his "passions spin the plot." Both men were strong-willed, filled with a sense of mission, and (in terms of the ethics of the Sermon on the Mount) prideful and vain. Churchill tried hard to be the honest broker in his relations with the two men, but as he frankly told de Gaulle, when he had to choose between what the Americans wanted and what the Gaullist French wanted, he had to choose the American way. Both Roosevelt and Churchill felt themselves to be friends of France, and, as high international politics go, so they were; but both were so molded as "Anglo-Saxons" in de Gaulle's meaning of that word that they could not sympathize with or understand so very French a person as de Gaulle.

Above all, Roosevelt and his aides right up to D-day and

beyond misunderstood the situation in metropolitan France. Their initial diagnosis of 1940–1941, a not wholly erroneous one, that the Gaullists had little or no support in France, was not sufficiently corrected to cover conditions in 1944. Gaullist propaganda, which had for some time insisted that nine Frenchmen out of ten would support the CNL, was distrusted by high American authorities as simply propaganda. It turned out to be substantially correct, not in the sense that a majority of Frenchmen had repudiated Pétain—a good many held that *both* Pétain and de Gaulle were good Frenchmen—but in the sense that an overwhelming majority of Frenchmen had repudiated Laval and the other collaborators, regarded the old Marshal as a prisoner of the Germans and their collaborators, and looked for the CNL to assume power as the Allies advanced.

It is no doubt unfair to suggest, though it has been suggested quite firmly by those hostile to Roosevelt, that the root difficulty in 1944 was that he thought of himself, not de Gaulle, as about to play the role of Joan of Arc in the liberation of France. It is not quite so unfair to suggest that Roosevelt, who was both a gifted political manipulator and an earnest political idealist, took seriously a kind of simplified version of Rousseau's general will: once French territory was entirely freed, some thirty million adult French men and women, under no pressures save those of their own conscience, faced by no Gaullist fait accompli, no Communist take-over, would choose in democratic freedom how and by whom they should be governed. Under these conditions, Roosevelt almost certainly believed, they would not choose de Gaulle. Meanwhile, France would be governed . . . well, by some kind of government under AMGOT.

To de Gaulle, who was fully aware of Allied plans and indeed thought these plans were firmer and had more solid backing in both British and American governing circles than they had in reality, such a provisional government would have merely substituted collaborators with the Anglo-Saxons for collaborators with the Germans. But "collaborators" has not for Americans anything like the depth of meaning that *"collaborateurs"* had for all Frenchmen at the time; one must use the undignified but highly accurate Americanism "stooges." It must not be forgotten that to de Gaulle the France he had never ceased to embody had never ceased to fight the Axis, never abandoned the alliance with the Western powers. To have carried out Roosevelt's plans would have been to treat France as an enemy, like Italy, not as an ally. Fortunately, in the short as well as in the long run, these plans came to nothing. Today their very existence, not widely known among the masses of Frenchmen at the time, is no longer in the minds of most of those who govern France or form French opinion anything but history as most Americans understand history— that is, the dead, or at least moribund, past. There is, however, at least one very important exception: for Charles de Gaulle these old plans, these old exclusions, in all their heaped-up weight are history as he understands it—the living present.

3. Although the euphoria of the first few weeks of the liberation could not last, the next few years were years of generally good Franco-American relations, both between governments and between peoples. The United States through the United Nations Relief and Rehabilitation Administration (UNRRA) and through other agencies at once set to work to aid in the task of rebuilding all over the world, including, of course, war-torn France. The French set to work effectively to do their own rebuilding, a fact masked for many Americans by France's failure to avoid in the new Fourth Republic the splinter-party system of the Third and its frequent cabinet changes. This failure finally in 1946 forced de Gaulle himself

into retirement from active politics in face of what was to him unbearable parliamentary squabbling, a retirement quite generally held at the time to be permanent. The retirement at least made continued Franco-American collaboration easier, and it reached its peak in 1947 with the Marshall Plan, under which the American Congress authorized the spending of some twelve billion dollars in what came to be called "foreign aid." In the late 1940's this aid vastly benefited France and Western Europe generally, giving the initial thrust to the great economic growth that was to follow and to the development of the "new Europe" and the "new France." Concomitant with help from the Marshall Plan, which had been at once rejected by the Russians and their allies, was the development of the alliance system that we built up to oppose the Russian system. That system, the now familiar North Atlantic Treaty Organization (NATO), was put together quite rapidly and effectively in 1948 in a Western Europe exhausted by war and fearful of Communist aggression. To the historian, NATO must seem a normal and expected expression of traditional balance of power politics. France was from the start, and in spite of its formal withdrawal from NATO in 1967, still is, to be numbered as one of this coalition of "free world" states.

Under the Fourth Republic, which lasted until 1958, Franco-American formal relations continued to be relatively serene. The chronic realist will say that France was still weak, its governing circles still aware of its weakness, and that the Russians, not yet fully aware of the possible menace to them of their Chinese ally, were still a threat to Western Europe, a threat reinforced by the importance of Communist parties in Italy and France. In short, France was a good ally because those who governed her thought she had to be.

The difficulties that arose after de Gaulle returned to power —real power this time—with the Fifth Republic in 1958 can therefore be explained simply: de Gaulle does not think France is weak, does not fear Russia, does dislike the United States, and therefore is not a good ally, perhaps not an ally at all. To generalize beyond a single personality, even so powerful a personality as de Gaulle: France when weak was manageable, but now that she has unquestionably recovered, now that she is probably stronger materially, stronger in morale, than at any time since 1870, she is no longer willing to follow our lead so readily. It would be absurd to deny that there is truth in both these statements. De Gaulle probably "determines" French foreign policy to a greater degree than any single man since the first Napoleon, and he is unwilling to accept much of current American foreign policy. French public opinion on the whole would appear to back him up.

The decade of the Fourth Republic was, however, by no means an era of unalloyed good feelings in Franco-American relations. For one thing, these were the years of the final decline of the old French Empire in spite of efforts to bolster it, even to liberalize it, as the French Union. Of the two sorest spots, Indo-China and North Africa, the first had to be given up, in spite of late and to a degree covert American support, after the French defeat at Dien Bien Phu in 1954; the second, long festering, burst in that same year into open revolt in Algeria. Our official government stand, in its contemporary form inherited directly from Roosevelt, has been, in principle, moral support for the anti-colonial movements even in the empires of our British, French, and Dutch allies. It will not do to maintain, as our Communist enemies do, that this stand was hypocritical, but the policy did have to be adjusted at least to a degree to spare the feelings and preserve the collaboration of these allies. No such restraint has ever been possible in our American free press and radio-television. American liberals of all shades, who do much of the writing even for conservative newspapers, magazines, and other mass media have been almost as outright as the Marxists in condemning imperialism everywhere; but even the Rightists themselves, if only because as good Americans they have to employ the vocabulary of the democratic revolutions of the eighteenth century, have seen clearly and pointed out vigorously the imperialist crimes of our allies, particularly in the last few decades, those of the French.

Yet our condemnation of imperialisms, which was far from purely verbal, never gained us much credit in France with that important segment of any Western nation, the intellectuals. French intellectuals, writers, artists, scholars, scientists, teachers, also anti-imperialists for the most part, have had their doubt about us for a long time. With the coming into the open of Russo-American hostilities in the Cold War, the outright Communists, numerous in French intellectual circles, lined up solidly against us; but we had little credit even with the uncommitted majority of intellectuals. Briefly, once more, in the honeymoon days of the liberation, we were the generous liberators, collaborators in the work of rebuilding France, not only materially, but more profoundly, as a new France of social justice. It was this aspect of the Resistance and Liberation that not only our American policymakers, but our press, our public opinion, either ignored or underestimated. When it began in the later forties to be clear that the Fourth Republic might be going "socialist," many Americans were shocked, as they had been shocked by British "socialist" government. The clandestine press under the German occupation had been no mere press devoted to newsgathering; it was a press devoted to an extraordinary degree to planning for a new France, making blueprints for a France no longer straitjacketed by the obsolete politics of the anticlerical, *rentier*-bound Third Republic, no longer exploited by the "two hundred families" of finance and industry, but a *planned* society of social justice for all. Americans, who have long since lived down their Revolution of 1776, who tend to regard Utopian planning as an illusion, if indeed they do not feel that *they* have attained in the only way possible something like Utopia, found it hard to understand this state of mind.

In France the desire for a radical change was not at all limited to the old Leftist parties. Already in the years of the occupation many Catholics, who under the Third Republic had never, save in the crisis of 1914, really rallied to the governing group, were preparing to make the great step to a welfare state, and were organizing the nucleus of a Catholic democratic party willing to experiment with "socialism." The Fourth Republic proceeded to nationalize the electrical industry and the great Renault automobile works, the owners of which had completely collaborated with the Germans—in short to set up a mixed economy with a strong "public sector."

It is true enough that the great achievement of the Fourth Republic, the creation of organs of West European supra-national cooperation, which culminated in the treaties establishing the Common Market (European Economic Community), had the blessing of the makers of American foreign policy and of American public opinion. It is also true that up to de Gaulle's return to power in 1958 Franco-American relations were on the whole good. Yet it is not quite fair to attribute the present difficulties between the United States and France wholly to the overwhelming personality of de Gaulle. At a minimum, I must insist that the France of 1967 is in so many ways so different from the France of twenty years ago that under any form of government, under any rulers, its stance, its policies, in international relations could not possibly be what they were in 1947.

Chapter Five

The New France:

The Material Basis

1. Who is this new man, this Frenchman? It is inaccurate, perhaps misleading, and certainly impious for an American writer thus to tamper with the familiar phrase of St. John de Crèvecoeur, whose *Letters from an American Farmer* (1782) are among the most touching tributes a literary Frenchman has ever paid us. The tribute was paid a long time ago, however, and its "new man, this American" was never quite so new— brand-new, manufactured new, totally unlike a European—as many American publicists have made him out to be, and still do, witness Daniel Boorstin and other contemporary writers. Old and new, permanence and change, however absolute the metaphysician can make them, however mutually exclusive our feelings and our everyday language are bound to make them, are hopelessly relative, mutually confounded in the world we have to live and die in. The Frenchman of the second half of the twentieth century is in many ways a new man. Because we Americans have been brought up to think of ourselves as young and new, of Europeans as old and worn out—and of Frenchmen in this respect as the most European of Europeans—no doubt too arresting reversal of Crèvecoeur's phrase may be allowed to stand.

If, however, you find it outrageous, I am willing to drop comparisons with America and state simply: France in the last two decades has undergone a revolution in many important respects much more complete and significant than those symbolized by Bastille Day, the July Days of 1830, and the focal dates of 1848 and 1870. This contemporary revolution in France is a revolution by consent, though not of course unanimous consent, relatively free from violence, relatively slow, and by no means finished today. It is a revolution which has changed much in the lives of ordinary Frenchmen of all classes and in particular the many usually denoted by the French word *peuple*, more precise than our "people," less scornful than our "masses." Many of these changes, specific, concrete, petty, undignified, likely to be neglected by political philosophers, historians, and other writers concerned above all with the "high culture" of their societies, are certainly important for those who experience them and may even have a value here, as revealing the infrastructure on which the imposing superstructure of national government and international relations has to be built.

2.   A sampling of these changes must begin with a very specific, concrete, indeed perfectly quantifiable change of great importance even for the loftiest concerns of the high culture. France was in 1939 almost at the point of actual decline in total population. Her net reproduction rate that year was ninety-three. This figure is a statistical measure based on the number of children born each year per hundred women of childbearing age in a specific country. Because the figure required to maintain a stationary population with no net immigration and no increase in life expectancy is one hundred, the French net reproduction rate of ninety-three meant that had it not been for immigration, mainly from Italy, Spain, Poland, and North Africa, the total population of France would have actually declined. Yet by 1949 the net reproduction rate had

reached one hundred thirty-three. France in 1939 was an old country, not just in the nice, conventional sense of old in history, but a country with many old and middle-aged people and few young ones. And yet, unlike young Irishmen, young Frenchmen were not leaving their homeland in significant numbers. France seemed to deserve the not infrequent American editorial comment: "Dying."*

The human stuff of the new France is not now reproducing itself at anything like the maximum rate our species seems to be able to attain in less developed countries, but its crude birthrate has been in the last two decades roughly in a class with the British, German, and, in the mid-sixties, the American. As a result, the demographic projections made by the experts in the 1930's are extremely far off the mark. Metropolitan France has in 1967 slightly over fifty million people instead of the barely over forty million predicted for it by the experts of the 1930's. Perhaps a million or so represents immigration, especially of *colons* who fled from Algeria. But the bulk is made up simply of millions of babies whom no one as late as 1945 could have predicted, babies arriving in numbers and above all in continued supply far in excess of the usual temporary postwar increase as the men return to their homes. They were certainly not usually unwanted or unplanned, because the reputation of the French people for addiction to, and skill at, various methods of contraception was certainly not undeserved and was well borne out in statistics as well as in literature.

Why this population growth took place is a fascinating problem. Certainly the problem is not to be solved by insistence on any single factor. Of the many variables involved, not even the

* These figures are quoted by C. P. Kindleberger, "The Postwar Resurgence of the French Economy," in Stanley Hoffmann and others, *In Search of France* (Cambridge, Mass.: Harvard University Press, 1963), p. 133. The net reproduction rate of France in 1963 was 136.4, which *with all other variables remaining constant* means a net annual increase in population of 1.14 percent, some half-million a year. See the *Annuaire statistique de la France* (1965), p. 50. This rate of population increase is falling somewhat.

one most popular among Americans as an explanation of all
work, the economic factor, will do as a sole cause. France was
from the early fifties on clearly prosperous, but the population
increase began in the mid-forties. A family allowance from the
government for children in a large family counted, but this is
certainly not the sole variable involved when under the Third
Republic such measures had been tried in a vain effort to
increase the birthrate. The highly intellectualist and existentialist explanation sometimes given by the pessimists, that
French men and women leading lives of cosmic despair no
longer gave a damn about how many children they had, is
nonsense. "Fashion," that greatest of multipliers, certainly
helped in the continuing process of population growth through
increased birthrate. Also, public health measures are today
somewhat better, but not very much so in comparison with the
1930's.

Population growth and economic growth in a developed
country like France are probably mutually supporting, although in an underdeveloped country population growth may
hinder economic growth. The important thing is that some
millions of French men and women decided to bring children
into this harsh world. They did this in spite of long-established
French tradition in all classes, a tradition of childless marriages,
of one- or at most two-child families, and of all sorts of accumulated cultural influences that helped lower the birthrate, from
laws requiring the equal distribution of property among all
children to middle-class postponement of marriage even among
the well-to-do until the groom was fully "established" in a safe
job or career in his middle thirties at the youngest. Most of all,
fashion in the old France reinforced all these influences: one
just did not have a large family.

Millions of French men and women today want many other
things their parents seem not to have wanted. One of these new
wants, or needs, will start a list of the little (or at any rate not

lofty, not always dignified) facts of ordinary life that are changing in France. The French until yesterday were not great
travelers. Travel is expensive, it is not an obvious addition to
one's capital equipment, not a form of investment as the typical
Frenchman of the clichés understood investment—indeed, it is
a sheer waste. And if the French did travel, they traveled
inexpensively within the hexagon, for they often really meant
what to us Americans was an apparent rationalization: Why
should a Frenchman leave France, a land that has everything
a civilized man could want?

Recently, however, when I was vacationing in Austria I saw
at the end of a forest road, rough and forbidding, two parked
cars, both bearing the familiar registration numbers for Paris
and both clearly belonging to French citizens. (The road
actually continued unbarred, but there was a conspicuous sign,
Eintritt verboten—entrance forbidden—which the French travelers, contrary to one of the clichés of their national character,
were duly obeying and which the American observer on the
scene promptly disobeyed.) Or there was the luncheon in an
American city for four visiting French academic deans, all from
provincial universities, at which two of the deans discussed
which, given clear weather, was the more impressive, the airplane flight over the Rockies, including the Grand Canyon of
the Colorado, or that over the Andes from Chile to the Argen-
tine. It is true that the deans' trips had been subsidized, but in
part by their own government, in itself a remarkable innovation. In the old days it was almost impossible to get French
academic personnel to go out for a term or so to French
colonial universities, let alone to lands where they might not be
able to speak French.

Finally in the field of travel, there was the effort made by the
French Commissariat of Tourism in the summer of 1965 to
counteract the relative decline in numbers of foreign tourists
coming to France, a decline especially noticeable in contrast

with big increases in Italy and Spain. The effort was an elaborate and expensive "campaign," American style, with roses and a small flask of perfume for every traveler (female) arriving at the Paris airport at Orly, a Léonard "pull-over" for each ten-thousandth lady arrival; and for each lucky one hundred-thousandth, a "robe de haute couture offerte à tour de rôle par Balmain, Chanel, Dior, Lanvin et Patou." It also seemed necessary, in view of the reputation of the French as ungracious and grasping hosts, to do something to encourage the French personnel catering to tourists. So the Commissariat set up two national contests, one for hotel or restaurant keepers, the other for waiters, gas-station attendants, policemen, customs officers, and others in direct touch with the tourists. For the first, there were distributed in hotels and restaurants blanks to be filled out by tourists and returned postfree to the General Commissariat of Tourism with the name of the establishment in which they had had the best reception in France. For the second, tourists on their arrival in France were given a little booklet of "chèques-sourire"; when the tourist received a notably amiably rendered service, he was asked to fill out one of these "smile checks" and give it to the person who rendered the service. The most remarkable thing about this campaign is not how well it succeeded—it had a mixed reception and was abandoned during the next tourist season—but rather that a French government should undertake it at all. At this juncture, however, what must be emphasized is the nature of the prizes awarded to the French amassers of the most in smile checks. These were not money, nor even valuable objects, but *travel* tickets, the first prize being four round-trip tickets to Tahiti, followed by four from Paris to the Antilles, two to New York on the "France" on down to tickets to Corsica, to a degree a foreign land.

The fact is clear. French people, from deans to shopgirls are spending their own, their government's, or their company's money on foreign travel. Especially in the summer, and even more especially in August, the French now spill southward by the hundreds of thousands into Spain, Italy, Greece, where living is fairly cheap, but also in lesser numbers into more expensive lands north and east. Students, businessmen and government officials come in considerable numbers to the North American continent and so does a trickle of mere tourists, attracted by off-season rates for air travel. Indeed French travel agencies offer package tours to the United States. The most popular always include New York, Washington, and Niagara Falls, although a number push on to those magic spots, the Grand Canyon, San Francisco, and Los Angeles.

The French are also, of course, traveling much more at home. Here under the headline "A Riviera Revolution" is a dispatch to the New York *Times* of September 11, 1965:

These days, when an affluent tourist in Cannes, Nice or Saint-Tropez tells you he is going down to the casino, it does not mean that he is going to risk family fortune in the devilish whirl of the nearest roulette wheel. He is merely going to the supermarket. He wants to buy cheese and sausages packed in plastic bags for a picnic on the beach or a precooked dinner for the wife to heat on the hotplate of the family trailer that evening. . . .

The big thing on the Riviera this year has been the trailer camp.

They have sprung up everywhere—in the pine forests behind Saint-Tropez, in the vineyards of Provence and on the rocks near Monte Carlo. . . .

A man who operated a country inn known for its exquisite food has closed his kitchen, turned the grounds behind his house into a camping site and now sells sandwiches, wine and beer over a counter.

A Chinese businessman has opened a stand for souvenirs at the entrance of a camp. And an enterprising Algerian has imported a camel and is offering children a ride near another camping area.

In the years before 1945, the French would at most spend a few weeks in a French seaside or mountain resort, or take the cure at Vichy, Vittel, or one of dozens of other watering places.

Such indulgences were confined to the upper and middle classes. Industrial workers, peasants, and artisans could rarely take real vacations. Nowadays paid vacations are the rule, in business and industry, and even the self-employed are likely to permit themselves some relaxation. It is true, and characteristic of the rigidities of the old that survive in the new France, that the great majority of vacations are taken in the month of August, with resultant untoward pressure on accommodations and travel everywhere. Attempts to stagger vacation periods have not achieved much success. All this new travel is part of the great increase in consumer demands that has marked the French economy since 1945—and that always carries with it the danger of monetary inflation.

By 1966 only a little over thirty percent of the average family income was spent on food; as recently as the mid-fifties this figure was forty percent, earlier a bit more. This is of course a statistic, an average. It is always possible that some Frenchmen are undernourished, that the not wholly mythical average Frenchman—better yet, Frenchwoman—has lost weight to follow fashion, and so on through the many other factors that get summed up in these statistics. In short, it is just possible that the decline in the proportion of income spent on food may not indicate an increase in real income for most French people. Sociologists take such a decline to be at least an evidence of "modernization," and economists have their "Engel's law," which says that the higher per capita income the lower the percentage of that income is spent on food.

Yet the French still make much of *la cuisine française,* still often take substantial and leisurely mid-day meals, still expect their bread to be fresh-baked, and unlike the sanitary, air-filled, wax-paper-wrapped American substitute for bread, to taste as bread has tasted for centuries. Worried Frenchmen of conservative taste will, however, tell you that there are many shocking signs that the good old French culture is breaking down even in matters of good eating and drinking. The bread is too white, too dry, too clean, and too tasteless—once more, Americanized; you cannot get old-fashioned bread any more. Supermarkets are springing up all over, not just on the Riviera, full of frozen food and other conveniences and short cuts good for a hurried cook, but disastrous for the gourmet. The Frenchman of really high standards of good eating in past days held that even refrigeration in the home spoiled food, which should never be kept in an "unnatural" temperature; *frozen* food was unthinkable. Now refrigeration is common, and the woman of the home tends to shop less often (she rarely now has a maid to do it) and to preserve foodstuffs longer. In the bigger cities, even the lunch hour—which is normally two hours long, from twelve to two—ceases to be sacred; all sorts of quick lunches, *snack-bars* in French, are springing up, patronized not just by American and British tourists but by the French themselves. Mendès-France, a radical political leader of the Fourth Republic who was returned to the Assembly in the Leftist swing of 1967, when in office dared institute a "campaign" to encourage grown French men and women to indulge not in wine but instead in that gloomy American beverage, milk. It must be admitted that the campaign was not a success. But, a fact even more shocking, without any formal campaign beyond conventional advertising, the young are increasingly addicted to what to a gourmet is an even worse American habit, soft drinks. Especially in the matter of cuisine, Frenchmen who do not like such changes blame them on us and talk of the regrettable Americanization of French eating and drinking habits, or even of "*la coca-colasation de la France.*"

Even during the period between the two great wars, the French were closest to Americans and overseas British in widening the ownership and use of motor vehicles, though, in 1939 they still were far from having attained almost universal distribution of such ownership. Since 1945 French production and French ownership of automobiles—to say nothing of minor vehicles propelled by internal combustion engines, motorcycles, *motovélos* (bicycles assisted by a motor), tractors, and the like —have continued to increase rapidly. In automobiles France has now reached about the American degree of ownership of the late 1930's. The tractor has largely replaced the horse in French agriculture. It is now possible to see workingmen's cars parked, though not in American numbers, outside the factory they work in. The statistics show for motor cars as for refrigerators, television sets, telephones, and other regrettably necessary apparatus of modern national—and personal—greatness a France still quite a distance behind us—and in many fields, but no longer in all, behind Britain, West Germany, and the virtuous little democratic countries of Western Europe.

The important things to note are, first, that France has in these fields been catching up rapidly in the last two decades and, second and even more important, that *psychologically* a great many French consumers and French producers are nowadays adjusted to—*want,* in good simple terms—all that goes with modern material culture from motor cars and color television on down to wine in individual tin cans, although this last recent development may have hard going with consumers. One striking piece of statistical evidence among many about recent rapid growth is the larger number of telephones in use, 3,700,000 in 1959 and 5,340,000 in 1963. Even more striking is the increase in households with television sets, once national television was introduced in the early 1950's; in the decade from 1954 to 1964 the proportion of French households possessing television increased from one in one hundred to more than one in three. It continued to rise rapidly as possession of a television set became a status symbol and, no doubt for many, a pleasure.*

* *France Actuelle,* September 15, 1964, p. 8. This semimonthly in English is published by a "private association of French businessmen." The statistics in this chapter are mostly from it and from other "propa-

As for the second point, the psychological adjustment of the French masses to wanting, and getting, the superfluous as well as the necessary, the following statistics compiled by the *Centre de Recherches et de Documentation sur la Consommation* (CREDOC of course in "alphabetese") make the point clear. With the price index of 100 for 1950 and with due adjustments for rising prices, the French in 1960 were spending well over 100 for almost everything, for this was a decade of great economic growth. In 1960, however, the index for food was only 138, but for clothing 152, for housing 157. For transportation, including touring and vacations, the figure was 205, for hygiene and personal care, including cosmetics, 219, for games, toys, and musical instruments, 271, and for what is listed in rather vague terms as "leisure-time activities," 178. These figures come to life if one leafs through a copy of *Paris-Match*, a French illustrated magazine something like our *Life* or *Look*, and actually on sale in this country at a few big-city newsstands. The advertisements in *Paris-Match* are opulent indeed, often in color, and given French tastes, French psychological preferences, technically effective. No doubt many French readers cannot afford the things they see advertised in their magazines and do no more than think wishfully about that Renault, that expensive and certainly seductive perfume, that electric dishwasher, that television or hi-fi set. Their fathers and mothers, exposed to less advertising, and that less modern,

---

ganda publications" by the Press and Information Division of the French Embassy in the United States. Of course these publications display the rosy side that their sponsors think Americans want to see, but the common opinion among both American and French liberal intellectuals that these statistics are falsified is not correct. They do somewhat exaggerate the completeness of the "modernization" of France by neglecting the surviving remnants of the old France of small-scale business and industry and aristocratic tastes—which only the privileged could enjoy. Even those who distrust the accuracy of the picture these publications paint should be impressed by the fact that, contrary to old French habits when printing in English, these propaganda periodicals and pamphlets are admirably done in a purely technical sense.

in their reading matter, did not even dream of such indulgences; but rather, if they turned their minds all to motor cars
and other luxuries, reflected indignantly as militant radicals on
the fact that those rich swine in power did have them.

3.   The step on the part of the many from envying and perhaps hating the few to the hope and then to the belief that
they themselves could have some of the things the few have is a
critical one indeed, tied, though in no simple, one-way, casual
sense, to a society's attainment of economist Rostow's famous
"take-off point" toward a fully modern American-style economy. As far as economic statistics go, the critical intellectual's
protest, that what the many get even in that land of plenty,
the United States of America, is only an inferior copy, an *ersatz*
luxury, not much better than the "cheap and nasty" that Carlyle
railed against in the early days of the first Industrial Revolution, is quite beside the point. At any rate, it looks as if in
France most of the many are content with what they are getting
and with the prospects of getting more of the same.

Since the end of the eighteenth century the material basis
for French national strength in terms of almost all the yard-
sticks that the economic and sociological statisticians use has
in relation to that of her main rivals been falling quite steadily
until only yesterday. The fall, even in terms of population, has
been relative, not absolute, though as I have noted earlier there
was a moment in the 1930's when it looked as though France
were in for an absolute decline in population. France at the
end of the eighteenth century was still clearly the strongest
nation in the West, inferior in population only to Russia and
perhaps to the Austrian empire, both then backward lands by
almost any standard of measurement other than population.
Even by the very early nineteenth century statistics had not
yet advanced far enough to permit the historian to go much

beyond population, rough estimates of trade, strength of armed forces, and the like. Probably in average per capita terms England and Holland were more prosperous, wealthier, than France at that date, although the addition of Scotland, Ireland, and Wales to form Great Britain in what was after all the competing political unit in international politics would bring the per capita figures for Britain down quite a bit. On the whole, it is not misleading to compare the position of France under the empire of Napoleon with that of the United States today— call it what you may, primacy, leadership, hegemony, top of the peck order—with Britain the rising challenger in second place, like Russia today.

Again taking a general view, it may be said that in the course of the nineteenth century almost all the statistics of material strength and capabilities show that France was passed, roughly in succession, by Britain, Germany, the United States and in the twentieth by Russia and in many fields by Japan. In simplest terms, the French did not adapt themselves completely to the latest and most efficient large-scale industry. Once again, this was only a relative not an absolute failure. France has not been a backward or underdeveloped country in the last two centuries. Frenchmen in these centuries have pioneered in pure science—the list is long, from Lavoisier and Cuvier through Pasteur to Becquerel and the Curies. There was a striking falling off in such individual achievement by French scientists in the years after 1918, a fact explicable at least in part (as are many other French failures in those years) by the incredible destruction of men in the war of 1914–1918. But the French were before 1914 also pioneers in many fields of applied science, technology, or just plain business enterprise. They were surpassed in large-scale industry of course. Yet the great marvels of the end of the last century, the internal combustion engine and its applications, the motion-picture camera and its applications, the airplane, and much else owe a great deal to the French. And in some forms of large-scale organization the French were by no means backward. Though the small shopkeeper and the small *rentier* were stock French figures, duly described in all the books about France right down to the 1950's, the great Parisian department stores founded in the nineteenth century were pioneer experiments in large-scale retail marketing, no whit inferior in size to their British and American counterparts. The French steel industry, though seriously lamed by the loss of Lorraine to Germany in 1870, remained a major and relatively efficient large-scale industry. Finally, France has in the last century or so enjoyed several periods of rapid and substantial economic growth, the two decades from 1850 to the early 1870's, the first decade of the twentieth century, and the 1920's.

Economists, economic and social historians, sociologists, and political scientists, French and foreign, have for generations wrestled with what we nowadays call the problem of why French overall *economic growth* has been so slow and so irregular relative to that of British, American, German, Japanese, and other peoples, or put in more journalistic terms, the problem of why France, once first as a "great power," has in the last two centuries fallen to fifth or lower, depending on how you rate the capabilities of the populous nations of Asia. Obviously, France, especially after the loss of the Empire, was simply not big enough to sustain comparison with the developed United States or with contemporary Russia. But it was and is roughly the same size as Britain and Germany, behind both of which it fell conspicuously in the last two centuries. The social sciences are nowadays at least far enough advanced to reject the concept of a single causal factor; on the other hand, they are at a loss when it comes to arranging in a universally accepted pattern, let alone an equation, all the causal factors that have been suggested for the failure of France to keep up with her rivals in material strength. The list of these is long and disparate:

purely material factors, such as shortage of coking coal, lack of petroleum and other natural resources; weaknesses in economic organization, such as predominance of family enterprises recalcitrant to innovation and industrial research; banking difficulties; tiny inefficient farms; shortage of, and excess of, labor supply (these contradictory explanations have been put forward by different economic historians for different times and places); excessive class tensions, with an unyielding capitalist class and a surly revolutionary working class deprived of its due share of the national product and hence not consuming enough to promote economic growth; slow population growth; vaguer sociological considerations, such as a French national character addicted to *mesure,* aristocratic tastes, preferring handwork over machine work, quality over quantity; and others, right down to the simple but not infrequent Anglo-Saxon verdict: the French are an inferior people, lacking in energy and enterprise, corrupt, commercially dishonest, lazy, sensual, and unmanly.

At any rate, the most recent spurt in the French economy has been real enough. In the decade 1950–1952 to 1960–1962 the rate of growth in the per capita product was 41.9 percent; for the same period the figure for Great Britain was 24.4 percent and for the Netherlands 41.3 percent. The "economic miracle" in West Germany and in Italy was even greater. In all Western Europe there was in 1967 some falling off, but still, the record is clear and remarkable.*

Lest the reader tire of statistics, I may here content myself with a few specific examples of French material achievements with emphasis on big engineering tasks: the middle-range passenger jet, the Caravelle, in use throughout the world by airlines, even including American airlines; the projected super-jet, the Concorde, to be developed in partnership with Britain;

---

* See Simon Kuznets, *Postwar Economic Growth* (Cambridge, Mass.: Harvard University Press, 1964), p. 129.

the great project of harnessing the tides for hydroelectric power, at which we failed in Quoddy, now achieved in the Bay of Mont St. Michel on the borders of Brittany and Normandy; a pilot plant, not yet economically profitable (and unlikely ever to be so), harnessing the direct rays of the sun at Font Romeu in the Pyrenees; attainment of a French atomic bomb and an accompanying nuclear fission industry, an achievement sneered at in the American press as pretty small-scale stuff, but none the less a real achievement in view of French exclusion from the know-how developed in Anglo-Canadian-American work from the very beginning of the Second World War; desalination of many acres of land in the desolate reaches of the Rhône delta by planting them with rice, which turned out in itself to be a profitable crop, so that France is now self-sufficient in that cereal; discovery and development of a very large field of natural gas at Lacq in the Basses Pyrénées with, as a by-product, a sulphur industry in competition with our own; the building, in cooperation with Italy, of a seven and a quarter mile vehicular tunnel under Mont-Blanc; the construction of a tanker, the *Dolabella*, only one step away from complete control of the whole ship by one man at one center; and much more, including many commissions abroad requiring collaboration of French architects, engineers, financiers, industrialists— and bureaucrats.

French agriculture deserves a page or two by itself. A great deal of what all the commentators, French and foreign, have said about "backward" French agriculture is still true. Farms of ten hectares (24.71 acres) or less are 56 percent of the number of farms, though only 16 percent of the total area farmed. Moreover, the old medieval survival of separated strips or parcels is great, so great that the 2.3 million farm units number 76 million parcels of land, an average of 30 per farm. Too many farms grow cereals or wines, too few grow high quality products, meat, fruit, vegetables suited to modern prosperous urban tastes. There are still hidebound conservative peasants, still difficulties in the way of agricultural credit. Yet in spite of all this, the fact is that France is now a land with agricultural surpluses much like those we have in this country, with problems of subsidies and the like much the same as those we live with, and certainly with a well-organized "farm bloc" capable of political action. Somehow or other her inefficient backward farmers manage to raise more, and especially more wheat, than she can use—hence the difficulties over agricultural tariffs in the Common Market, especially with Germany, where agriculture today in that land of industry and efficiency is as a whole less efficient than in France. Finally, as in other sectors of French life, there is a new spirit among French farmers, particularly among the young. The young welcome innovation in methods, want more and better vocational education, and to a surprising degree for Frenchmen are willing to cooperate among themselves and with government agencies. New men, new ideas, are getting results, short of miracles, but still amazing to those who knew the old France of the story-book peasantry.

The whole agricultural problem in France is nicely illustrated in concrete detail in an admirable study of Chanzeaux, a village in Anjou in western France.* A team of young Americans under the guidance of Professor Laurence Wylie of Harvard University lived at various times in this small agricultural village, studying it with the best of modern sociological techniques. Chanzeaux is in a region naturally endowed as far as fertility goes, nearer the best rather than the worst of French lands; it is far from the stony infertility of the *causses*, though not so rich as the best of truck-farming, wine-growing, or large-scale grain-farming lands. It has some largish farms and some much too small farms. The important things that come out of

* In the chapter "The Farm Problem" in Laurence Wylie, ed., *Chanzeaux* (Cambridge, Mass.: Harvard University Press, 1966).

this study are that the younger farmers want very much to close the gap between their net incomes and those of city workers; that they are at least beginning to consider and practice co-operative methods; that they are aware of the problems of marketing farm produce (the middlemen in France usually get too large a share of the final retail price of farm products) and are trying to do something about them; and that fewer farm workers are working larger farms with machines rather than with animals and hired help, with a consequent loss of rural population as the unneeded workers emigrate to the cities or merely make Chanzeaux a dormitory town while they work in nearby Angers or Cholet. All this is by no means unique to France; we in this country are still going through some such processes, having started rather sooner than the French.

Perhaps a final, important factor in Chanzeaux is less vital in this country, although anyone who knows much of farming in the American East will not find it altogether unknown here. This is the persistence of the old conservative farmer, usually but not always a poor one on a marginal farm. From Wylie's study of Chanzeaux here is M. Menget, not a poverty-stricken farmer by any means because he owns a large farm, but, as the American commentator notes in italics, one who actually *likes* to work: "He does not own a tractor, though he could easily afford one. . . . He is not interested in modern breeding practice. He does not concern himself much with breeds, and his herd is a mixture. Consequently, his cows give lower-quality milk and bring in less money than Arrial's [a "modern" farmer]: Arrial realizes 1,750 francs a year per cow milked, Menget only 820 francs. . . . Arrial has saddled himself with a debt nearly equal to his annual income. Menget would never borrow a penny. He thinks French farmers are too deeply in debt and that millions of them will be dispossessed in a second great depression. 'In ten years there will be no more than 300 people

in Chanzeaux. It will be like *The Grapes of Wrath.'"*" An
interesting man, M. Menget, though the future no doubt
belongs to the Arrials. The reference to Steinbeck's book is
certainly surprising. But the French peasant has long since
ceased to be the stock figure of Zola's *La Terre,* if he ever was
such.

Explaining the current French economic advances, agricultural, industrial, financial, gives the experts at least as much
trouble as any they have met in their efforts to explain past
French advances and retreats. The American economist
Charles P. Kindleberger in his interesting essay, "The Postwar
Resurgence of the French Economy," lists briefly various
attempts to explain French economic history since 1850 (including all those noted above), weighs the evidence carefully,
and comes to this conclusion: "The economic recovery of
France after the [second world] war is due to the restaffing of
the economy with new men and to new French attitudes. . . .
To conclude that the basic change in the French economy is
one of people and attitudes is frustrating to the economist. . . .
It is true that capital has grown and technical progress has
been made, but these are accompaniments of a more far-reach-
ing process rather than exogenous variables." Kindleberger
doubts whether sociologists and economic historians have fur-
nished much in the way of explanation: "The family firm and
deep-seated fissures in the social structure fail to explain the
rate of progress in the past, and exist today even when growth
is again rapid."**

The unchallengeable facts are that many, many Frenchmen

---

* Wylie, ed., *Chanzeaux,* pp. 130–131. This book and Wylie's earlier
study of a Provençal village, *Village in the Vaucluse* (Cambridge, Mass.:
Harvard University Press, 1957) together make a fascinating study in
illuminating detail impossible for a writer concerned with the whole of
France.

** Kindleberger, in Hoffman *et al., In Search of France,* pp. 156–157.

have come to want a great deal they may not have wanted and certainly did not have in the past and that they are now beginning to get these wants satisfied. It would seem that what they want is substantially what many, many Americans apparently also want and have in great numbers attained. The French economy, in short, has become a demand economy, a consumer's economy. The ten million babies of the French baby-boom alone would have added vastly to demand; their parents and grandparents also make new and greater demands as consumers.

4. The present regime in France quite naturally takes full credit in its publicity, which is copious, modern, and almost like the American, for the economic growth. The various statistical tables compiled by the French and nowadays generously distributed in this country usually—and not unexpectedly —start with the year of the founding of the Fifth Republic, 1958. Actually most of the leading persons in the French economy today in their more serious writing and speaking freely admit that the bases for their prosperity were laid in the now much maligned Fourth Republic. Unless they are violently anti-American or just plain Communists, French experts will give full credit to Marshall Plan aid from the United States begun in 1947 for making possible the repair of war damages and the initial steps in building the new economy. Almost all the institutions of the new economy, the various national Plans, the coal and steel agreement (Schuman Plan) and other forerunners of the Common Market, the Common Market itself, many of the great new technical achievements, the development of hydro-electric power, the full nationalization of gas, electricity, and most heavy industries, coupled with the cooperation of private industry in the French variant of modern "mixed economies"—all this goes back to the late forties and

the early fifties. Above all, in these years there were developed the "new men" of the French economy mentioned by Kindleberger, symbolized in American opinion by Jean Monnet, who during the worst years for the Gaullist government in London and Algiers quietly did much in the United States to gain the confidence of the American business and political communities. There were many of these new men, most of them quite young, some of them bureaucrats if you like, but adventurous bureaucrats, some of them "managers" in the new "mixed economy," some of them trained engineers and scientists, some of them businessmen, even bankers.

Here is a paragraph in which Kindleberger summarizes admirably these early signs of what was to come in the French economy: "The change in attitude toward economic expansion was universal in France. The proof is that the net reproduction rate moved in a big jump in violation of normal causation as recognized in social science. There was vigor in many sections of society: in the resistance leaders themselves; in the Communist Party which organized the revival of coal production; in the neo-Catholic Centre des Jeunes Patrons; and among geographers. Economists organized the Institut Scientifique d'Economie Appliquée with its focus on national-income accounting. The Confédération National de Patrons Français gradually abandoned its protective attitude toward little business. The family firm looked for outside help. One significant index: the demand for youth in business expanded rapidly. The Ministry of Labor stated in 1951 that the top hiring age for middle-rank executives (cadres) declined from sixty in 1898 to fifty in 1945, forty-five in 1950, and forty in 1951."*

Granted that no full causal explanation for French economic development and certainly no single one-way cause can be established, I must nevertheless assert that this development has at least been accompanied by, can perhaps be symbolized

---

* Kindleberger, in Hoffman *et al., In Search of France,* p. 153.

by, a great change in the attitudes of the French elite, the ruling classes, in good democratic French, the *cadres*. These men are no tiny minority like the old "two hundred families" but all told number several thousand, leaders in many fields, educated, not infrequently risen from the ranks. The Frenchman it used to be said, above all the ambitious Frenchman, wished for a literary, artistic, or at any rate professional achievement in something demanding verbal and manipulative skills—law, letters, art, music, politics. If he did go into business or industry, it was in the small "family firm" and he looked forward to early retirement and the pursuits and prestige of aristocratic leisure. He was not so likely as his opposite numbers in other Western lands to go in for the hard work of the engineer and scientist; he disdained the skills of the modern "manager" or "technocrat," large-scale industry, and the risks of technological and economic innovation. But these new men are different. In French higher education, liberal arts students outnumbered students of science and engineering until 1957, when for the first time the enrollment figures were reversed. During the 1960's the great rise in the proportion of the total population continuing into higher education has meant that once again the "easier" subjects have become more popular than the tougher sciences. But there is no doubt that a bright young Frenchman is nowadays by no means as scornful of a business or managerial career as he used to be; and even if he aims at and attains a relatively secure "government job," he is not much like the bureaucrat of tradition, custom-bound, unenterprising, an irremovable petty tyrant.

5.   The new French economy of the 1960's is, like that of Britain, Germany, the United States, Sweden, indeed all the Western world, a "mixed economy." Many Americans, members of an old conservative society clinging to attitudes

toward their own economy that are not in very close relation to the facts of their economic life, find it hard to understand this mixed economy. The degree and nature of the mixture between the "public sector" and the "private sector," between "collectivism" and "individualism," between governmental or quasi-governmental controls and free individual or corporate initiative varies of course with different countries. It is tempting to flirt with the notion of an arithmetical scale from say one hundred for the fully collectivized society to zero for the fully individualistic society. Neither extreme has been quite attained even by any subsociety on this earth, not one hundred by any Utopian socialist society of the American 1840's, not zero by the wilder American frontier societies of the same period. Such a scale, however, cannot be made for any Western country, if only because the kinds of government or at least collective social controls vary so greatly from outright nationalization as with the American post office to tight regulation as with our Interstate Commerce Commission, Food and Drugs Administration, and many like controls to those many forms of monopoly or oligopoly found in modern society. In short, the French economy of the 1960's is in respect to the degree of "laissez-faire" practicable within it much more like than unlike that of the United States, although in terms of planning and nationalization, France is much more "public."

The most striking difference is the much greater extent of French nationalization of industry. The intellectuals of the Resistance had made many plans for nationalizing certain industries. During the year or so after the war in de Gaulle's most radical government—there were ministries held by socialists and communists in what was a government of national union—there was carried out nationalization of coal, electricity, and gas and some rather complicated arrangements were made for government participation in the oil industry, later to become important with the discovery of oil in the

Sahara. Similar participation in air transport has now reached the point where the great air line, Air France, is nationalized; there remain, however, two smaller private companies in the field of air transport. The stock of the two major shipping companies, the Compagnie Générale Transatlantique and the Messageries Maritimes, is owned by the state in a majority, and the state appoints their ruling officers. The most important industrial nationalization involving a finished consumer's product was in a sense accidental. The management of the well-known Renault automobile works had been conspicuously and cynically collaborationist with the Germans during the war and was therefore taken over completely by the state in the enthusiasm of the Liberation. Finally of course the government, especially through the Ministries of Industry and of Public Works and Transports, has the kind of regulatory powers even the American government possesses and uses, as well as a hand in national planning (in French, *planification*) and promotion. The railroads had previously been nationalized in 1936.

After nationalization, planning is the most striking difference between the French and the American economies. The planning commissariat was another product of the Liberation and was formally set up in 1945. There have been four Plans since the first was actually put to work in 1947; a Fifth Plan, to cover five years instead of four, began in 1966. The General Planning Commissariat is for a contemporary government agency modest indeed in size: even with the recent addition to its ranks of the Productivity Commissariat, its personnel, professional and clerical combined, was in 1963 only about two hundred; moreover, many of the professional members have been seconded to the Commissariat from their own ministries. It has been a highly flexible and undogmatic group, of which the Anglo-French couple, John and Anne-Marie Hackett in their excellent study of French planning say might take as its motto: power through persuasion.*

It persuades largely by careful consultation with representatives of the public grouped in commissions. For the Fourth Plan ending in 1965 there were twenty-two "vertical" commissions by industry or social function—for example, chemicals, steel, culture and arts, school, university, and sport equipment —and five "horizontal" commissions, General Economic and Financial, Manpower, Productivity, Scientific and Technical Research, and Regional Planning. The extent to which the various sectors of the French public were consulted comes out clearly in the following table of the members of the various commissions and working parties under the plan.

Employers (including the nationalized industries)	715
Farmers	107
Employers' professional associations	562
Trade unionists	281
Civil servants	781
Other (university teachers and other independent experts)	691
Total	3,137**

The planners do not dictate to private industry and indeed do not have the legal power to do more than guide and set certain limits. The "private sector" of the French economy remains most important. Moreover, many of the great nationalized industries over the last two decades can be fairly said to have *behaved*—a perfectly good word for the economist as well as for the psychologist—more like great oligopolist or monopolist private firms than like traditional government departments. All hands, even the most conservative economic

* J. H. and A. M. Hackett, *Economic Planning in France* (London: George Allen & Unwin, Ltd., 1963), p. 35.
** Hackett and Hackett, *Economic Planning in France*, p. 47.

royalists, agree that the Régie Renault has had to pursue producing, marketing, advertising, and wage policies quite like those of its big private competitors, Peugeot, Citroën, Simca. Unreconstructed advocates of private industry insist that the evils of bureaucracy have crept into the Régie Renault, that it is inefficient and bound to fail, but to the layman's eye these do not appear obvious. At this writing Renault is doing quite as well as the other three. It has achieved a special agreement with the Soviet Union and is attempting to recapture its American market by a daring and highly American advertising campaign in this country, a campaign described by one Frenchman as "très Madison Avenue." There may be in the offing a crisis of "overproduction" in the French auto industry, but it is a crisis shared among all producers of motor cars. As for the Electricité de France, the railways, Air France, and the rest, they have a generally good reputation among the French public, whom they seem to serve well. They are in fact public corporations with technical and managerial staffing by the new breed of French civil servants, and they bear comparison with so virtuous an American private institution as the Bell Telephone semimonopoly rather than with that unhappy butt and victim, the American Post Office.

It must not be thought that the old French multanimity, which of course extended to matters economic, has given place to unanimity and regimentation. Right and Left, advocates of laissez-faire and advocates of complete nationalization exist and can and do express themselves freely. The C.N.P.F. (Conseil National du Patronat Français), the French equivalent of our National Association of Manufacturers, issued in 1964 an economic policy declaration in fourteen points, a number perhaps chosen with French ironic intent to recall the fourteen points of Woodrow Wilson. The second of these asserts roundly, "The free establishment and the free growth of businesses in consonance with natural economic laws are irre-

placeable factors for the improvement of man's existence."*
On the other hand the French Communists, numerous and
vocal, however much they have lessened their intransigence in
some respects, remain firm in their formula: no private ownership of the means of production. And in general the French
Left presses for an extension rather than a retraction of the
public sector of the economy.

Employer and employee do not yet lie down together like
the biblical lion and lamb. But, perhaps to abuse the metaphor,
we must note that it is no longer quite so clear as it used to be
which is the lion and which the lamb, a circumstance that
makes for compromise and a degree of toleration, if not of
mutual affection. Management and labor do sit down nowadays
at the same table and negotiate from strength on both sides
and with at least some mutual respect and understanding. The
French businessman and the French labor leader are not in
that euphoric state of mutual confidence that some of the bright
young men of *Fortune* and other Luce publications have suggested is true of our American "permanent revolution," but the
old French class struggle between capital and labor is not so
deadly as it used to be. As for planning and further nationalization, the Hacketts can say almost in an aside that "it is striking
to note the extent to which the debate is now based on practical, rather than ideological, considerations and the general recognition that other types of policy measures can often be more
effective than nationalization in implementing the Plan."**
Finally, if the second of the C.N.P.F.'s fourteen points was
pure Rightist laissez-faire, the first was piously democratic
enough to have been asserted by our N.A.M. "The economy
should serve men so that they will find in the performance of
their work a higher standard of living, opportunities for ad-
vancement and personal development and the pursuit of a

* *France Actuelle*, March 1, 1965.
** Hackett and Hackett, *Economic Planning in France*, p. 348.

better future for their children." In short, there would seem to be, even on matters economic, an *approach* to consensus in France, that land where of old no one agreed with anyone else on matters of principle—ideologies if you like—but everyone held that his own principles were true, great, and should prevail.

As of 1967 and in fact among some commentators all during the last two decades of economic growth, there is a tendency to worry over its continuing. As did the old Corsican mother of Napoleon I in the midst of the luxuries of the imperial palaces, some experts say, *"pourvu que ça dure"*—if only this lasts! Inflation, apparently always a threat in an expanding free or mixed economy was a very serious problem for the Fourth Republic, which never quite solved it and was brought down in part because of this failure. Devaluation of the franc in the first days of the Fifth and the creation of the new "heavy franc," formally equal to the twenty cents it had been worth in the distant past of 1914, resulted in fairly stable prices for the next four years, but prices rose alarmingly toward the end of 1962. De Gaulle's government in 1963 took steps to insure a relative stabilization. These steps were mostly orthodox restraints on credit, attempts to increase exports, regulation of prices including wages, but not significant cuts in total government expenditures.

These measures have been at least partially successful. The retail price index, the best measure of inflation as it affects ordinary citizens, after a 4.2 rise in 1963 from the base of 100 in 1962, was 2.9 for 1965 and about the same for 1966. These last two are somewhat under the average American price rise in 1966. Yet industrial production from a base of 100 in 1962, after a brief initial drop to 94 in mid-1963 as measures for "stabilization" took hold, had by June 1966 risen to 123. As of 1967 the French economy seemed to be maintaining, not a "heated" growth, but what one of the new French economists calls a "normal and middling growth" threatened, he holds, by a domestic policy too much on the expansionist side.*

French labor is certainly in no mood to put up with any radical restrictions on its share of the national income. There are still enough Frenchmen on fixed incomes to insure some public protest against even the two or three percent annual rises in price level so good an economist as the late Sumner Schlichter held were inevitable in a modern Western economy. Among economists the chief worry is whether or not a sufficient proportion of the Gross National Product is in fact being set aside and used for investment in ways that will insure continued growth. Perhaps too much is being spent on the good life in the American style, which, it cannot be sufficiently emphasized, is for many French intellectuals the worst possible life. Perhaps wages are, as consumers insist, going up faster than the productivity of labor. This is a complaint not unknown in the United States. Finally, in view of the current policies of de Gaulle's government, there are grave doubts as to whether France will continue her collaboration with her five partners in the Common Market, a collaboration which has been commonly held to be of great importance in the achieved economic growth of France itself.

The difficulties over the future of the Common Market are perhaps rather more political than economic and will command attention in a later chapter. In 1967, though there are various signs of lessening growth rates as well as the usual worries noted above, worries surely common to most of the free world today, France seems economically well-placed, much better at the moment than her old rival Britain. France is threatened no doubt by a dip in the statistical curves, by what in this country is called a "recession" but not a "depression." If contrary to

* S.E.D.E.I.S., *Chronique d'Actualité*, October 20, 1966. See also the optimistic article "La France Déstabilisée," *L'Express*, September 5–11, 1966. *L'Express* is by no means a "Gaullist" organ.

expectation France undergoes an economic crisis as serious and prolonged as that of the 1930's, one may safely conclude that she will not encounter it alone and that prediction of what will happen to a free world subjected to any such crisis is not possible.

There are limits to French economic growth and to the place France can attain in our contemporary rank order of great powers based on material strength and capabilities. I have not here attempted to brush off the obvious hangovers of the old France of *mesure,* caution, and small-scale enterprises; such will long endure. But an even more obvious limitation to French greatness is the simple physical one of size; neither in territory nor in population is France—even granting her a certain persistent influence in some of her former colonial dependencies—comparable with the "superpowers." Metropolitan France, smaller than Texas in area, cannot rival the giants, the United States, the Soviet Union, China, and, perhaps some day, Brazil and India. Even a thoroughly industrialized France, populated as densely as England or West Germany now are, could not approach these giants. A full federal union of all the Western European countries in a single unit would be a giant indeed, one which in the total of material resources that military intelligence likes to call "capabilities" would be at least as strong as the United States or the Soviet Union. But no such union seems remotely possible in our time; and if and when it is achieved, France could be no more than a "region" within it. All this the present leaders of France know well. De Gaulle's apparently accurately reported sigh, "If only we had a hundred and eighty millions!" was no more than a sigh. It does reflect, if only in the closeness of that figure to the actual population of the United States, his dislike and envy of American "gigantism."

Chapter Six

The New France:

The Fifth Republic

1. The instability of French governments since 1870 has been if not actually exaggerated at any rate dealt with superficially, not treated as part of a whole by most foreign critics and by many French critics with a special cause to plead. The Third and Fourth Republics were parliamentary democracies with a decorative president who fulfilled the functions of constitutional monarchs in lands like Great Britain, and with a ministry or cabinet headed by a prime minister exercising supreme executive powers. The ministry was, however, at bottom an executive committee of the democratically elected lower house of the legislature, the Chamber of Deputies, which could dismiss it at will by a majority of actual votes. The deputies represented about a dozen organized parties, no one of which ever commanded a majority. Ministries were therefore established and supported by fragile coalitions negotiated among leaders of these splinter parties. Any ministry could be overthrown if some groups not members of the coalition joined with discontented—or merely ambitious—individuals within the governing coalition. The result was a very brief life for a ministry, on the average less than a year, which meant

in effect that the responsible chief executive of France was changed every few months.

Yet those favorite words of hostile or uncomprehending columnists and editorial writers on French politics, "chaos," "anarchy," "irresponsibility," miss the mark. France seen as a political whole was far more stable than its critics would admit. In times of great crisis France did indeed suffer if such a crisis coincided with a ministerial crisis, and there was for perhaps several days or weeks no prime minister. But over the lives of the Third and Fourth Republics such crises were few and not in themselves fatal. Two important factors, as well as a good many lesser ones, helped to counteract the instability of ministries. First, there was a striking continuity in the ranks of the higher civil service, men who were not mere administrators, but who were also policymakers. The French civil service at this level was well served indeed. And of course the important daily work in the courts, in local government, in special functional agencies went on as usual no matter what man was prime minister or what coalition of parties had put him in office. Second, ministries were never entirely changed in personnel. Those who attacked the system wrote indignantly of the "republic of comrades," or complained—to use an Anglo-Saxon figure of speech—about the game of musical chairs that went on when ministries were changed. The same men did indeed reappear in different, sometimes even the same posts in a long series of ministries; usually only a few marginal changes were made each time a ministry fell. In effect therefore, the men who governed France—the politicians, if you like—were not by any means inexperienced tyros, but old professionals. One can easily work around to argue that the trouble with the Third and Fourth Republics was in fact the *lack* of real change in the ranks of the leaders.

Much more important than these superficial criticisms of the working of the French parliamentary system is the fact that the compromises of political life necessary in a modern mass democracy were made in parliament *after* the general elections in which the many splinter parties (which did after all usually "stand for" something) all presented candidates for the people's approval. For in this world all free societies are politically pluralist, never, not even in the model Anglo-Saxon democracies, with two simple parties; all, to be provocative, have splinter parties. In the United States, for instance, the necessary compromises are made *before* general elections, through our complicated party machinery with its culmination in the national conventions to nominate candidates for president and vice-president and to draw up those remarkable ideological compromises, the party platforms. Even so, the threat of a "third party" or more is rarely absent here or in the British democracies. In France and indeed in most continental free societies, these compromises were made in the actual workings of the legislative body, after it was elected, and were consummated in the structure of cabinets.

There is, however, also a sense in which all free societies, all modern societies that have "government by discussion" among their citizens, have two great parties, Right and Left. The simple polarity of Gilbert's guardsman in Iolanthe will not hold.

> For every boy and every girl
> That's born into this world alive
> Is either a little Liberal,
> Or else a little Conservative.

But there is a rough polarity as on our globe, with most voters dwelling in temperate zones on each side of an equator. In France, as in other modern democracies, the Left has since the last quarter of the nineteenth century pushed, or been pushed, toward the welfare state and a goal of socioeconomic Equality; and the Right has in these years moved more and more toward what was once a goal of the Left, a maximum of laissez-faire individualism and an emphasis on Liberty. In France, as elsewhere in the free world, the last hundred years have seen by the struggles and compromises a fairly clear and in our time apparently irreversible trend toward the goals set by the new Left, toward the welfare state and the mixed economy. In the light of this great general movement, the continental European phase of splinter-party party government and cabinet instability looks less important than it does if studied in isolation.

Nevertheless, democracies probably do work better when the compromises necessary to life—or certainly to an orderly society—are made as quietly as possible, even if they are made in our familiar "smoke-filled room." However this may be, there is no doubt that the Third and Fourth Republics, though their great failures of 1940 and 1958 cannot reasonably be attributed wholly or even largely to their form of government, their "constitutions" in actual practice, have suffered at home and abroad in public opinion from just this reputation for irresponsibility and instability. De Gaulle himself has made full use of this reputation in his attacks on "the parties" and the sins of government by parliamentary coalitions.

2.   Historians will no doubt long debate the reasons for the fall of the Fourth Republic in 1958. The conjuncture of, first, the presence of an unoccupied and available "strong man" in de Gaulle, second, the threat of a galloping monetary inflation, and third, the deep rifts made in French society at home and in Algeria by the revolt of the native Algerians—these afford, if not a full explanation, at least a clear frame of reference. The three must be seen in the light of the long-drawn-out struggle in Indo-China, the defeat at Dien Bien Phu, and the forced withdrawal of the French from this major colony in 1954, the year the Algerian revolt began. There was then in 1958 a compounded crisis, which the leaders of the Fourth Republic proved unable to weather. It should be noted that in

all our national history, only the crisis of 1860–1861 was at all comparable to this French crisis in the depth and intensity of the challenge it offered to constituted authority. We by no means solved that crisis in a nice, quiet Anglo-Saxon way. The equivalent of the firing on Fort Sumter was for France the seizure by a small group of extreme Rightists, not to say fascists, of the General Government headquarters in the city of Algiers and consequent wild rioting. But this *Treize Mai* (May 13, 1958) was merely the irrevocable firing of a charge long preparing. Of the three major factors in the situation we have just noted, the threat of serious price inflation is endemic in modern industrial economies and needs no more analysis here as a contributory cause. More attention must be directed to the Algerian situation and to the personality of de Gaulle. Of these two the Algerian situation, with all its complexities, is surely the simpler.

In 1958 the French had held Algeria for almost a century and a half as a "possession"; its flanking lands, Tunisia and Morocco, which together with Algeria made up most of ancient Roman Africa, the Arab Maghreb, were acquired later and were no more than "protectorates." Tunisia and Morocco, after much nationalist agitation but little actual violence, had by 1957 both been granted formal independence, although French influence remained strong in both. Algeria, however, had technically been integrated with metropolitan France, organized in departments, given direct representation in the legislature in Paris, and left with no more than minor marks of separate status, such as an appointed Governor General and a General Government staff in Algiers. Save for a few assimilated Algerians, suffrage was limited to those of European stock, the *colons*. Between the Moslem masses and the *colons* there was a great cultural and economic gap.

In the course of some five generations, Algeria had to a degree become a true colony of settlement by Europeans, the only one in the great nineteenth-century French Empire. In the rest of the colonies (save for tiny St. Pierre and Miquelon!) a few, often a very few, white French administrators, planters, businessmen, and missionaries stood over against a large, colored, native population. The French, doubtless for a most complex set of causes, do not emigrate in numbers. Even in Algeria, the million or so European *colons* who held the best lands and the most profitable enterprises, were probably in blood at least as much of Italian, Spanish, and other Mediterranean stocks as of French. By 1958, however, they all had been brought up as Frenchmen, spoke French, and felt . . . well, not quite French, in spite of their insistent slogan, *Algérie française*, but rather French colonialist. They were outnumbered by the nine million or so nonEuropeans of mixed Berber and Arab stock, Moslem by cultural inheritance from a long past, and by no means a simple monolithic block. There were a few almost wholly Gallicized Moslems of the *effendi* class familiar in other Middle Eastern lands, no longer professing Islam, but rarely Christians either—just good French secularists. There were native intellectuals, most of them also no longer of very strong Moslem faith, but more or less Marxist. These latter were in fact the leaders of the national liberation movement. The French had after all brought a great deal of modernization to North Africa—economic historians hold that the Maghreb had never been so prosperous as a whole since the best of ancient Roman days—and there were the beginnings at least of a native middle class. Nonetheless, the great majority of the Moslem population was composed of peasants, agricultural and industrial workers, and, in some regions, nomadic grazers. They were certainly for the most part better off materially than were their ancestors before the French came, and they were not subject to any high-pressure religious or cultural attempt to make them French.

Yet as events were to show, they for the most part rejected the French and welcomed independence. The revolt that broke out in 1954 was the work of a determined minority, and the whole liberation movement followed a pattern by now familiar—guerrilla raids, plastic bombs, killings, terrorism, and counterterrorism by the governmental authorities. Whether an earlier series of concessions by the French government might have prevented much of this violence and gradually brought Algeria to a more comfortable independence is an interesting, but idle, question. If you wish to speculate in the not-very-well-explored field of the comparative sociology of revolution, you will find an analogy not so much in the recent freeing of colonies like Burma or the Philippines, with few white inhabitants, but in Ireland. In that country the British "garrison," numerous indeed, were in fact *colons*, differing from the native Irish originally in language, later in religion—a most important factor—and in social and economic status. There are obvious differences between the two revolutions, Irish and Algerian, but there are quite as obvious similarities. Not the least significant of these last is the fact that at the climax of the resistance by Protestant Ulster and the English "garrison" throughout the island to the legally enacted Home Rule Bill of 1914, the British officer corps, law-abiding gentlemen brought up in the tradition of obedience to civil authority, not unruly Frenchmen, began a mutiny against their king, which was halted only by the outbreak of the World War of 1914–1918.

The *Treize Mai* in Algiers was in part an army mutiny that went much further than that in Ulster and, with de Gaulle and his followers aiding and with a hesitating and divided government in Paris putting up no effective resistance, overthrew the Fourth Republic. I shall not here attempt a detailed account of what went on in the fortnight between the thirteenth and the twenty-ninth of May 1958, when de Gaulle entered the

Elysée Palace as *président du Conseil* and the Fourth Republic
ended. Hundreds of messengers and thousands of messages
went back and forth between Paris and Algiers. As Jean Lacouture picturesquely puts it, the two cities "hanging on to
each other like two old boxers in a clinch" were stalling for
time.* De Gaulle in that fortnight exercised all the skills at
handling delicate situations and tough opponents that he had
learned in his years with the Free French. He would, he insisted, come back from his self-imposed retreat at his estate in
Lorraine only on condition that he be given, not quite a
dictatorship, but the kind of presidential powers an American
president enjoys. He was backed in the necessarily complex
negotiations that followed by a nucleus of faithful Gaullists, by
Algerian *colons* and metropolitan Rightists who believed he
would save *Algérie française,* and by a few farsighted or lucky
liberals, socialists, and kindly internationalists who believed he
would turn Algeria over in the end to the Algerian nationalist
revolutionaries. Whether de Gaulle made specific promises to
the *colons* and the Rightists to keep Algeria French or whether
they merely inferred from his early background of French
Catholic conservatism that he would so act will be debated
for a long time, but almost certainly not settled, by publicists
and by historians. It looks from here as though he could not be
wholly cleared from charges, if not of purely Machiavellian
double dealing, at least of judicious ambivalences. I must
attempt the exceedingly difficult task of judging the character
and the aims of this extraordinary man, without whom France
would not be altogether what it is today—and without whom
almost certainly Franco-American governmental relations
would be somewhat different.

* Jean Lacouture, *De Gaulle* (Paris: Editions du Seuil, 1965), p. 154.
This, one of the best of the many books on de Gaulle, has a very fair
account of the *Treize Mai.*

De Gaulle was born in 1890 into a family background conservative indeed, in fact royalist. His father was of an aristocratic family, but relatively not very well off; his mother was of upper-middle-class stock and an even firmer Catholic and royalist than her husband, perhaps because she was of a firmer character. The father was an intellectual, a *clerc* as the French say, a teacher and later head of his own private school. Charles and his three brothers had the strict conventional upbringing of their kind in French conservative families at the turn of the nineteenth century. Above all, they were brought up in the conviction that the real France—the France which throne and altar in alliance had over the centuries endowed with the best of civilizations—had under republican secularist control gone astray and been beaten by a culturally inferior Germany in 1870. Neither parent was an activist *revanchard,* and all the boys in adult years accepted the Republic as their fatherland. Charles de Gaulle clearly, however, always felt differently about France from the way freethinking, anti-clerical Clemenceau, with whom he has some traits in common, felt about *his* France. De Gaulle's France was a less cerebral, a mellower and more tolerant *patrie* than that of the Jacobin Clemenceau. A Rightist's ideal France need not be such as de Gaulle's, witness the France of the bitterly intolerant and rigid *clerc,* Charles Maurras. For Maurras, royalist by conviction and Catholic by political convenience, the ideal Roman France was so far from the Third or any possible Republic that he was to find himself a full collaborator with the Nordic, romantic, impossible Germany of Hitler.

Charles de Gaulle chose the army, not the academic life of his father, and went through the usual training of a French officer, being graduated from the officer's school at St. Cyr thirteenth in his class. He was wounded three times in the War of 1914–1918 and spent two and a half years in a German prison. Between the two wars his actual military career was not marked by striking promotions, though fate cast him under the command of Marshal Pétain, the hero of Verdun, with whom he was for years in close, friendly relation. Indeed Pétain served as godfather (or held later that he had so served) for de Gaulle's son Philippe, who was certainly named for the Marshal. De Gaulle's very choice of a military career is evidence of one important phase of his personality, for which the worn and often misunderstood Nietzschean "will to power" will have to do. No one works his way up to the very top of competitive politics without this quality, which often seems to those who merely write about such persons self-centered arrogance or, worse, megalomania. Certainly the Big Three, who never allowed de Gaulle to join them as a Big Fourth, Roosevelt, Stalin, Churchill, at times displayed their wills to power in quite unattractive ways.

De Gaulle's career as an officer during the twenty years' truce shows evidence of a master-element in his make-up that neither Roosevelt nor Stalin possessed, and Churchill had only to a slight degree. De Gaulle is an intellectual and a rebel, compatible things in a Marxist and in academic revolutionaries generally but rarely found in heads of state even at the crisis stage of revolutions. He is intelligent—not an exact synonym of intellectual—a cultivated man well-read in French and classical literature, and the possessor of a prose style always clear when he wants it to be and, what is more surprising, capable of Voltairean irony and malice. He can also make public pronouncements in a sententious, bumbling, oratorical manner that lends itself beautifully to satirical imitators. That he can at will employ so cliché-ridden a style is in itself an example of his complexities; but good authority has it that he enjoys very much listening to recordings by his parodists; he certainly reads and laughs at the weekly *Canard enchainé*, in which he is mercilessly attacked and caricatured in the style of that periodical, so determinedly and ceaselessly allusive and full of *l'esprit français* as to be in the end rather boring.

Admittedly, "intellectual" is a shopworn and imprecise word, but it will have to do. The intellectual usually shares two important attributes: he has an impatient discomfort about many things-that-are, and he can be very articulate, often by use of irony, in expressing that discomfort. De Gaulle's two controversial books of the 1930's, *Le Fil de l'épée* and *Vers l'armée de métier*, are attacks on the complacency and lack of intelligence of a high command that could trust the defensive Maginot line and mass armies in an era of armored divisions and dive bombers. They help to explain why de Gaulle was no more than a colonel when the second war began. He was of course obviously too gifted to be left in routine assignments. But when in 1924 he had had his chance at the advanced *Ecole de Guerre*, he there attacked official doctrines relentlessly and was ranked unfavorably by his superiors. Lacouture tells an anecdote that should serve to confirm the description of de Gaulle as a rebel—and an arrogant one. "At the War School Captain de Gaulle maintained, against the official teaching of Colonel Moyrand, founded on *a priori* conceptions, his own theses inspired by 'circumstances'. . . . The unfavorable grade he received surprised only himself. His classmate Chauvin commented on it to him at the moment of leave-taking in the courtyard of the school, 'you've stuck enough darts [banderillas, as in a bullfight] in them in the last two years to deserve this sentence of execution.' At which de Gaulle replied in exasperation, 'I'll not come back to this filthy hole except as its director!' "*

There is then nothing surprising in de Gaulle's supreme gesture of rebellion in June 1940. This was mutiny, treason; but so too in 1776 was the action of a sworn officer in the service of his Britanic Majesty named George Washington

* Lacouture, *De Gaulle*, p. 62.

when he assumed command of the Continental Army. It is unfair to Washington and de Gaulle, and to others like Robert E. Lee to suggest that the subsequent empirical test of success or failure establishes the difference between virtuous rebellion and wicked treason. De Gaulle saw clearly through the horrid days of June 1940 what had to be done, but he has confessed that the final decision to keep France in the war in just the way he did cost him hours of anguish. There is no doubt that he has preached and practiced realistic and pluralistic politics in ways that shock the pure in heart and head. He does not, however, like a Talleyrand, rejoice in the practice.

The experiences of the war and the liberation taught de Gaulle much, but they also deepened, if that were possible, his feelings for—self-identification with is not quite fair—the greatness of France. That greatness, he held, had been not merely diminished, but almost lost by a failure of intelligence, character, and will among those in all fields responsible for the entity "France." His later difficulties in 1945–1946 in getting his France restored in just the way he wanted it restored intensified his already firm conviction that in the essential *political* phase of that restoration the "parties," those quarrelsome, unrealistic, wordy splinter-parties of the Third Republic, were making the task impossible. When he could no longer control them and when the Fourth Republic began to look exactly like the Third, he resigned power and went into opposition. His attempt through a Centrist party of his own, the *Ralliement du Peuple Français* (RPF—the "Gaullists" of the Fourth Republic), to further his policies never was very successful and soon petered out. For a while in the 1950's de Gaulle was in a sort of voluntary exile at home in Lorraine. There were those at the time who habitually wrote about him in the past tense, the French preterit or historical past.

To sum up: the de Gaulle who came to power in 1958 was a strong-willed, practical, political leader, an authoritarian but also a rebel and in some senses an intellectual, formed in youth as a Catholic and royalist, molded by circumstances into one kind of "realist" and therefore no dogmatist, no absolutist, not at least in the give and take of politics. His France indeed has, for him, always been an emotional absolute. We all escape from this world somewhere; de Gaulle escapes into his own private France. Such escape ordinarily does not change this world appreciably; but when the man who so escapes into a private and, surely to a degree, unreal France is Charles de Gaulle, the consequences to the France of this world are great—and as usual in this world, both good and bad. History will probably judge that, for June 1940 and for May 1958, the good outweighs the bad; for the 1960's and later the verdict is still uncertain.

The transfer of power now irradicably recorded as one from the Fourth to the Fifth Republic was almost a legitimate one. Had de Gaulle wanted to, he could probably have retained the title "Fourth Republic," which might have helped the reputation of France in the United States, a land where public opinion is hostile to the implications of revolutionary change. There was indeed a great deal of violence in Algeria and in France itself during the next four years as the *colons* and the extreme Right in the *Organisation de l'armée secrète* (OAS) took to terrorist tactics with plastic bombs, shootings, and riots, together with milder ways of propagating their cause. Would-be assassins missed de Gaulle on several occasions, once by a matter of inches. He managed, however, to hold the loyalty of the conscript army and many of its younger officers. Negotiations with the native Algerian revolutionary government (FLN) were difficult and protracted, but in the end complete political independence was granted to Algeria, with residual economic rights to Saharan oil and a good deal of real influence left to France. The events of 1958–1962 are still too near for a full explanation of why the terrorism of the OAS failed in a world where so much terrorism has succeeded. On the record, Rightist terrorism has in the last two decades been rather less successful than Leftist terrorism. At any rate, it is clear that in

1958–1962 most Frenchmen did not want the OAS to prevail and were ultimately reconciled to, even pleased with, the loss of Algeria. Unlike the loss of Alsace in 1871 and 1940, the loss of Algeria made no occasion for the *revanchard* spirit among the masses of the French people.

3.   The constitution proposed by de Gaulle and his experts was approved four to one in a referendum in September 1958. It has been amended significantly only once when in 1962 instead of election of the president by a large electoral college of over 70,000 national and departmental legislators and other notables, direct election by universal suffrage, male and female, was substituted. The constitution provides for a president who is the real as well as the symbolic head of state, and who is elected for a term of seven years and can be re-elected. He appoints the premier and other ministers, who may not hold seats in the legislature. It is, however, an interesting survival of parliamentary prestige in this supposedly wholly presidential régime that many ministers run for a seat, with a specifically named *suppléant* on the ticket, and when elected resign the seat in favor of the *suppléant*. The president may dissolve a legislature any time after the first twelve months of its life and order a new general election. By a controversial article (number sixteen), he also has great additional powers that amount to a right to govern by decree in times of great national emergency. The legislature, composed of an Assembly directly elected and a Senate indirectly elected, has according to the constitution the usual powers of making laws, raising taxes, and approving treaties; furthermore the ministers are "responsible" to it. Clearly this is a constitution based on separation of executive and legislative branches to a very high degree. The executive has been strengthened, the legislative, which under the last two republics was really supreme, greatly weakened.

The legislative power and in particular the popularly elected lower house, the Assembly, have by no means been eliminated. Save when article sixteen has been evoked in a national emergency, it must pass on all legislation. Because the cabinet is "responsible" to it, it can overthrow a prime minister, though only by a majority vote of its full membership. The Assembly cannot, however, force a *president* to resign. Clearly in this constitution there is the possibility of an American-style conflict between a president and the legislative branch. De Gaulle's prestige and skills, the obvious willingness of most Frenchmen to accept the political stability offered them by the occasion, and no doubt much else has meant that so far no such direct confrontation has occurred. The new France may conceivably have new politics.

The Left and to a certain extent the extreme Right have long complained about de Gaulle's "dictatorship," about the "rubber-stamp" legislature, the lack of public interest in political life. Many of the leading figures in the old days of parliamentary supremacy and chances for all—well, all who mattered—to attain that glamorous title *Monsieur le ministre* have of course had to suffer, often in near obscurity. Just how the new constitution will work out in the long run is very hard to say. The one previous attempt at strong presidential government, the constitution of the Second Republic after the Revolution of 1848, fell foul of a Bonaparte, Louis Napoleon, who used his presidential powers to achieve imperial ones. This ultimately disastrous experiment gave presidential government so unhappy a name in France that no such experiment was tried again until the Fifth Republic. De Gaulle has now been president for nearly a decade, and no *coup d'état*, no Empire, is in sight.

Of French practice in political life in that decade one thing at least is very clear. France has not been a totalitarian society, but a democracy. De Gaulle has not suppressed the old parties, though they are unquestionably evolving, perhaps to some approximation of a two-party system. At present the realities of French party politics are perhaps best reflected in the general election of 1965, the first in which the president was directly elected by popular vote. There were four serious candidates and two very minor ones comparable to our own minor party candidates in presidential elections. In the first voting on December 5, 1965, de Gaulle received 45 percent of the vote, his leftist opponent Mitterand 32 percent, the Catholic—*democratic* Catholic—Lecanuet fifteen percent, the Rightist Tixier-Vigancour about 6 percent. Because no candidate received an absolute majority, there had to be a run-off between the two top candidates, de Gaulle and the Leftist Mitterand, which de Gaulle won on December 19 with 55.2 percent of the vote. The total vote in the second election was less than in the first, for several million Frenchmen and women apparently wanted neither candidate and therefore abstained.

The revealing thing about this election, however, is what it shows about the party situation in France. Behind de Gaulle there stood his well-organized party, the Union pour la Nouvelle République (UNR—Union for the New Republic), formed in 1958 and essentially *his* party, like him moderate conservative or centrist for the most part. Behind Mitterand there was a temporary and loose "federation of the Left," including Communists, Socialists, Radical-Socialists, these last, as the old saw goes, neither radical nor socialist. Actually the Radicals are the characteristic old-fashioned anticlericals of the Third Republic, descendants of the Jacobins of the great French Revolution, and all for as much free enterprise as possible. This united front of the Left was difficult to build, and in an earlier unsuccessful attempt at building it the popular socialist mayor of Marseilles, Gaston Deferre, was a victim of this failure and thus was unable to stand for the presidency in 1965. Lecanuet was the man of the postwar

French democratic Catholic group, Mouvement Républicain
Populaire (MRP—Popular Republican Movement), which,
just because it was Catholic, gained the votes of many of the
faithful who in the old days—and today—could hardly be
labeled liberals. Tixier-Vigancour was the man of what was
left of the old royalist Maurrasian Right (very little was left),
plus the still disgruntled fighters for *Algérie française,* and
perhaps a remaining fragment of the Poujadistes, the little businessmen, farmers, and *rentiers* against taxes, the welfare state,
the modern world.

Now to many Americans this may not sound like the beginnings of a two-party system. But note that in the run-off there
was a confrontation of ins and outs and, though imperfectly,
of Right and Left, conservative and progressive, to use nice if
inaccurate terms. What is really important is, first, the fact that
a good many Frenchmen, though unable in that election to vote
for the precise ideological shading they could have voted for
in the old days, did vote; and, second, that the separate parties
of the Left came together, it is true with great difficulty, in a
coalition a bit more "structured" than usual.

This trend—it is no more than a trend—toward two-party
politics was confirmed by the legislative elections of March
1967. The Gaullist UNR, the party in power, was confronted by
a kind of revival of the Popular Front of the late 1930's, this
time however an even firmer coalition. This Left had but two
parties, a Federation of the Left running from Radicals through
two different groups of Socialists, and the Communists, a separate party formally outside the Federation but bound by an
agreement with the Federation that each side withdraw their
candidate in favor of the other in the run-off in any district
where such withdrawal seemed the surest way to beat the
UNR. The agreement was kept with remarkable discipline on
both sides, Federation of the Left and Communists alike. As a
result, well over three hundred of the four-hundred-odd elec-

toral districts had run-offs, "duels," as the French call them, between two candidates only, one Rightist and one Leftist. In fact, shockingly inexact though the comparison may be, there was in the first election on March 5 something like an American primary, with five or six candidates in many districts, and in the second on March 12 a run-off between two surviving candidates, one conservative and one radical, almost like our Republicans and Democrats. Furthermore, these two "parties" in France, like our own two, are neither of them composed of individual representatives in complete, monolithic agreement; both the UNR and the Federation-Communist groups have themselves Left wings, Right wings, and centers.

Again to use a not wholly inappropriate analogy with the realities of American politics, the French election of 1967 was an off-year one, with legislative but no presidential elections, since the presidential term is seven years and the legislative term five years. (Barring dissolution or some other horrid crisis, the two will coincide in 1972.) This off-year election, as was expected, was a very close one and resulted in a considerable diminution of the number of seats held by the UNR. The "Gaullists" by themselves—they were not all solidly UNR—secured a bare majority of one, 244 seats in an Assembly of 486 members.

There is even in France much confusion about the actual labels for some of the political parties or groups in the Fifth Republic. Many of the old habits of parliamentary politics have clearly survived de Gaulle's displeasure. Moreover, there has been a tendency, going back at least to the Fourth Republic, to experiment with labels incorporating even for Rightist groups magic terms like "democratic," "progressive," "modern." This tendency is certainly not limited to unstable France, witness the adoption in stable Canada of the label *Progressive* Conservatives for a party once frankly called just Conservative. In the Fourth Republic the Catholic center was known as the

Mouvement Républicain Populaire (MRP—People's Republican Movement), which became the Centre Démocratique (CD —Democratic Center) and then—although the term seems not to have taken on—Progrès et Démocratie Moderne (PDM— Progress and Modern Democracy). The press commonly uses the term Center, or Democratic Center, but even in the late 1960's MRP still crops up.

The official diagram of the parliamentary parties in the Assembly elected in 1967 issued by the press service of the French embassy in this country used for the majority party centered on the old UNR the unwieldy term Union Démocratique pour la Cinquième République (UD V^{e}R—Democratic Union for the Fifth Republic), but the old label UNR continued in universal use, though individual candidates were occasionally labeled (Ve Rép).

The old terms for the parties of the Left were much the same as in the earlier Republics—Radical-Socialists, usually simply Radicals, the Section Française de l'Internationale Ouvrière (S.F.I.O.—the French Section of the Worker's International); the orthodox socialists, if there is such an orthodoxy, the Parti Socialiste Unifié (PSU—the United Socialist Party), a dissident group; and the Parti Communiste Français (PCF—the French Communist Party). Of the recently formed dissident groups the most important is a Rightist splinter off the Gaullist UNR, centered around the young and ambitious Valéry Giscard-d'Estaing. In the press this group of several dozen is usually called the *giscardiens*. They commonly support the government, but they do not like de Gaulle's anti-American policy, nor do they see eye to eye with him on economic matters. In local elections—no doubt a hopeful sign—one occasionally finds a group (*liste*) with the label *liste apolitique*.

It may be noted here that these March elections of 1967 were not quite so severe a rebuff to de Gaulle himself as the American press generally made them out to be. For one thing, his foreign policy, and in particular his policy toward the United States, was tacitly approved by every Communist vote and by many other Leftist votes. Just as in the United States in off-years, this was an election in over four hundred electoral districts with all sorts of specific local issues at stake and with candidates of varied degrees of charismatic attractions—and no one's coattails to ride in on. Finally, the French, like other democratically conditioned peoples, have a good many individuals who like to turn out those in power just because they are in power, and do so for many different and sometimes ignoble motives and often for no good reason. That such individuals are more numerous proportionately among Frenchmen than among Anglo-Saxons, itself a firm belief at the level of the stereotype among Anglo-Saxons, is surely not quite proven. The fact remains that the number of seats lost by the UNR in the election of 1967 is almost exactly the same as the number of seats in the House of Representatives lost by the Democrats in 1966.

A more significant survey of French political postures than any single election can offer is afforded by a recent expert public-opinion poll in France.[*] The poll, conducted by modern methods on a sample of some 10,000 voters, finds that no politically active group in France has a majority. The pollsters are willing to list only three (not the old dozen) effective "parties," Right, Center, and Left, though admitting that there are extremists at both ends of this spectrum; but no combination of Center with either Left or Right had a majority, because of the existence of an unorganized collection of human beings, numbering about a third of the whole body of voters, which SOFRES calls the *marais* (marsh). This word, definitely pejorative, goes back to the Reign of Terror in the French Revolution.

[*] E. Deutsch, D. Lindon, P. Weill, Société française d'enquêtes par sondages, *Les familles politiques aujourd'hui en France* (Paris: Editions de Minuit, 1966). The society, of course, is known as SOFRES.

The legislative body known as the Convention (1792–1795) had Left and Right wings, but a much larger unorganized group of deputies, moderate, cautious, perhaps merely cowed, called variously by the immoderates and the committed, the Plain, the Marsh, or—most scornful—the Belly. This big group, actually a majority, simply shrank into silence during the Terror. Deutsch, Lindon, and Weill are clearly French intellectuals, and they seem at bottom to dislike and possibly to regret the very existence of the voters who form the *marais*. In the United States, a land which finds the euphemism useful, many of these voters would undoubtedly be called "independent." They have no specific, steady party identification. To the enquirers they made such shocking avowals as these: "The best policy is the beefsteak on my plate, the bigger the better. . . . Improve my own situation, that's what I want from politics. . . . I don't have time to read my newspaper, only the sports pages."*

But the members of the *marais* are not for the most part abstentionists. Their often vulgar cynicism does not lead them to refrain from voting. And in the France of today they incline to support the government, or at any rate to accept the Fifth Republic. They incline in a majority to support the kind of measures the Right supports, limitation of the right to strike by government employees, reduction in the amount of aid France gives to underdeveloped countries; they find the loss of the Empire "lamentable," and in general they are mildly nationalist. But on the big and often abstract questions, such as whether or not to "build socialism," they are indifferent. Fifty-one percent of the *marais* have no opinion on the subject of Franco-American relations, and fifty percent are indifferent to Communism as well.

If the pollsters have correctly analyzed their *marais,* cor-

* For these and other quotations, see *L'Express,* October 31, 1966, p. 44.

rectly isolated this third of the voting population from the true believers, one may at least conclude that there is little immediate danger of another of those shocking political overturns that have given France its reputation for political instability and untrustworthiness. These people do not seem to be of the stuff of revolutionaries, not even of the fascist stripe. Even more clearly they are not Frenchmen who conform to the stereotype of the addict of logic, abstract ideas, lively debate over ultimates of faith, but lacking the stupidity and practicality of the English. They are unquestionably not the kind of people who can bring about a French equivalent of Lyndon Johnson's Great Society. But the conclusion of the high-minded authors of this study of SOFRES, that their *marais* is politically amorphous, uninformed, and dangerously unstable, would seem to be, if seen in the total balance of political forces in France today, quite wrong. In ordinary political life—and the French, after the troubles they have been through in this century, deserve a little such—a certain amount of indifference to the big questions is probably necessary.

Such is neither the opinion nor the practice of most of those French men and women who have to be called intellectuals. This regrettably disputable term here includes those whose vocation, or main interest in life, lies in the pursuit of one or more of the arts, pure and even to a certain extent applied science, scholarship in the humanities and the social sciences, journalism, and in general "intellectual" concerns. If you think of "class" in any simplistic terms, they are not of course a class. They are certainly not a uniform group, and they must not be considered as by definition more *intelligent* than those in our Western society not commonly numbered among the *intellectuals*.

In France today the intellectuals—the conspicuous ones most certainly, the writers, the painters, the other artists, many of the academic community—are to be numbered on the Left and very frequently as Communists. They are against de Gaulle. There are certainly Gaullists among them, and it is probable that a good many public school teachers and other civil servants, once pretty solidly anticlerical and radical, have been won over to the UNR. On the other hand that unattractive pair, Sartre and Beauvoir, for whom "bourgeois" and "American" are completely synonymous and completely adequate descriptive terms for all that is wrong with the universe, are not to be taken as wholly representative of French intellectuals. Still, like their American opposite numbers with whom they have a good deal in common, these run-of-the-mill French intellectuals do not like things-as-they-are—or rather, they are torn between their belief in democracy and a democratic society based on the magic trinity of *Liberté, Egalité, Fraternité* and their dislike for the things that the great majority of Frenchmen seem to like and want. To them the word "Americanization" is a threat to all they hold dear, a threat to good cooking, good literature, good art, good living. Perhaps somewhat more of them than of their American fellow intellectuals hold fast to the belief that the lower classes, the nonbourgeois common man, have been corrupted by the wicked commercial characters who exploit them. Almost certainly somewhat more of them believe that the Russian experience holds great promise and should be followed as far as possible in France. They hold this allegiance in spite of the reign of "socialist realism" in art and literature in the Soviet Union and in spite of what looks to be the lesson of the Russian experience, that the proletarian in command wants to be, and succeeds in being, a bourgeois in most of the horrid connotations that word has for the intellectual.

How much political influence the French intellectuals have is still another one of those hard questions no one ought to be dogmatically certain about answering. There is a firm and not altogether incorrect belief especially strong among some Americans that in France as in Greece and a few other countries, the intellectual is held in high honor by his fellow-countrymen, not scorned as a fellow who has never met a payroll. Certainly there are outward signs of this in France, statues of artists and of writers, even poets, everywhere, almost as common as statues of great captains, and far more common than statues of mere politicians; streets named for these and other culture-heroes as well as from historic events and even abstract ideals; a system of education that puts a clear premium on scholarly and scientific achievements, one in which an athletic scholarship would be unthinkable; a general interest in discussion of ideas, something hard to measure but probably real enough, if hardly universal in France.

In the narrower sense of purely *political* influence, however, it looks now as though at this juncture the French intellectuals have not been much more effective than their American, and rather less so than their British, compeers. They have obviously not succeeded in seriously undermining the hold that de Gaulle and the Gaullists have over the French masses; they have not lessened the affection that those masses have for the products of commercialized industry; nor have they succeeded in communicating to most Frenchmen not of their number their anti-Americanism.

4. French politics under the Fifth Republic exhibits a kind of interplay, not quite pure conflict, but not pure harmony either, between the old and the new characteristic of most things French today. The parties themselves would not seem altogether strange to their adherents and opponents of thirty years ago, though some would seem much more so than others; some parties of the thirties are dead or moribund; and almost all those remaining have suffered injections of change; and finally, some parties are essentially new ones. A brief review of the spectrum should summarize the French political situa-

tion at the moment. But first I must note again the existence among the mass of French voters of a probably larger group of independents and indifferents than was usual under the Third and Fourth Republics, these for the most part oriented toward the "new France" and its material blessings and certainly oriented toward what we Americans aptly call in politics the bandwagon.

No one should be surprised that the French Communist Party of the mid-sixties looks, at least in ideology not unlike itself when young in the twenties. Communism is a well-regulated set of beliefs and attitudes, not to say dogmas, a secularist Church with an orthodoxy firmly established and administered. There are indeed heresies and schisms. The French party lost some members in the repression of the Hungarian revolution, the repudiation of Stalin, and the growth of the Maoist heresy. There is a Maoist group, strong in the turbulent city of Marseilles. On the whole, however, the French party has remained loyal to Moscow. Numerically it has never equalled the 38 percent of the popular vote it attained in 1946. Yet even now it tends in favorable circumstances to poll some 20 percent of the total vote in France. But though its leaders and its numerous intellectuals follow the line as directed from Moscow, a line much softened in the 1960's, its rank and file are a mixed lot. There is a nucleus of workingmen, "proletarians" of a sort, firm believers in but nowadays less firm practitioners of the class struggle. Prosperity, that two-horsepower Citroen or that Renault Dauphine, yes, even that little house well outside the "Red Belt" of nearby Parisian industrial suburbs, have made inroads on these.

The Communist party organ, *L'Humanité*, which has a nationwide circulation, is a good index of contemporary French Communism. Its editorial comments and its big news items are so conventionally Marxist that anyone familiar with French politics could predict their contents in advance; for the most

part, and barring the specifics, they could have been written
forty years ago. But *L'Humanité* also has sports pages, much
less hostile to the sports "establishment" than those of many
American newspapers; it has all sorts of "features" that show
little if any class-consciousness—or rather, that sound quite
bourgeois. Naturally the big national advertisers do not use a
medium so verbally hostile to private enterprise, but the little
annonces are as revealingly bourgeois as are some of the features. There are even advertisements for summer homes, a most
unproletarian form of consumer goods. An issue of *L'Humanité*
recently picked at random advertised three *maisons de cam-
pagne* and under the rubric *"Special Week-End"* (sic) lists
some dozen or so houses or building lots, one of which is as far
away as Thonon in the Alps of Savoy.* One house is called
Mon Toit, "my roof" literally, but with the possessive pronoun
practically a French equivalent of "the Englishman's home is
his castle." It is hard to imagine a Communist buyer of *Mon
Toit* submitting to its nationalization. Faced with advertising
boycotts, *L'Humanité* in 1967 actually took time on the air
waves to advertise itself through the extraterritorial and very
bourgeois radio station "Europe Number 1."

The French Communists from the very start of their Resistance activities made a special and not quite honest appeal to
the peasants. It is a rare French peasant, even of the poorer
sort, who would be content to be merged into a collectivized
farm, but the party has won over many of them simply by
promising something of the sort of help and regulation that the
old Farmer-Labor party promised in Minnesota and the Dako-
tas. The French Communist Party has not in the main changed
its propaganda or its programs, always in France more eclectic
than a strict Leninist could approve. It just isn't growing and
has little chance of greatly improving its position in French
politics. It finds the ideological compromises necessary for the

* "La Tribune des Annonces," *L'Humanité,* September 16, 1966, p. 6.

creation of a unified Left difficult to make the more since its leadership is pretty well on in years. An injection of youth in its leadership (*cadres*) could conceivably help matters; but any great abandonment of its collectivist aims would take the heart out of communism. It is significant that in the 1967 election the PCF definitely maintained its own identity and did not submerge that identity in the Federation of the Left.

Moving from Left to Right on the spectrum, the next group is the Socialists. Their core is the French Section of the Workers' International (SFIO). Since this "International" is the Second of the title, founded in 1889, it is clear that the Socialists too are not exactly new-born. They have been torn apart by dissensions, the most recent of which was brought about by the adhesion of one of their ablest leaders, Guy Mollet, to the cause of de Gaulle during the crisis of May 13, 1958, and the forming of the Fifth Republic. Mollet's group and some others formed the Parti Socialiste Unifié (PSU—Unified Socialist Party), a splinter group which will work with the SFIO and did so in the elections of 1967. The Socialists are certainly more pliable, more willing to work with "capitalists" than are the Communists, but they too are tied to some old habits of mind, class-warfare, anticlericalism, nationalization and collectivism at all costs, and the like. Their leaders, even the younger ones, yearn for the days of parliamentary supremacy and, collectivists though they are, show some distrust of the new breed of bureaucratic and business planners and their kind of planning in general.

Finally, the Radical-Socialists are certainly for purposes of a Federation of the Left, or revived Popular Front, to be regarded as belonging to the Right side of that whole Leftist spectrum. They were the great party of the Third Republic, the party that won the Dreyfus case and separated Church and State at the turn of the last century. They too have a heavy inheritance from the past. Their two great articles of faith, out-

side their patriotic feeling for France, which to be fair was
never aggressive or militarist, were, first and emotionally fore-
most, their great hatred for the Roman Catholic Church and
their accompanying faith in a secularist and rationalist Enlightened Church, and, second, their economic individualism
and its accompanying distrust of much that the welfare state
does. The Radical-Socialists were supposed to have been buried
by the Resistance and Liberation, but apparently there is just
too much of the old France in them for that to have happened.
They emerged from the tomb and are still in being, with no
more than some thirty to forty deputies, but with a good deal
of power in local politics, especially in the Southwest region
from Limoges to Toulouse. It is very hard indeed, and not surprisingly so, to get the Radicals and the Communists to work
together. Even in 1967, there were some Radical candidates
who defied the discipline of the electoral agreement between
the Federation of the Left and the Communists.

It looks from this hasty review as though the French Left is
in fact rather more a part of the old France than of the new,
and this conclusion is to a degree correct. In 1967 poor old
Pierre Cot, a scapegoat for the sins of the Popular Front in the
late 1930's, was elected to the Chamber of Deputies and
promptly went on the air for a correspondent of the Columbia
Broadcasting System with the assertion that he had been
elected by the votes of the oppressed poor against the filthy
rich of the Gaullist party. There are, however, in spite of ap-
pearances, important new elements in the French Left. The
most important group, though one that does not to any great
extent supply *cadres* for the parties and is not in fact very fond
of the Left, is what I have called the "new breed," the mostly
young or middle-aged men who have guided French economic
growth in the last decade. Many of these men, especially those
in business rather than in the civil service, vote centrist or
moderate rightist. But a good many of them would certainly

vote for a New Left, and, in a pinch, in order to further French participation in an extended Common Market, to promote a unified Europe and a *détente* with the United States, even with the present Left.

Still another new element, more closely bound to the old Left, is the "clubistes." As an inheritance from the Resistance, and specifically as a rallying point for those, mostly intellectuals of one sort or another, who felt strongly the need to show more political imagination than the old Left as revived was showing, there grew up, often quite definitely on the model of the Jacobin Clubs (*sociétés populaires*) of the French Revolution, voluntary groups meeting for discussion and planning, but not as political parties putting up candidates for office. Since 1958 the clubs have often claimed to offer a haven for the sort of free discussion essential to a democracy and, according to them, not afforded by the rubber-stamp parliament of the Fifth Republic. But if the many are indifferent to parliamentary debates, they are equally indifferent to what goes on in the clubs. The ancestors of these clubs, the Jacobins, were effective pressure groups from their begnnnings and at their height in 1793–1794 an essential adjunct of the revolutionary government. The clubs are sometimes treated as a fourth constituent of the Federation of the Left, the other three being the organized parties, the two kinds of Socialists, and the Radicals. In principle the clubs, led by active younger men committed to a political career might serve as the catalyst for a really united new Left. So far they have merely added a fourth element in a not wholly stable mixture or, counting the Communists, a fifth.

It is tempting to treat the UNR as no true party, but a bandwagon for de Gaulle's varied following. Almost always in writing about France the term "Gaullist" will crop up as a synonym for this party. Yet the UNR is the best organized, the most "modern" of French political parties, at least in its electoral techniques. It prepares candidates for general elections in seminars presided over by trained public-relations experts and makes full use of the kind of electioneering tactics familiar to Americans, including of course television. Some commentators believe that in fact the experts of UNR in 1967 overdid the Madison Avenue approach to wooing the voters and that their losses in the general election were due in some part to back-firing from excessive pressure of salesmanship *à l'Américaine.* The UNR is certainly no well-knit totalitarian party, not even "crypto-fascist." It has not even really maintained, as it legally well might, a monopoly on broadcasting time, but has permitted the opposition rather more than mere token appearance on the air.

Unquestionably the party is the work of de Gaulle and his close collaborators, and it may well not survive its leader. It is almost certain on de Gaulle's death or retirement to face a crisis, for it has within itself a right, center, and left. These terms may well be too precise for the heterogeneous and ambitious men who make up the national and local leadership of the party. Yet its general stance is centrist in domestic affairs, not really worlds apart from the position of "moderate Republicans" in the United States. Critics have exaggerated the extent to which de Gaulle himself neglects domestic policy to concentrate on foreign policy. Even in foreign policy, the Gaullist position is not unfairly classified as centrist, and certainly is not the simple, old-fashioned, Rightist nationalism of "la France seule." De Gaulle himself has lately shown an interest in measures to promote workingmen's participation in profits of enterprises that employ them (the Vallon amendment), as well as to encourage them to invest in their companies' stocks. His opponents on the Left have seen in these measures a menace of "corporatism" on the fascist model and have made full use of this effective charge against him, because the great majority of the French people want nothing of fascism.

There are of course some echoes of Vichy and the old Right in what the UNR tries to achieve. A good specimen is the campaign—it is nothing less—to encourage physical training and competitive sport among the young. There is even a Ministry of Youth and Sports. Once more, the basic motivation behind this campaign would not seem to be the one that inspired Mussolini and Hitler, the hope of raising up a tough generation of good soldiers. This purpose was surely not wholly absent, but the compound of purposes includes a desire to combat the image of France as overly intellectual and artistic, to improve public health, and, perhaps above all, to enhance the prestige of France in that form of international competition which William James somewhat too accurately perhaps called a moral equivalent of war. In many fields of international competition in sport the French have succeeded very well. They have led the world in Alpine skiing, save for the jump; they have had world track champions, not as might be expected so much among *les sprinters* as among *les stayers*, especially milers; their rugby is now so good that they sometimes win the five-nation championship playing against the national teams of England, Scotland, Wales, and Ireland; they have never quite recaptured their long Davis Cup supremacy of 1927–1933, but they continue to figure in the great international tennis tournaments. The long-drawn out bicycle road race, the *Tour de France,* holds the attention of all France and its neighbors. The climax of attention to sport in France—a climax that profoundly shocked some conservatives and all Leftist intellectuals—came in 1966, when de Gaulle in person at a special ceremony, well televised, decorated six chosen sports champions with the Legion of Honor, hitherto reserved for less vulgar, less "American" achievements.

For the rest, it may be said simply that the UNR has become, if not by any means the party of the French masses, at least the party of those who on the whole are contented with the economic and social gains they feel they have made and hope to continue to make under the Fifth Republic. These people are not to be catalogued in any simple Marxist manner as *bourgeois*—a term which has in France a long historic past associated with membership in an urban patriciate. Yet like most Americans who do not resent the appelation "middle class," the bulk of the UNR would presumably accept themselves as members of *les classes moyennes*. The more cautious or less principled of the old royalist and/or fascist Right has gone along with the UNR. Nevertheless, French and American liberal criticism of the Gaullists as essentially fascist or unreconstructed extreme Rightist is not justified. French politics in general has never come up in practice to the best standards set in the literature about English nineteenth-century politics or about the New England town meeting. Neither has much actual American political reality. The Gaullists have nothing quite so formally paramilitary and fascist as the Hitlerian stormtroopers or the varied shirt-wearers of the prewar days; they have nothing quite like the *Camelots du Roi* of the old *Action Française;* they have nothing, even in Corsica, quite like our city "machines." But they do have groups organized to shout down opponents at political meetings—and shout up their own candidates. They do occasionally rough up opponents —and get roughed up themselves. In the election of 1967 there were some fine rows between crews of Communist bill-posters and Gaullist crews determined to tear down Communist posters and put up their own, and vice versa. Television time was not equally divided among government and opposition. Once more, however, all this adds up to much less than totalitarianism. It adds up, in fact, to the spotted reality of democracy.

Allied with the UNR in much that has come out of the Fifth Republic, but still a separately organized party, was the Popular Republican Movement (MRP), called briefly the Democratic Center and as a parliamentary body after 1967, the party of Progress and Modern Democracy. It emerged from the Resistance as a Catholic group similar to the older centrist parties in Germany and Italy. There were Catholic elements in France before the second world war which might be described as Christian socialists or liberals, but organized Catholic opinion was overwhelmingly rightist and conservative. The Resistance and the Liberation gave a new impetus to the liberal elements in the Church, and in the early years of the Fourth Republic the MRP was, save for the Communists, the strongest single party. It lost a good deal of ground to the UNR, but the recent popularity, in part due to his successful appearance on television, of its leader Jean Lecanuet gave it a lift. The Democratic Center disagrees strongly with de Gaulle's foreign policy, and has always supported the Atlantic alliance system (NATO) as well as measures for strengthening European institutions such as the Common Market. Like the UNR however, it is by no means united on domestic policy, for many of its members are sincere and conventional Catholics who distrust state intervention in the common life; others are indeed Christian socialists anxious to further the work of the welfare state and rescue it from Enlightened secularism. The party took some not unexpected losses in the general election of 1967, because the photogenic Lecanuet could not overcome the handicap of leading a centrist party at a time when Left and Right were engaged in a clear-cut duel. But its power, and the comparatively youthful Lecanuet's, may increase just because the Gaullists will need its support.

There are still remnants of the old Right, but Charles Maurras would hardly recognize them. In the election of 1967 even the voters who had supported M. Tixier-Vigancour for president in 1965 and gave him some six percent of the total vote had little or no success. It is true that their almost complete failure in 1967 was due in part to abstentions from the run-off, abstentions largely motivated by Mercutio's "a plague o' both

your houses." Many Gaullists are in fact fairly far to the Right.
It seems possible that in the near future a true Rightist or Conservative party will in fact be constituted.

The problem of the succession to de Gaulle is much discussed, but there are few who think that there will be the kind
of murderous struggle for power that took place in the Soviet
Union at the death of Lenin and that was freely predicted—it
turned out inaccurately—at the death of Stalin. On the other
hand, sound prediction of just what will happen when
de Gaulle leaves is difficult indeed. The constitutional machinery for orderly succession certainly exists. De Gaulle has
so far not committed himself to any "Dauphin" and is unlikely
to do so. The two candidates from the Center and Right Center
most often mentioned are the present prime minister, Georges
Pompidou and his predecessor, Michel Debré. Both are com-
petent, neither is a popular figure, nor even very photogenic.
Lecanuet, who seems to have some of the assets needed for
leadership in a modern Western democracy, might, if he can
rally the votes of the non-committed and the *marais* of
SOFRES, succeed as president in keeping the Fifth Republic
on an even keel. So, for that matter might a Leftist like Mitterand or Deferre, or one of those once buried and now ex-
humed characters of the Fourth Republic, Mendès-France and
Guy Mollet.

The importance of one single charismatic leader tends in our
world to be exaggerated. A basically more important set of
questions about the future of political democracy in the Fifth
Republic centers on the possibility of a really effective opposition to the party in power. The party in power since 1958—
I must repeat that such a party is a reality, that the personality
of de Gaulle in itself in isolation is no full explanation of what
has happened in French politics—this party is basically and
conventionally conservative. For the forseeable future, an effective opposition party must be more radical, in the special

American sense of the word, more liberal, in French usage, more Leftist. But in the Fifth as in earlier Republics, it has been very hard to get the Left to unite effectively in actual long-run electoral and legislative practice. The gains made in 1967 are no proof in practice of a really united Left. At the moment, there are no clear signs that much progress is being made at the core of the difficulty, which is how to bring Communists, conditioned to work for a revolutionary overthrow of the basic institutions of France, together with the rest of the Left on any sort of program to put before the voters. Agreements—logrolling—about specific *candidates* in run-off elections is an old habit among French parties, but the fact would seem to be that something like what in this country we call a "platform" (and can afford the luxury of being ironical about) has also to be put before the French voters. No such agreement has yet been made, and for good reason; the little Radical shopkeeper, the "compromisist" and peaceful Socialist schoolteacher, close in many ways to a British Labour Party voter, are not going to accept a Communist platform of full collectivism in industry, services, and agriculture, the abolition of "capitalism" and all kinds of private property. Many knowledgeable commentators on the French scene today hold that in fact the PCF has ceased to be *really* Communist, that Communist members of a national ministry would go along with a "revolution" no more thorough-going than that achieved by the British Labour Party in 1945. This is unlikely in the near future, but quite possible in a not extremely long run, especially if the Soviet Union recovers sufficiently from its great revolution and compromises further with the rest of our unheroic Western culture.

French public opinion would seem, if the polls can be trusted, to confirm this analysis. In a poll professionally conducted in December 1965 those polled were asked whether they thought that at that time there was any chance that a

Popular Front (that is, a real union of Radicals, Socialists, and Communists) could be realized in France. An identical question had been asked in July 1964. Here are the results:*

	July 1964	December 1965
Yes	23%	22%
No	24%	45%
No opinion	53%	33%

There is from the same source a slender straw that seems blown in the opposite direction. Asked in the same year whether they thought the Communists in France (PCF) were getting tougher (*plus dur*), more conciliating, or not changing at all, only 3 percent thought they were getting tougher, a whopping 60 percent thought they were getting more conciliating, 22 percent thought they were not changing at all, and 15 percent had no opinion in the matter.**

To sum up briefly: France under the Fifth Republic is still a land of many opinions on political issues. Yet there has clearly been established a modern right-and-centrist informal consensus with a backbone in the Gaullists. This consensus is certainly not unanimity. The Left continues in practice formally splintered, but there has been a real attempt, slowly progressing, to achieve a working union on the Left. In domestic politics, though there are many old divisive sentiments still alive, many slogans and hangovers from "le cléricalisme, voilà l'ennemi" to "la gueuse" (the slut, the royalist name for the Third Republic, from its symbolic female figure, Marianne), there is one fundamental set of issues: Is the recent economic

---

* *Sondages*, no. 1 (1966), p. 47. In French the question was: Croyez-vous qu'à l'heure actuelle un front populaire a des chances de se réaliser en France? It is unlikely that many of those polled understood the question to ask whether a popular front could *win* an election. The key phrase *se réaliser* clearly means no more than whether such a union of the Left could be constituted at all in actual political legislative life.

** *Sondages*, no. 1 (1966), p. 71.

growth to be continued, what are the best ways of doing so, and above all, are its benefits at present equitably divided among all Frenchmen? Almost all who would call themselves Leftists would answer that last question with a no. But they are still very far from agreement as to how to achieve this more equitable distribution of the new national wealth—and how to maintain economic growth. Many Frenchmen would like to work out a middle way between that of the Russians and that of the Americans, but rather nearer the American than the Russian way. They may just possibly succeed.

5. There must remain for the political scientist attempting an unbiased analysis of the degree of stability attained by the Fifth Republic some very specific doubts about two provisions in its constitution. Perhaps the first, concerned with Article 16, which gives the president powers to govern in a grave emergency by his own decrees, is influenced by the sad example of the failure of Brüning's government by decree in the last years of the Weimar Republic. Yet in itself the provision is probably harmless; if conditions in France got to be as bad as were conditions in Germany in the early 1930's no democratic constitution could stand up under attack. The really difficult provision lies in what may be an unworkable compromise between French traditions of parliamentary control of a ministry and the institution of an independent, popularly elected president.

By Article 49 the lower house, now known officially as the National Assembly, can by a majority vote of its total membership force the resignation of a ministry. There are various provisions designed to prevent the old snap votes that used to upset ministries—the requirement of a formal notice of intent, a forty-eight hour delay before the roll call, and the like. Still, if a cabinet is overthrown in this way, the president must appoint a new one. Should he attempt in the style of the earlier republics to make only minor changes, he risks finding the Assembly after prescribed delays passing another vote of no confidence. It is true that after the first twelve months of life of a legislature he may of his own initiative dissolve the legislature and go to the country for a new one in a general election. If that election still returns an Assembly hostile to the president's policies, he must either give way, or resign, or attempt something like a coup d'etat, because continuation of a ministry condemned by the Assembly is clearly illegal. Should there be out-and-out opposition of president and Assembly immediately after a general election, the prescribed twelve-month delay would involve a stalemate exceedingly trying on both sides. There will indeed have to be a revolution in French political habits for such a crisis to be endured.

The French have had, in spite of a few interruptions, some four or five generations of parliamentary government. This was not parliamentary government in quite the manner of the British, but nevertheless it was a government to which the French have got well used, conditioned if you like. They are simply not accustomed to a situation that we in this country, under presidential government (Woodrow Wilson called it "congressional" government), take more or less in stride. If Congress turns down an administration bill or amends it out of all resemblance to what the administration proposed, the president either accepts amendments or gives up on the bill, usually with the intention of trying again in the next session. The French administration after the general elections of 1967 had so slim a majority that, although a formal vote of no confidence seemed almost impossible and was indeed in effect fended off by the failure of an opposition maneuver in the new Assembly, a given bill sponsored by the administration might well be defeated in the Assembly. There is no reason, so far as the machinery of government set up by the Constitution of the Fifth Republic is concerned, why the president and his prime minister should not simply accept the defeat of such a bill or make a few concessions and try again. But there is no precedent for such behavior. The great test of the new constitution will probably occur, not when a president's cabinet is formally voted down in a motion of no confidence, but when an important measure proposed by the administration is turned down. If the Fifth Republic can stand a few such incidents, it may well survive for some time.

Perhaps my opinion is unrealistic. Perhaps French public opinion, increasingly desirous of a degree of political stability for the sake of the national image abroad, would somehow force a compromise. But the possibility of a disastrous struggle between legislative and executive was there, written into the Constitution. In the opinion of many publicists such a possibility was increased by the remnant of the old complete dependence of cabinet on parliament provided for in Article 49. It would be better, they said, to go all out for an American full separation of powers and leave the president master of his own cabinet, with both president and cabinet fully free of any form of direct control by the legislature. Presumably in such a case some specific equivalent of the American institution of impeachment of a president by the legislative power would have to be made. Whether the French could tolerate a situation like that which developed in the presidency of Andrew Johnson is surely doubtful.

All in all, however, this "bastard" or "hybrid" constitution of the Fifth Republic as amended in 1962 would seem to deserve a trial in the kind of reasonably good conditions of the economy prevailing since 1958. It can be amended, as the introduction of direct popular election of the president in 1962 showed. The fate of the one similar constitution the French have had, that of 1848, hardly threatened in the mid-sixties. Had de Gaulle wished to assume a crown of any kind, he would have made the attempt long since. Offensive though the comparison may be to some Americans, de Gaulle's real power is hardly greater than that of many of our "strong" presidents. His personality, his style, the trappings of his power are certainly quite unlike anything American. Its substance, in spite of the cartoonists, is not at all like that of Louis XIV, or even Napoleon III. No one on the French political scene in 1967 seemed likely to attain such a position, not even in the only form it has hitherto taken in the twentieth century, that of an uncrowned dictator or "princeps" in the style of Augustus Caesar, in a totalitarian society. If a modification in the constitution was going to come, one could guess that it would be in the direction, offensive though that was to de Gaulle himself, of the old parliamentary republics. The big test would come if a united Left gained a solid majority in the Assembly.

Chapter Seven

The New France:

The Cultural Revolution

1. The current revolution in France cannot be encompassed by its politics, not even by its economics. A great many French men and women, and children too for that matter, are quite simply thinking, feeling, and behaving in ways few would have predicted a mere twenty-five years ago. There is no master key that explains this process, and no attempt will be made here to find one. Sufficient to note that what is happening in France is merely the French phase of a great and complex series of changes which have their beginnings far back in Western history, changes first made really evident to the world in the American, French, and other "democratic revolutions" of the late eighteenth century. These have now widened their scope to cover the world. France, a major initiator of this great revolutionary movement, is now undergoing its own twentieth-century phase of the "revolution of rising expectations" throughout its cultural life. Consideration of these changes may begin with that critical social experience—and nowadays certainly *experiment*—education.

The French have long prided themselves on the fact that in their language the word *éducation* means the whole process of bringing up the young, a process involving training in morals, taste, and judgment even more than in academic studies. Moreover in this process what goes on in the home, the church, in peer groups and other informal groups is more important than what goes on in school classrooms. For what goes on in schools of all sorts the French use the word *instruction,* and for teachers, *instituteurs.* This distinction between *éducation* and *instruction* has, however, never been rigorously used, and one has the impression that *éducation* has come to mean in French what it means in American usage, the process of training in an organized system of schools: primary, often called by the French the "first cycle," secondary or second cycle, and higher or third cycle.

Ever since the great French Revolution there has been a struggle between Church and State for the control of elementary education, a struggle with many ups and downs, with the State usually in control of the great majority of schools. What we call "private" schools, in France almost always Catholic schools save in the Protestant regions of Alsace and the Cévennes, have never, even during the "secularist" triumph of the State after the victory of the Dreyfusards, quite vanished. After 1918 and even more after 1945, the tide turned a bit, and under the Fifth Republic the *loi Barangé* afforded Church schools a degree of state support. Many even of the younger and presumably more "modern" of the Left still take the *loi Barangé* very hard indeed.

The French educational system has since Napoleon's neat bureaucratic centralization in the first decade of the nineteenth century been carefully planned and administered by a Ministry of Education in Paris. Yet Anglo-Saxon critics have probably exaggerated the deadening effects of such bureaucratic centralization on French education. At least the striking inequalities which have accompanied American local control of public schools have been avoided. Even in France, however, no minister of education has been able to close the gap between the school in the decaying agricultural village and that in the thriving industrial city. The basic job of making France a literate nation has long since been accomplished. How successful the effort to inculcate in these public primary schools attitudes to morals, ethics, and politics as the anticlerical heirs of the Jacobins have tried to do is another matter. The prescribed textbooks in what we should call "civics," written a generation ago by such *bons républicains* as Professor Aulard of the University of Paris, historian of the French Revolution, are not the sort to impress children of this generation. Nevertheless over the years a good many children exposed to this official *instruction* and to *instituteurs* who were almost all convinced secularists have grown up *bons républicains* themselves and thus have helped keep alive the divisions produced by the French Revolution.

Yet there is much new in French primary education, both public and private. Materially, new glass and steel single-story buildings, gymnasiums and all, not unlike those we are building in this country, are going up all over France. More important, there are among the "educationists" all sorts of stirrings. These professionals are no doubt for the most part less extremely permissive and progressive than in the United States, but they do base their positions on contemporary international work in the psychology of learning. French is a language with its own irrational spelling—not much better in this respect than English—and one hears complaints that children exposed to these new methods read with difficulty and cannot spell. But the most striking novelty is the steady growth of coeducation. The old France, which for so long denied the vote to women, had from the beginning separated even the very young boys from the girls. The old buildings even in small rural schools had separate wings marked *école de garçons* and *école de filles*. Educators—and parents—inclining in these matters to conventionality, have tended to resist so dangerous an innovation as coeducation. Nevertheless, the situation in fact is well put in an unpublished report of planning in education: "Primary schools are coeducational when the enrollment only justifies one class. Where the opening of two classes is justified, boys and girls are separated in principle, but exceptions to this rule are more and more frequent." Note the economic motive evident here in "justified"; whatever the motive, the number of single-class schools separating boys from girls dropped from 23,000 to 5,000 in the five years 1960–1965, presumably turning many pupils into coeducational classes, though consolidations certainly lowered the number of single-class schools.

In secondary education the major public institution is the *lycée*, commonly held to be a year or two more advanced than our high school. The graduate of a *lycée* is probably more or less at the level of an American college sophomore or a graduate of a junior college. There are also private secondary schools, usually called *collèges*, and usually administered by a religious order. All cities have *lycées*, with boarding pupils from surrounding regions as well as day pupils from the city itself. Recently transporting pupils in buses from outside the city has made it possible to widen the socioeconomic base of secondary education. Still, although even in the past very bright boys of the poorer classes have been able to attend a *lycée*, there is no doubt that secondary education was on the whole a middle-class affair. It costs money to keep a son or daughter in these secondary schools, public or private, though once more in the "new" France the authorities are making a real effort to broaden the socioeconomic base of secondary education.

The traditional curriculum of *lycée* and *collège*, strong in the liberal arts, mathematics, and the established sciences, made no serious attempt to encompass "practical" studies, let alone the student "activities" of our American youth culture. These schools were and still are excellent in this great tradition. They have recently broadened their activities to include various forms of physical training or even competitive sports, but not in the American sense of schools against other schools with cheering sections and the like. Finally, in this second cycle in French education are included teacher-training schools and a great variety of special schools for technical training for all sorts of life tasks important in this modern world. For such tasks French educational experts do not yet feel that "higher" education is necessary or desirable. It is just possible that the modernization or "Americanization" of France will stop well short of the creation of higher education for the millions.

At the end of their formal secondary education, all French young men and women from public and private institutions alike face a standardized national examination, that for the baccalaureate, for years abbreviated to the "bachot" and now almost universally to the "bac." The baccalaureate is essential for admission to almost all forms of higher education and in particular to the most prestigious institutions that prepare for the traditional liberal professions, law, medicine, and the arts, sciences, teaching, and research. For many institutions, notably those two nurseries of intellectual élites, the Ecole Normale Supérieure and the Ecole Polytechnique, and also for the military and naval academies and others, a strictly competitive further examination is necessary to gain admission. Without the baccalaureate, a young Frenchman or Frenchwoman today is still condemned to a career in such undignified pursuits as business, routine mechanical jobs, service jobs, and farming. The very gifted, particularly in the nobler pursuits like the arts, can succeed even without the baccalaureate; and more important, the pursuits just described as undignified are nowadays, as part of the current French revolution, steadily gaining in prestige.

Yet the baccalaureate remains a high hurdle that the ambitious youth (and his parents) feels has to be cleared. One of the liveliest subjects of universal discussion in France today is the needed reform of the baccalaureate, a subject so prominent in newspapers, periodicals, and broadcasting as to confirm the cliché of French national interest in matters intellectual. There has been great experimentation in the actual substance of the examination, which of old was indeed heavily weighted in favor of the *bon élève* with a good memory and an ability to feed back to his teachers what they had fed him. Some experimentation has been in the direction of more emphasis on what in the United States is called the "essay question" in an effort to separate the good minds from the merely recording minds. Here the pattern has probably been the British university honors examinations, especially at Oxford and Cambridge. Certainly the essay questions on the 1966 examination were geared to the bright but also informed and inventive mind, and they would have left most American high school seniors bewildered. Of recent years the mathematics examination has been even tougher. It would be surprising if the increase in failures in these examinations were not—and perhaps subconsciously— an effort on the part of the graders to reduce the overwhelming numbers now trying to enter the universities and the other institutions of higher education.

Even more important than the problem of the nature of the baccalaureate examination is this vast rise in sheer numbers of those who want the degree and the education that prepares for it and makes a university degree possible. There are not enough buildings, not enough teachers, not enough laboratory space, not enough library books. Almost certainly this increase in numbers means also a relative decrease in the proportion of students interested in or capable of effective work in the classic academic curriculum; it means a dilution of intellectual interests. This difficulty is not unknown in the United States, where it is commonly solved by the big high school which provides something for everybody in one institution. The French tend to separate at the secondary level the "practical" or the technical school from the traditional school based on what is after all a curriculum descended from the trivium and quadrivium of the Middle Ages. Americanization has in fact not got very far in French secondary or higher education. In no French school—certainly in none within the "system"—is it possible to obtain credits for playing in the band (there are no school bands), preparing for a happy marriage, making model airplanes, or learning to dance, or to drive a car. There are indeed sports and clubs of all sorts, but these are voluntary groups, not part of the curriculum.

There is, however, if only so far on the margin of formal French *instruction* in these schools, a beginning of something like our American "youth culture." In a recent report by a committee set up by the Ministry of Youth and Sports the sober *Le Monde* writes: "As far as leisure time goes we learn from the investigation that there is among the young a more marked taste for sport than had been supposed. One boy out of three takes active part in a sport, one girl out of twelve. Among the sports swimming, football [soccer] and track are most prominent. . . . Some 20 percent of the young are members of clubs other than those for sports, such as photographic clubs, movie clubs, orchestras, choral societies, or religious groups. All told, one girl out of four, one boy out of two take part in some kind of group activity."*

All this, though remote from our American ways, still shocks the older generation, for whom Homer and Vergil in the original tongues definitely will not mix with soccer or even with a choral society. Of course there is in France as elsewhere an almost complete abandonment of compulsory Greek and not much more insistence on compulsory Latin.

The basic problems facing French higher education are the same as those facing secondary education. French universities and special schools at this top level are in fact what in the

* *Le Monde,* February 26–27, 1967, p. 14.

United States are called graduate professional schools. There is no attempt at "general education," a process assumed to have been undergone in the *lycée* and to be continued at the initiative of the individual student throughout his life. The universities proper, again a Napoleonic institution, are divided among the major centers of the geographic regions, but with the University of Paris heavily outweighing in numbers of students and in prestige even the greater provincial universities like those of Lyons, Strasbourg, or Aix-Marseilles. They and the various special professional schools at the top level did until only yesterday a good job in taking care of national needs, though the progressives criticized them severely as too bookish, too conventional. But today all of them, and most especially the University of Paris with its 106,000 students enrolled (many of course no more than enrolled, not really studying), are unbelievably overcrowded. The University of Paris has added three suburban branches, which ought at least to keep overcrowding from getting worse as the unforeseen "baby crop" of the late forties comes to enroll. Since 1952, new universities still in the Napoleonic tradition involving new "academies" administering all public education within their area, have been added to the earlier sixteen in seven cities: Amiens, Limoges, Nantes, Nice, Orléans, Rheims, and Rouen.

In Paris students unable to get into a lecture room listen to loud speakers over public address systems seated in corridors and/or staircases. Many never go to classes, for just as the continental universities never tried to house students in dormitories, so they never tried to take class-room attendance. Faced with a similar crisis, it looks as though most other Western countries have done rather better than France in making room for the sudden vastly increased number of students in higher education. But the present French government has worked hard to do something about the crisis of numbers, which came to a France that was not prepared for it and had little reason from its past experience to expect it. Leftist critics are certainly correct: the millions spent for the French *force de frappe* would go a long way toward solving the housing problems of French education and its other problems as well. But Americans, with their vastly superior material resources, ought not to feel justified in throwing the first stone in this situation.*

For the admittedly inadequate material state of the French plant in higher education and to a degree in secondary education does not even now explain the present state of mind of the French student body or at least that of a conspicuous and certainly lively portion of it. The problem of the cultural generation, ill understood in terms the social scientist considers necessary, would seem to be in the mid-sixties especially acute everywhere. The gap between fathers and sons, better perhaps between grandfathers and grandsons, seems abysmally deep and almost impossible to cross. It is especially deep in France, where the family was a much firmer unit than in this country, and where moreover there was something close to rule by the old (gerontocracy). Now the young are disrespectful of their elders, share almost none of the tastes for *mesure,* the classical graces, *douceur de vivre,* not even the taste for good food, of their elders, and in general behave, in the words of one of their critics who clearly finds that standard French is no lan-

* The following table makes clear the great rise in sheer number of students that faces French educational authorities (figures in thousands):

	1951–1952			1964–1965		
	Public	Private (*écoles libres*)	Total	Public	Private	Total
Primary	4,336	1,022	5,358	6,308	1,098	7,486
Secondary	830	351	1,181	2,383	738	3,118
Higher	151.8	10	161.8	390	22	412
Totals	5,317.8	1,383	6,700.8	9,111	1,900	11,011

Source: Statistics from the Ministry of Education.

guage suitable to describe such behavior, "comme des yé-yé beatnik teenagers."*

To those who remember the French academic world of forty years ago there has been a striking transformation which most Americans will find good. Professors, during the "Twenty Years Truce," victims of inflation and shockingly small salaries, and often addicted to nourishing a not wholly uncomfortable feeling of martyrdom about their status, have now attained greatly better salaries and a better status in the new France. Few of them exhibit that pride in poverty, that contempt for physical exercise, that obsessive drive toward scholarly perfection that their predecessors used to show. Many, as good Communists, continue to dislike the *bourgeoisie* and to behave like a *bourgeois* except in politics. Some of them begin to go to excess in the opposite direction and, like their American equivalents, begin to look like successful businessmen—and even to play golf. Almost all of them drive their own cars. Moreover, the present French government, in addition to its patronage of *la vie sportive*, has begun to spend more on scientific research and therefore also on researchers, to encourage travel abroad for teachers and students, and in other ways to encourage members of the academic world to emerge from their long isolation in the role of unworldly *clercs*. The very wealthy French, who are, as are their likes all over the world except perhaps for the United States, fewer proportionately and less wealthy than of old, have never gone in for endowing colleges and universities. No doubt the semimonopoly of the state in secondary and higher education is largely responsible. There is in France nothing like our continuous drives to raise money from alumni.

---

* *L'Echo touristique,* September, 1966. I shall come later to the contemporary linguistic penetration of French by English, even more by American, which the reader will find very completely, if very indignantly, covered in a bestseller, Etiemble, *Parlez-vous Franglais?* (Paris: Gallimard, 1964). The "yé-yé" above is French for what they think is a typical American chant.

French scientific research has improved since World War II. The government is spending money on such research; some American economic aid has helped; and the old ferocious French individualism is yielding to the necessity for teamwork in this area. There are academic "imperialists" and enterprisers —in short, modernization, Americanization, much that would horrify Julien Benda, whose *Trahison des clercs* is only a generation old.

On the whole education in the new France seems to be thriving. At least the French, a people not given to great satisfaction with things-as-they-are, are surprisingly satisfied with the education their children get. In a poll taken in 1963 in answer to the question "Are you satisfied or dissatisfied with your children's education," 67 percent said they were satisfied and only 14 percent were dissatisfied.* Much of the credit for this state of affairs must go to French planners and administrators, educationists, working teachers, and economists, all no doubt to many Americans people damned in advance as "bureaucrats." These people have, however, worked together successfully even in matters involving budgets and the building of new plant. They have consulted with and indeed themselves number among representatives of local interests. This has not been a Napoleonic centralized operation, and most importantly, it has been inspired by a desire quite unknown to Napoleon and his aides to make education available to all who want and deserve it. There has been a generally successful attempt to retain the best of the older classical tradition and its standards while trying to provide technical and other sub-

---

* *Polls* (Amsterdam), Spring, 1965, p. 62. The missing 19 percent answered "Don't know." This Gallup international poll was taken also in Britain, West Germany, Norway, Denmark, Switzerland, and the United States. The American figures were 66 percent satisfied and 27 percent dissatisfied. France ranked third in degree of satisfaction with education, behind those contented little democracies, Denmark and Switzerland. For more subjects of satisfaction or its opposite, in which the French rank much lower in satisfaction, see below, Chapter Eight, p. 235.

jects not dreamed of when our Western classical tradition was begun. Above all, there has been a frank acceptance—on the part of the planners at least—of the pluralistic character of the new French society for which this educational system is planned.

2.   Some comprehension of the state of religion in contemporary France is essential if one is to go beyond the surface of everyday international politics in an effort to guide our relations with her. Yet, in the present juncture, such comprehension is peculiarly difficult in the United States, where religious conflicts have apparently been almost stilled and certainly softened. Those for whom American history is at all real will, however, realize that such was not always the case. An irrational fear and hatred of Catholicism persisted in this country from the earliest times to quite recent ones; sectarian passions were strong among the Protestants; and that complex of secularist or substitute religions here called simply Enlightenment has had firm and often influential representatives from Franklin and Jefferson to Colonel Robert Ingersoll, the "atheist," who during one of his lay sermons was heckled to say what he would do if he were God and announced simply, "I'd make health contagious instead of disease."

Few French atheists would have made so good-natured, hopeful, and thoroughly American a reply. The basic fact of French religious life is that there the division between Christians and anti-Christians has long been deep and bitter, far beyond American experience. Moreover, in France the believers in the pure (that is, anti-Christian) faith of the Enlightenment are no small minority, as they probably always have been in this country; they are a very numerous group, a majority at least among males in some parts of the country. Oversimple as the statement is, it is not misleading to say that, although Protestantism did not take hold in France, Enlightenment as a surrogate religion certainly did.*

The immediate origins of the religious quarrel in France lie in the Reign of Terror in 1793–1794, when there was a concerted attempt to "dechristianize" France by closing churches and convents, confiscating ecclesiastical property, and banishing priests. These acts were supplemented by an attempt to devise a surrogate religion with appropriate dogmas and rituals, such as the cult of Reason, the cult of the Supreme Being, or that curious hodgepodge known as Theophilantropy. The effort failed, and Napoleon in the Concordat of 1801 with the Pope restored state support for the Roman Catholic Church —and, sign of the times, also for Protestantism and the Jewish faith. What I here call Enlightenment was at least tolerated in practice and increased in numbers of believers and in influence as the nineteenth century wore on.

The French have no single word for the Enlightened. *Anti-clérical* is a good loose term, but it can be used of Catholics who simply do not want clerics interfering in matters that they hold are not proper priestly concern, like politics: *Laïque, laïcisme* are simply *lay, layman,* that is, men and matters concerned neither with church nor with religion, but, especially in a phrase like *école laïque,* very close to what is here called Enlightenment: *Déisme* and *positivisme* are more specifically philosophical or theological: *Humanisme* in French has not yet at any rate the meaning it has in Yellow Springs, Ohio. *Sécul$arisme* in French is not quite our secularism. But the thing is certainly there and important, whatever sectarian name its devotees prefer.

Since Napoleon's Concordat in 1801, the conflict between Catholics and Enlightened has gone on, now relatively sub-

* I have done my best to make clear what I mean by classifying Enlightenment as a form of religion, and not as *irreligion,* in my *History of Western Morals* (New York: Harcourt, 1959), pp. 293–307. This is, however, a view strongly challenged both by Christians and by secularists.

dued, now bitter and open, sometimes with one side or the other in control of the central government, sometimes with neither having assured control. Both as respects governmental control and acceptance among the ruling classes and the *peuple* the high point for Catholicism was the Restoration, 1815–1830, and for the Enlightenment the first decade of the twentieth century, when the Concordat of 1801 was revoked and Church and State separated in the aftermath of the Leftist victory in the Dreyfus affair.

In France the conflict has not since the Reign of Terror been a really bloody one—not seriously so even during the so-called White Terror when the Bourbons came back in 1814–1815. Though at times many of each side have felt persecuted by their triumphant rivals, it is not sensible to speak of "perse-cution" in its literal or even its legal sense. And even with regard to the much more unavoidable form of pressure from fashion, from those who hold formal social norms as Christians, "atheism" has never been so disreputable, so scandalous among the upper and middle classes as it is in much of the United States. Nevertheless the pressures were there. In the old upper classes, in the officer corps of the army, it was proper to be Catholic, improper to be ostentatiously Enlightened. Many such *bien pensants* among the upper classes were at the turn of the century strongly anti-Semitic, and such sentiments have not entirely vanished in France today. But the horrible example of Nazi anti-Semitism has certainly made their expression today unfashionable. The governmental class of the Third Republic constituted an Enlightened upper class, and their likes were by no means unknown in the business world. There were even a few generals like Marshal Franchet d'Espérey in the First World War, who were *bons républicains* (that is, anti-cler-icals). Clemenceau, the "tiger," was of course the great hero of the non- or anti-Christians.

The religious situation in the Third Republic is well depicted in many of the novels of the time, most readably in the work of the skeptically Enlightened Anatole France. His *Penguin Island* is a brief satirical history of France; *The Gods Are Athirst*, an historical novel of the great French Revolution; and a series of novels center on M. Bergeret, who is Anatole France himself as a quiet provincial intellectual. It is, incidentally, symptomatic of the degree to which this Catholic-Enlightened conflict has abated today that Anatole France is no longer read by the young, is regarded as *vieux jeu*, old hat. That conflict was nicely symbolized in the usual small town or village of the Third Republic by the two inevitable leaders of each side, the priest and the *instituteur*. In this role the priest fits naturally enough for an American; but rarely indeed in this country has the public school teacher been an avowed opponent of Christianity of any kind. These French teachers, however, had been formed in teacher-training schools under government control, had quite possibly chosen their teaching career because of their sympathies for the anticlerical Left, and were often terrible simplifiers, like the familiar M. Homais of Flaubert's *Madame Bovary*.

It would be absurd to deny the bitterness and the divisive consequences of this struggle between the two Frances, the France of throne and altar and the France of the Great Revolution. Still, as human conflicts go this was not, even under the Third Republic, a *combat à l'outrance*. It had perhaps among the many some of the aspects of a sporting competition, and it had its lighter side. This last is well brought out in a best seller of the 1930's, just because it was a best seller and no masterpiece perhaps a better source for the mere sociologist and historian than more enduring work. The trigger-pull for the struggle in the town of Clochemerle was the decision of the anticlerical town government to put a needed urinal as con-

spicuously close to the church as possible. The novel ends
peacefully as the ardently anticlerical schoolmaster is softened
by a hint, just a hint, from the Senator that the red ribbon of
the Legion of Honor lies ahead if he keeps the peace of compromise in Clochemerle.*

The Resistance and the Liberation initiated in France a
revival of Catholic faith in some ways stronger than the revival
which followed the excesses of the French Revolution. The
revival certainly was centered in the younger generation, and
in particular among the younger intellectuals. Among those
intellectuals the start had come as far back as the early part
of the century, in the writings of such Catholics as Péguy,
Claudel, and Mauriac. But this revival later spread much more
broadly in all classes and, unlike the revival of the 1800's, took
and retained for many of the faithful a democratic, not to say
socialist tinge. One result has been the current success, short
of course of majority status, of the MRP, now CD, a Catholic
party whose leaders at least try to keep a bit left of center (as
the previous chapter detailed). Above all, there are signs that
among the masses, the ordinary people who have certainly
benefited from French economic growth, people who are not
very much like what the Sartres and the bulk of the intellectuals would like them to be, and perhaps at bottom actually
think they are—there are signs that the masses are no longer
greatly excited about the old conflict, signs that the conflict is
dying out. De Gaulle's own firm Catholicism seems not to have
diminished his hold over the many. There has perhaps been
some long-term survival of the collaboration between Catholics
and non- or anti-Catholics begun during the Resistance. Under
the Fifth Republic the monks have come back to the Grande
Chartreuse in the Dauphiné whence they were banished after
the separation of Church and State in 1905, and a few have

* Gabriel Chevallier, *The Scandals of Clochemerle*, English translation
(New York: Simon and Schuster, 1937).

trickled back to that lovely but barren museum, the abbey of Mt. St. Michel. I have noted already the *loi Barangé*, symbolic of the return of the teaching orders and the renewal of Catholic educational opportunities.

In short, it is possible that in this matter of religion there are no longer two warring Frances, but a more pluralistic France, with differences, with variety, indeed with conflicts, but no deep and unbridgeable chasm. Yet one must not exaggerate. The Communists, old-fashioned and reactionary in their tastes, and bound by rigid dogmas, if not precisely in the state of mind of wishing to see the last king strangled with the entrails of the last priest, are nonetheless firmly anticlerical. There are signs of such sentiments among the new élite of the political clubs. But then, very little indeed in a complex modern society wholly dies out, and certainly not religion and religious conflicts.

3. I have noted that France, like the United States, is an old society, very greatly influenced in its social structure and beliefs by the democratic revolutions of the late eighteenth century. In both our revolutions—look for instance at those great condensed statements of ideals and purposes, the preamble to our Declaration of Independence, the French Declaration of the Rights of Man and the Citizen, Bills of Rights federal and state—the great word "equality" is almost as frequent and as important as "liberty." In both countries certainly there has been an emphasis on many aspects suggested by that powerful word "equality," an emphasis not found to the same degree elsewhere in continental Europe, or in England. In both France and the United States there are fairly simple social symbols of a kind of equality perhaps not very deep-rooted and yet indicative of a common feeling for the dignity of man. In the United States all men are Mister, if not Hey, you,

Charlie; in France all men are Monsieur; in England by no means all men are Mister, let alone sir. There remains in the England of socialist triumphs a great deal of the old deference of lower for higher, or in Miss Mitford's now familiar terms, some consciousness on both sides of the gap between U and non U.

These little signs have their importance. In no Western society is there perfect social equality; in all there are complex peck orders, orders of rank, prestige, even privilege. In all, however, even in the most conservative, there is today a strong current of at least superficial egalitarianism, part of the great revolution of modernization—or, if you dislike it enough, the revolt of the masses. In France, this current is nearly two centuries old, and though it has had to run against many obstacles from the days of the ancient régime, it has gained strength from the force of tradition over the years. The kind of social sentiment, and the generally accepted social stratification that goes with it, exemplified for instance in Molière's *Bourgeois Gentilhomme*, whose leading character, M. Jourdain, tries ludicrously to behave in a way above his rank in the peck order, hardly exists in France today. A young Frenchman would find it almost as hard as would a young American to understand emotionally the attitude of the faithful servant arrested during the Reign of Terror for smuggling in a roast chicken to his imprisoned master when he answered the questions of the court with a spontaneous "but M. le Marquis was born to eat chicken." In both countries the difficulty of understanding sympathetically would be compounded by the fact that chicken is no longer a luxury in either.

The traveler in France today, if he remembers the France of prewar days, can see clear evidence of this social revolution. As late as the 1930's, one never saw in a good hotel or restaurant French patrons unsuitably dressed by conventional standards of dress for such places. Today one sees men without neckties, in sweaters, in various informal dress; and even their women, if a trifle *mieux soignées,* shock the older generation by appearing almost anywhere any time in slacks and "revealing" sweaters. No doubt some of these are youthful members of the upper classes in conventional revolt against convention. But at least to the foreigner it looks as though many of them are *peuple,* newly prosperous, able to afford comparative luxury, and apparently not very self-conscious—less so, in fact, than many Americans in a similar position. It is true that one does not yet see in the restaurants, as so often in this country, the sign "Come as you are." They come anyway, without the sign, being good democratic Frenchmen.

The foreigner must always find it hard to understand the subtle distinctions of "class" in contemporary Western societies. Indeed, since that term has been so excessively oversimplified in *Vulgar-marxismus* and in other forms of belief that man is a rational economic animal a good many sociologists try to discard it altogether. But "peck order" too has its deficiencies, for it suggests that who pecks whom is always reasonably clear, and that both parties to a pecking are always aware of the process. The important thing in a study of French society is first and most obviously, not to simplify crudely, as do those French—and not only French—commentators on the American scene who announce that the only thing that distinguishes one American from another is how much money he has, and second, to keep aware of the bewildering variety and fluidity of whatever, in a modern society like France, gives the individual status, or statuses, in that society.

The Frenchman today almost certainly has wider choices, in the common-sense meaning of choice, of what his station in life will be than his father had. This is clearly not the place to confront the problem of free will versus determinism. Of course the child of a French urban slum has many limitations, many impossibilities ahead of him; so too has the child of the aristocratic quarters of Paris, different ones, but not always easier to overcome. But even seen in the simpler terms indicated by such familiar expressions as "career open to talent," "equality of opportunity," "circulation of the elite," or by that horrid hybrid, "meritocracy," France today is a relatively open society. One of the difficulties in the way of American understanding of the rest of the Western world is the not uncommon American belief that we have a monopoly on the career open to talent, that all other Western societies are really caste societies, and decayed ones at that.

No neat measure of the degree of openness of a given society is available. Once more, and in spite of the despair of many of the intellectuals—including sociologists—there are today throughout the West so many talents, so many ways of living —and believing. Of old one might have generalized roughly to the effect that in France the gifts, whether from constitution or from environment, that make an athlete, a salesman, to a lesser degree those that make an engineer, a business executive, a modern, large-scale farmer-entrepreneur, were not so readily and successfully developed as for instance in this country and that the gifts that make an artist, a musician, a soldier, a great chef, a great and conspicuous courtesan, and to a lesser degree a writer, a scholar, a "pure" scientist, were more readily and successfully developed in France than in the United States. Such comparisons were always uncertain, always a matter of degree. They are now even more dubious, perhaps indeed no longer very valid. A born athlete in France cannot expect to earn as much money as the star professional athlete can earn in this country, but he can do pretty well for himself, especially if he wins the cycling *tour de France*. As for the "tennis bum" and other technically amateur athletes, the French are familiar with him and his expense account and have coined a phrase for it, *l'amateurisme marron*. The kind of talent that makes for success in business management and the no doubt closely related talent of the entrepreneur are both well regarded in France. There was always some mythology in the widespread notion that whereas France was full of honored *rentiers,* big and little, in the United States it was a disgrace not to work, so that even those Americans who could live on their unearned incomes worked at something. After all, there were "playboys" in this country before the word was coined. There are still *rentiers* in France, but two wars and a depression have been hard on them; and there certainly is growing up in France a general feeling that the status of *rentier* is not quite one in keeping with the progress of the new France.

Obviously one of the variables in the conditions of life sketched out roughly above, indeed probably the chief one, is the esteem in which a given activity is held. Here again there are abundant signs of change in contemporary France. It used to be held that one large reason for the failure of France to keep up in material achievements with her rivals in Germany, the United States, and Britain was the preference her brightest and most ambitious men showed for the esteemed pursuits of law, politics, art, literature, and warfare over the ungentle-manly pursuits of business, industry, and practical engineering. Even were these last careers taken up, there was in the old France an unwillingness to start from the bottom and do the hard, even dirty work, often necessary for real mastery of the enterprise. Never wholly true, this cliché has less and less application in the present France of rapid economic growth. There was not in France even in the nineteenth century quite the sort of feeling reflected in English Victorian novels against "trade" as a socially inferior activity. Today the atmosphere of the French business world, its creeds, its methods of publicity, its assertiveness, is by no means worlds apart from that of the United States. This business world is of course disliked by

French intellectuals, much as is ours by our intellectuals; and few young Frenchmen have yet dared to assert that the business of France is business.

Another test of a given society, harder to quantify even than that of social mobility within it, and of course not unrelated to social mobility, is the degree of conflict within it. Again one must note that in all modern Western societies there are innumerable conflicts among individuals and among all sorts of groups, with an enormous range of intensity, duration, and extension, from playful—well, almost playful—competition to murderous combat. In this respect, France has had a reputation, no doubt in part because of the cabinet instability of the last two republics, as a society rather dangerously rent by conflict of most serious kinds, class conflicts, religious conflicts, party conflicts, all heightened by the unfortunate French national tendency to take ideas, principles, seriously and therefore to push them to extremes. I must again insist that in the present state of the social sciences it is impossible to work out an overall numerical measure of the incidence of conflicts of all sorts in any society. If my diagnosis of the whole French situation so far has had any validity, it should be evident that France is tending toward a state of less rather than more internal conflict.

The details are not easy to fit in. Class conflict in something approaching the Marxist sense was certainly great—though not deadly—in the old France and is almost certainly diminishing in the new. The same is true of religious conflicts. The conflict between the generations, never even in the old France of family solidarity quite unknown, is in the new at least no more serious than in the rest of the West, perhaps rather less so. Sectional conflicts are now hardly more than sectional rivalries. As I have noted, the old ethnic or linguistic minorities on the edges of the hexagon—Breton, Basque, Alsatian, Flemish— seem in this world of angry minority revolts in Belgium,

Quebec, the Tyrol, Spain, the United States and elsewhere, positively irenic. The French have not as a matter of fact been so free from race prejudice as Anglo-Saxons, in praise or blame, have usually asserted. Neither in the old colonies nor in metropolitan France was formal marriage between whites and Negroes anything but rare. But there have not been any such race conflicts as those in the United States, or the recent ones in England resulting from immigration from the West and East Indies. Negroes in France are neither numerous nor concentrated enough to make race riots likely. There is at least the possibility of trouble over the several hundred thousand Algerians, conspicuously dark-skinned and for the most part poor and unskilled, still to be found in France. These people make up much of the heavy labor in road gangs or do other poorly paid work or peddle cheap merchandise. They are in economic terms even more fully proletarian than the Negroes in the United States, for the few exiled upper-class Moslem Algerians in France are worlds apart from them. Still, again in purely economic terms, they are usually better off than their brothers in Algeria, and unless they stay and multiply while remaining at the bottom of the heap they are not numerous enough to create serious disturbances. The white Algerian *colons,* the *pieds noirs,* who fled to France in much greater numbers— almost a million—were and no doubt will remain as voters a rather more serious danger to the internal peace of France. They have, however, been absorbed into the prosperous French economy in a way that would have been thought impossible under the unenterprising economy of the Third Republic, and though they have not forgiven de Gaulle for his "betrayal" of their cause, they seem to take out their feelings in no more serious way than by voting with the far Right.

There is indeed in France today a conflict between the older generation and the young, but this is a conflict common to the West and, if the news from Russia is accurate, even to parts of

the Communist world. France simply runs true to the pattern
of our time. Juvenile delinquency as measured in statistics of
conviction for crimes of all sorts has increased faster than the
population of the age group defined as juvenile. Specifically in
France, in 1959 there were 76,000 convictions of male delin-
quents under 20 years, 3,000 of female; in 1962, 82,000 males
and 6,000 females; in 1963, 120,000 males and 11,000 females.
No doubt there are variables, such as increased harshness by
the courts and growth of youth population, but nonetheless
there clearly are more young people misbehaving themselves
by the standards of their elders.*

Again what in the eyes of their elders is a less serious but
still unpleasant kind of behavior—sloppy dress, long hair, generally unkempt look, fondness for jazz, continuous jazz, dis-
respect for elders, the whole long catalogue—is to be found in
France. In fact a stroller in parts of the Latin quarter of Paris
might if he confined his looking to persons only, think himself
in parts of Cambridge, Massachusetts, or Berkeley, California.
There are in Paris and in other university towns student riots
and other forms of protest, perhaps a bit more purely political
than in the United States, and with an occasional extreme
Rightist youth group behaving as if this were the 1930's and
they *camelots du roi*. There is another side to this medal, worth
noting even though it is less interesting and more in accord
with the standards of ordinary dull people than the horrors of
alienated youth: the alienated, the delinquent, are in fact a
minority, conspicuous, often worth condemning, but also often
carriers of the new, the fecund, perhaps heralds of a new great
age. Most of the young are even in their modest subservience
to avant garde necessities at bottom conservative and solid
citizens, often not even unhappy.

France, then, seems in 1967 no more seriously divided, its

* For the statistics, see *Annuaire statistique de la France* for the years
cited, under the rubric "Justice."

internal stability no more seriously threatened, than any other Western state. In respect of ordinary crimes of violence, even juvenile delinquency, the statistics show France far more orderly than the United States. There is no clear-cut social conflict in France anywhere near so acute as the conflict between whites and Negroes in America. It is always possible, however, that the French have a much lower flash point than other peoples. Such certainly has been their reputation for nearly two centuries.

4. These statistics should not be allowed to suggest that France has settled down to an inconspicuous and unexciting cultural life such as one must assume goes on in Luxembourg or, such as, according to some observers who hoped for something more noteworthy after its ardent revolution, now goes on in the Republic of Ireland. There is plenty of intense political dispute in the Fifth Republic, both as to foreign policy and domestic programs. Granted that somehow the fires of parliamentary dispute have been banked, the French press, as I have noted, remains extremely free. As for culture in its widest sense—the high culture, art, music, literature, pure science, all those products of the human spirit that the French would describe, using a word far more resonant than our literal equivalent, as *sérieux*—over these high matters there is still intense debate. Contemporary or "modern" art of all kinds has been so far accepted in France that there has been no public riot over matters purely aesthetic anywhere near so violent as that which greeted the first performance of Stravinsky's "Rite of Spring" in Paris in 1913. But the French can still riot when art gets too much mixed with politics. All through its run at the Odéon theatre in 1966, Genet's bitter and certainly unpatriotic play about the Algerian War, *Les Paravents* (The Screens) was likely to be greeted with hoots and ripe tomatoes from patriotic

youth of the Right. And when a very anti-French Italian movie about the Algerian war, directed by a well-known Italian Communist, won first prize at the Venice festival in the same year, the whole French delegation walked out on the festival, with much publicity. Some, probably many of the French delegation must have been Communists or at least fellow-travelers above mere patriotism, for such allegiance is the rule in their circles. But everyone should by now be aware that save for a very few true believers in the purest Marxist faith, nationalism in a pinch will rise to the top anywhere in the world.

There is in France a low culture, a culture for the masses, to which, and to the problems of its relation to the high culture, I must shortly come. But the present state of French high culture and above all the state of mind of those who create and those who follow it are rather more important for us Americans, if only because there is much misunderstanding about the matter in this country. First of all, the intellectuals, the *clercs*, in France today are not a monolithic block. Even among the creative intellectuals one can find a whole political spectrum from Right to Left, and in matters aesthetic one can find a few conservatives, a few representational painters, for instance, a few old-fashioned realistic novelists. Still, the most numerous, the most successful, the most fashionable, are "moderns," experimentalists' avant garde in art and letters and Communists, fellow-travelers, or nihilists in politics.

Their political position is most certainly not that of the majority of Frenchmen, highbrow, middlebrow, or lowbrow. It is not even that of most consumers of ("audience for" would be a kinder way to put it) what the creative intellectuals produce. Still, it cannot be too firmly driven home to Americans that very few Frenchmen, even among the Christian Democrats or the remnants of the old Right, share any of our American crusading zeal against Communism. There are few, extremely few Frenchmen, let alone French intellectuals, who could share the feelings of Father Finian in *The Ugly American:* "The priest realized that here was the face of the devil. The Communists had duplicated the ritual, faith, dedication, zeal and enthusiasm of the Church. There was the same emphasis upon training, the same apostolic energy. . . . The only difference was that the Communists served evil. They served it so well that the priest knew that both faiths could not exist in this world at the same time.* A good many French people would accept Father Finian's analysis of Communism as a fighting faith, but possibly in part because of the disastrous efforts of their distant ancestors in the Crusades to prove that Christianity and Islam could not exist together in this world, and of more recent ancestors to prove that Christianity and the French Republic could not coexist, they would not accept his conclusion. At any rate, it is a fact that Communism in France is not disreputable, that most Frenchmen (not all of course) no longer fear it as a threat to what they hold most dear, even if that dearest thing is their property.

Among the intellectuals—the leaders in many fields, the Sartres, the Picassos, the Joliot-Curies—adherence to Marxist beliefs is a witness to their traditional dislike for the many, a dislike they delude themselves is a dislike, not for the unspoiled though misled many, *le peuple,* but simply for the middle classes and their bland, dull, unjust, and vicious culture. This attitude goes back a long way, to the romantic Bohemians of a century and a half ago, to the anti-Philistines, to the Flaubert of *Madame Bovary* and *Bouvard et Pécuchet.* There was a phase in the late nineteenth and early twentieth century when, with the anticlerical triumph of the Left the intellectuals, the artists turned away from such disappointing success, and briefly "la littérature était à droite." There were of course exceptions,

---

* W. J. Lederer and E. Burdick, *The Ugly American* (New York: Norton 1958), Chapter III.

but novelists like Barrès, Bourget, most playwrights, political philosophers like Maurras, and from many points of view even a Péguy, even a Georges Sorel, did belong on the Right. Only the great teacher of the normaliens, Alain, was a good Jacobin. But the wheel turned once more, and for some time literature and the arts have returned to the Left, but a Marxist, not a Jacobin Left.

It is of course a wholly traditionalist, indeed conservative, attitude, a rejection of most of what constitutes the new France. Among many of these intellectuals, more particularly among writers, artists, and a few well-known but aging scientists, the kind of "alienation" common among intellectuals in much of the West is clear enough. This alienation is no simple matter, and has no simple explanation. In France much of the bitterness among intellectuals springs from the inevitable failure of the great—the Utopian—hopes of the Liberation; some is disillusion with the course of Communism in the Russian fatherland; some has less noble origins, in the feeling of exclusion from the great if common world, in pique at the spectacle of the success, even the apparent happiness, of the vulgar. One of the younger and not alienated intellectuals, a sociologist, Michel Crozier, has summarized the plight of this "Sartre generation":

"All these attempts naturally led rapidly to the failure for which they were destined: the years of disenchantment, disillusion and abandonment. Such a result was inevitable because no one was willing to understand the necessities of action, that is, to admit the existence of a real society, in crisis to be sure, but very much alive and which could be transformed only if it was understood. The intellectuals wanted a new society, but one fallen from heaven, or at least one that would not be conditioned by the impure struggle that had to be waged against the old society. Misled by this profoundly conservative dream, they could not find a middle ground between the total liberty of the individual revolutionary and the total constraint of Stalinism, and they thus deprived themselves of all possibility of communication with others and therefore of constructive cooperation and rational action.

"However unjust such a brief analysis may seem, these positions sum up the general trend of the intellectual movement as expressed in its articulate existentialist wing. In addition, there were, of course, numerous more subtle and more solid works in process, but they had absolutely no influence. Outside of revolutionary moralism, Communist alienation and the existentialist attempts at conciliation, no one proposed anything. Between the rigid bourgeois society that they criticized and characteristically parodied without respite and the utopian society of which they dreamed, the intellectuals were incapable of conceiving or of shedding light on the society actually taking form, to which they themselves contributed without knowing it."*

Whatever the final judgment of the world on the high culture of the mid-twentieth century, there can be no doubt that the new France has had in the creation of this culture a place proportionately quite as great—given the world-wide extension of such culture in our time—as she has had in the past. Ranking in these matters is not quite so readily made in arithmetical terms as in economic fields, or military capabilities, or population. Still, it would seem that, after a lapse (surely in part explicable by the loss, among the millions lost in World War I, of many potential geniuses), France has made up generously for lost ground. She has not been in the forefront of one of the two major currents of formal philosophy in our time. The land of Descartes and the *philosophes* has not contributed greatly

* Stephen R. Graubard, ed., *A New Europe?* (Boston: Houghton Mifflin, 1964), p. 613.

to modern neopositivism, symbolic logic, the linguistic philosophy.* But perhaps again marking one of the great facets of the change that has come over her, she has led in the antithetical school of neoromanticism, existentialism. Sartre, Camus (who did not want to be called an existentialist), Gabriel Marcel, and others, working on ideas largely of German origin, have spread these ideas around the world, much as the French *philosophes* of the eighteenth century, working on ideas mostly of British origin, spread the Enlightenment around their more limited world.

These philosophers, themselves literary figures, have permeated French literature in all its forms, at least in those of the high culture. The pervasive despair over a world they never made, but would like very much to remake, the curious amalgam of stoic acceptance of this real world, this world that *exists,* and utter rejection of what most of their fellow human beings in this world want from it and often get from it, the beautiful clarity of their chaotic ambivalences, the energy of their drive to get beyond this world, somewhere beyond, and —to be fair—their willingness to try new forms and the depth and sincerity of their suffering in this time of troubles—all have contributed to the great mark that French philosophers, poets, novelists and antinovelists, playwrights, and movie directors have made in our time.

There is no need to make a catalogue of French names in contemporary high culture. Nobel prizes in medicine in 1965 and in physics in 1966 marked the return of France to this roster in the natural sciences. Nobel prizes in literature and for work toward peace had continued to come to France even during

---

* As H. Stuart Hughes points out, however, in his most interesting survey of French twentieth-century thought, some few French philosophers did come rather late, in fact not until after the Second World War, to logical positivism in the sense Wittengenstein, Carnap, and others have used the term, or something like it. Even so, they can hardly be said to represent a main current in French philosophy. H. Stuart Hughes, *The Obstructed Path* (New York: Harper and Row, 1968).

the lean years. Although the American middlebrow press, *Time* magazine for example, has been denigrating French achievement in all the arts ever since 1940, the fact remains that the *école de Paris,* never exclusively French in respect of its personnel, continues to hold a place of high esteem and continues to be productive.

Unquestionably most of the men and women who create this high culture and those who enjoy it, or at least consume its products, are at this writing to be listed as vigorously opposing American foreign policy, as disliking and fearing what they take to be the dominant culture in the United States. Yet it is not quite fair to say simply that they are anti-American. For one thing, many of them grew up on a diet of Scott Fitzgerald, Hemingway, and, above all, Faulkner. They listened to, and imitated, our jazz. They could not altogether avoid the vulgar America they were later to hate so thoroughly, for most of them were exposed from childhood to Hollywood movies. There was just after the Liberation a brief honeymoon when even the Communists were not outspokenly anti-American. But nowadays the ordinary French intellectual tends to agree with Simone de Beauvoir: the only bearable thing about the United States is that minority of American intellectuals who, like their French counterparts, are anti-American.[*]

Not all *sérieux* French intellectuals are anti-American, or even alienated. In what American academic usage knows as the "humanities" they are, it is true, overwhelmingly "modernist" and experimental. They as artists reject the representational in the visual arts and as composers reject the classic tonality—and in *la musique concrète* the classical instruments and classical notation. In literature devotees of the absurd, the violent, the tortured, the private prevail. No respectable painter would dare attempt what used to be called the academic portrait, though of course such portraits continue to be painted

[*] Quoted above, p. 73.

by the less ambitious or the more commercially minded. Still, and notably in criticism, much good clear standard French is written. And in what are hopefully called the social or be-havioral sciences and in historical scholarship, the French are doing very well indeed, following a comparatively thin two or three decades after the disasters of the first World War. These economists, political scientists, sociologists, psychologists, and the rest are far from alienated, and they often seem capable of a degree of optimism about the human condition. They are, however, by no means innocent rationalists or "reductionists." The avant garde among the literary and artistic, now in some senses perhaps really a rear guard, damn them as "technocrats." They have played and are playing no inconsiderable part in the new France of material prosperity. They reject what one of them, Raymond Aron, has called the "opium of the intellec-tuals," that is, dogmatic and simplified Marxism. They are, for the most part, unashamed pragmatists, chastened but not dis-illusioned rationalists, rather better democrats in real life than the literary and artistic intellectuals.

5.   France, like all Western countries, has a popular culture more or less sharply distinguishable from its high or high-brow culture. A comic strip—in French, *bandes dessinées*—has very little in common with an *anti-roman* of Robbe-Grillet's or a poem of Aragon's; a number of *Paris-Match* or *Elle* (French illustrated magazines of big circulation) could never be confused, quite apart from differences of format, with a number of *Esprit,* an admirable intellectual, not to say idealist, review or even with a number of the ancient *Revue des Deux Mondes,* now in its one hundred and thirty-ninth year; an audience listening to the music of von Webern is not for the most part the same audience as one listening to Georges Brassens, a popular *chansonnier.*

Yet this last comparison should give pause. Though very few low brows would be found listening to von Webern, a good many highbrows listen to Brassens, and for that matter, to the Beatles. The high and the low cultures are not wholly separate. The problem of their interrelations is one of the most difficult to face the sociologist of knowledge and in itself, as a matter of aesthetics, can hardly be faced here. I must, however, pay some attention to that aspect of the problem which concerns the degree of stability, "social peace," in the Fifth Republic.

In the United States we have long since been accustomed to hearing complaints about the "anti-intellectualism" of the American people, the distrust of the many for the thinking few, the horrors of McCarthyism, the John Birchers, the White Citizens' Councils, and the like.* No doubt the American intellectuals who have discovered this anti-intellectualism have exaggerated its depth and its extent. Nevertheless there is—and perhaps in a society that takes egalitarian goals seriously, there must be —some popular feeling against so privileged an aristocracy as the intellectual class. Yet even in the United States this feeling is by no means without its ambivalences; opinion polls show that writers, artists, and professors are thought to be high in the pecking order. In France, tradition says, *le peuple,* however antagonistic toward the merely rich, thought highly of the intellectuals, respected them, absorbed from them ideas and ideals. The amount of absorption has diminished of recent years as the ordinary Frenchman began to have time and money for such pursuits as spectator sports, travel, television, movies, and much else not approved by the intellectuals. Moreover, the contempt of the intellectuals for the many, clear already in the nineteenth century, sharpened as the evidence grew that the proletariat wanted nothing so much as what the philistine bourgeoisie already had.

* This is classically stated in Richard Hofstadter, *Anti-Intellectualism in American Life* (New York: Knopf, 1963).

There is then a degree of conflict in contemporary France between the intellectuals and the many. It is not, however, nearly so conspicuous as in the United States. Above all, though the hostility of the intellectuals to the ways of the newly emancipated many is at least as strong as the corresponding sentiments of the American intellectuals, the French many, *le peuple*, respond rather with indifference than with hostility. Of course the stock figures appear in popular culture, the absent-minded, impractical professor (who, however, is rarely if ever reproached with never having met a pay roll), the effeminate poet or artist, the arrogant and snobbish highbrow. But not even the Poujadistes of the Fourth Republic, a minority group against taxpaying, big business, and big government, made a major point of hatred for the intellectuals. Nor, carefully cherished myths to the contrary notwithstanding, has the Fifth Republic persecuted and suppressed intellectuals. André Malraux, the minister in charge of culture, is no McCarthy.

On the positive side, there is certainly ample justification for the usual label the intellectuals—and not only the intellectuals—attach to the popular culture of France today: Americanization. Although a good many American industrial enterprises, some of them producing consumer goods, have been set up in France since 1945, and although even French economists are somewhat worried about the phenomenon, this general "Americanization" is not basically the result of American initiative, not a deliberate and aggressive expansion of American economic "imperialism." Although there is no doubt much imitation, conscious and unconscious, of things American, the popular culture of the new France is simply the French form of the worldwide revolution of rising expectations. These forms are "determined" by no single country, not even by that giant of neocapitalism the United States, but by an enormously complex interweaving of men and motives from all over the world.

An interested American, even if he knows little or no French, can get a perfectly adequate idea of the "modernity" of the low or average culture of contemporary France by leafing through a few numbers of *Paris-Match,* which started out some time ago as an illustrated sports magazine (hence the Anglicism "match" in the title—the Americanism would have been "game") but is now a French equivalent of *Life* or *Look,* mechanically quite as up to date as they. The photographic coverage is worldwide, technically excellent. The advertisements would do credit—or discredit if that is one's way of looking at such things—to Madison Avenue. The range of goods and services advertised is quite as great as in a corresponding mass medium of ours, though there would probably turn out to be on careful analysis slightly less appeal to those worried over individual social inadequacy—that is, fewer advertisements of deodorants, mouth washes, greaseless hair oils, cosmetics generally. But there is still plenty of attention in the French mass media to ways of attracting the opposite sex and to all the comforts of the vulgar. The problem of advertising on television does not exist, because the government, which has a monopoly on broadcasting, does not permit ordinary advertising. There is, however, a certain amount of pressure exerted by commercial interests, so far without much success, to allow such advertising. Because of the geographic scale of Western Europe, radio and television broadcasts from neighboring countries can be picked up in most of France, and of course the French government has no direct control over these. Radio Luxembourg, for example, has for years broadcast with advertising.

The French newspaper press underwent a great change with the Liberation in 1944. All papers that had compromised themselves by collaboration with Vichy were forced to give up publication. These included almost all the newspapers with large mass circulations, among them the conservative and respectable *Le Temps* as well as those of popular appeal—many of them quite as shocking in the eyes of the intellectuals as our tabloids—*Le Matin, l'Echo de Paris, Le Journal,* and many others. The two most conspicuous newspapers to survive by suspending publication under Vichy were the conservative and highly literate *Figaro* and, naturally enough after June 1941, the Communist *l'Humanité.* In spite of its virtuous patriotic behavior under the occupation, *Figaro* remains under suspicion in dogmatic Leftist quarters as "cryptofascist."

The new press is, as might be suspected, quite like the old, although Anglo-Saxon stereotypes, never wholly justified, about the venal character of the French press are not nowadays heard quite so often. The whole political spectrum is represented, and papers are for the most part closely identified with a specific political party. The paper of largest circulation (about 1,300,-000), *France-Soir,* generally supports de Gaulle. The most interesting daily is *Le Monde,* staffed by and much read by intellectuals, and certainly not pro-American. Nor is it Gaullist, Communist, or anything quite so specific, just "independent" in pretty much the sense that word has for Americans. Most of the great Paris dailies have a national circulation and can be bought almost anywhere in France on the day of publication. There is a provincial press, with a very considerable circulation all told—some dozen provincial papers have each a circulation of over 100,000—but no one paper is very distinguished. Almost all, even in the provinces, pay due attention to European affairs and, nowadays, a surprising amount to what is going on in the U.S. The old *Action française* having died with the Liberation, there is no longer a ferociously nationalist daily of large circulation; in fact, to a casually sampling reader, no great French newspaper is so narrowly nationalist as many very prominent American ones.

The periodical press is, given the number of persons who understand French in the world, quite as varied and abundant as the American. A glance at a French newsstand shows some-what less cheesecake and sheer female nakedness than does an American newsstand. The old *Vie Parisienne* has vanished, to the regret of few. But a Russian would still be shocked at the display of capitalist immorality evident in the mass media in France. *Paris-Match*, its feminine partner *Elle*, *Jours de France*, and a number of others are typical enough of what lowbrow and middlebrow consume. On the highbrow side the range is perhaps wider than ours. *L'Express*, in format nowadays quite like an American newsweekly or the German *Der Spiegel*, is actually far to the Left of our *Time* and *Newsweek*. In this field the far Right has its organs, notably *Rivarol*, as scurrilous as the Leftist *Canard enchaîné*. The Communist *France Nouvelle* is suitably highbrow. The *Nouvel Observateur* is what Americans call "liberal" in outlook, but its format is much like that of other more popular magazines. All in all, the French periodical press is a good reflection of what I have in this study insisted upon, the pluralistic and open character of modern French society.*

Without accepting an Orwellian view of the horrors of an approaching uniformity for all men, it must be granted that the French form of modern popular culture is more like than unlike—at least under quantitative analysis—other national forms of popular culture. In particular, French devotion to the motor car, French television, French comic strips, French sport, French teenagers, French pornography, even French cuisine among the many, French vulgarity if you wish, are very much like the corresponding things American. Directly experienced, they are of course quite different, for they are experienced as wholes. The seasoning always changes the taste of the dish,

---

* A good brief but representative list of both newspapers and maga-zines can be found in W. H. Mallory, ed., *Political Handbook of the World* (New York: Harper and Row, 1966), pp. 94–95. The most impor-tant of these are now sent in thin-paper editions to the United States by air mail.

even though the main ingredients are the same. The likenesses of the new France and the old United States in this respect, however, ought not to encourage proponents of world peace. There are few if any signs that the spread of common tastes and aims among the many in itself diminishes conflicts among nations.

The most obvious and, to the purists, most annoying form of Americanization is the invasion of, the corruption of, the French language. Here is a random sample taken from *Paris-Match, Candide,* and a few other magazines, mostly, it is true, from the advertisements, which are lush indeed: steak-frites, flirter (both old borrowings), sexy, le cocktail présidentiel (de Gaulle serves cocktails?), un ranch de Seine-et-Oise, spécialiste du marketing, tee-shirts, Oh yeah! le drugstore, la tête du Hit-Parade, pour ses fan's (sic), une stripteaseuse, des thrillers, un best-seller, un Cow-boy, la démystification du western, aux gadgets, ce jerk. The list could be very long. It may be concluded with two items from the theater and concert page of that respectable newspaper *Figaro:*

> Deux récitals du nouveau programme des SWINGLE SINGERS—Jazz Sebastien Bach

> Texas Nous Voilà—1,000 Gags!

The linking of Bach and jazz will no doubt offend other than linguistic purists. The word *récitals* is itself an anglicism, so the plural is not *récitaux.*[*] In Professor Etiemble's *Parlez-vous Franglais?* such listings occupy page after page. But there has long been linguistic free trade both ways between French and English—hundreds of years of it—and moreover much of the above is a fleeting borrowing, mere slang, little of which will survive.

There are those who hold that all these innovations are superficial, that the Frenchman is still what he has long been,

[*] *Figaro,* February 20, 1967, p. 16.

unrevolutionized, still living in the nineteenth, if not in the eighteenth century. For example: "France in its great majority is not ripe for the great revolution of modernity in customary morals and manners (*moeurs*), in habitual ways of living. . . . There are all those Frenchmen who accept the technological revolution, who give themselves over to plastics, to gadgets, to the supersonic, to the interstellar, to the quick-frozen, to robot aids to housekeeping, but who continue to venerate 'the splendor of the sailing ships' and 'the softness of oil lamps' as far as their actual social and moral conduct goes."* Well, yes, perhaps. But one need not be a Marxist to hold that in the long run the material conditions of life affect the whole of life. The current social revolution in France seems as real, if somewhat delayed, as the revolution we Americans frankly admit we have undergone.

6. Such briefly is the new France, or rather, the present somewhat heady mixture of the old and the new in France. As of early 1967, the material prosperity and even the relatively high birthrate, which may have an important sustaining effect on that prosperity, have still held on a kind of plateau, by no means an absolutely level one, but still one without deep trenches. Economic growth, slightly lessened by stabilization measures to combat inflation, has remained still substantially in the range of four to five percent per year. (I must note once again that the Left out of principle and habit commonly challenges the accuracy of all government statistics.) At any rate, it is certain that the French, like the rest of the free world, have had their worries over the continuation of prosperity since the end of World War II. They have, however, not lacked skilled economists in posts of importance in the new and lively bureaucracy. Like anxious physicians these watch over the

* Paul Giannoli, "La France de Mireille Mathieu," *Candide*, September 19, 1966. Mireille Mathieu is a very popular singer (feminine).

health of the economy, but perhaps with rather less certainty and general agreement about therapeutic measures than is common among physicians today.

Yet I may here risk a no doubt far from certain generalization: the structure of French government, the long tradition of central control by bureaucrats (please let that term be taken as a neutral one) may well be better fitted to the needs of the modern "mixed" economy than Anglo-Saxon local self-government, especially when in the United States such government is reinforced by federalism in national government and an emotional if often largely theoretical addiction to free enterprise. There is of course always the possibility that salutary neglect, "do no harm," trust in the invisible hand, will work better to keep the economy healthy than the uncertain prescriptions of the economic physicians, who moreover have never met a payroll. But, not to overdo the analogy, just as the individual sick man *has* to have his remedies, so in the modern world, as the brief experience of the Hoover administration in 1929–1931 proved, the public insists that something be done. The present generation of French economists and sociologists are among the best in the world, not narrowly centered but fully willing to learn from other nationals, and with no inferiority complex vis-à-vis the businessman. In the partly planned French economy of today, they may have too much power, may be too able and too willing to try too many remedies.* The cynic, the skeptic, the man of common sense, may enter a caveat as to the dangers of such meticulous interference, but the possibility remains that, if only their science really is science and is reinforced by proper humility, the economists in power may at least keep France from another Great Depression.

* The reader who would like to see in detail how French administrators unhampered, or very little hampered, by political controls act in such matters should consult W. P. Travis, *The Theory of Trade and Protection* (Cambridge, Mass.: Harvard University Press, 1964), p. 224, especially his list of decrees (*arêtés*) instituting and modifying the export program between February 6, 1952 and August 12, 1954, some dozen in number.

As for a second great worry, this one largely limited to intellectuals, whether the rise of a mass culture in an almost affluent society will destroy what for so many centuries have been the distinguishing marks of French cultural achievement, one can do no more than hazard an opinion. In the long run, a really profound chasm between the tastes of the many and the tastes of the few is certainly inconsistent with the ideals of a modern democracy and may be disastrous to the approximation in real life of such ideals as men believe, or hope, they can attain. But in the short run, there would seem to be no reason why in a varied and free modern Western society a great diversity of tastes, a willingness to tolerate what seems bad taste in others, should not be possible and indeed desirable. Even in the long run, intellectuals should not wish and probably would not be able to convert all mankind to their ideas of the Beautiful and the Good—ideas moreover in this particular culture conflicting and inconsistent. As I have insisted, the acidulous quality of much of the intellectual life in France today, the great disgust with humanity, the incurable addiction of many intellectuals to the opium of the Marxist religion—none of this seems to have aroused among the many in France anything like as strong a class antagonism as the paler disgusts and snobberies among American intellectuals have produced in this country.

Finally, it cannot be sufficiently emphasized that all the obvious ills of our time, from air and water pollution and the other horrors of our strangled cities to alienation, identity crises, neuroses, psychoses, drug addiction, and juvenile delinquency, are shared by the United States and France, and most of the rest of the world. To France most of these ills have come conspicuously later than to us, just as the full thrust of "modernization" came later there. No historian would quite dare suggest that because of this the French might learn a bit from the longer experience of others, including ourselves. Yet there may be a tiny marginal gain for the French in coming rather later to these problems. At least their able experts of the new kind, well trained in the social studies and in the humanities, may spare France some grave difficulties, and their long and well-assimilated historic experience of times of troubles may give the French people as a whole a more patient and tolerant attitude toward them than we Americans, who have hitherto been spared the trauma of enemy occupation and defeat in war and who find our history either unimportant or rosy, seem as yet able to summon.

But France is not an island, and some—many—of the problems that confront her are not solely of her own making; they arise from the play of international relations of all sorts. Among these, her relations with the United States are of prime importance, not only to herself, but to the United States and to the world.

Chapter Eight

The United States and France:

The 1960's

1. Franco-American relations of the kind that make the head-
    lines—or at any rate page two—are relations between
relatively small groups on each side. These "formal" or "diplomatic" relations are not limited to members of the diplomatic
corps or even of departments of foreign affairs, for they include
many members of what Mosca called the *classe politica,* badly
translated for our egalitarian and libertarian United States by
"ruling class," because of unfortunate echoes of stratified society and privileged classes. This group, the policy makers,
ought to be understood in a wide sense to include, in addition
to those professionally charged with the business of diplomatic
relations, all those whose attitudes and behavior influence,
even if only indirectly, international politics—that is, journalists, television commentators, publicists of many kinds, academic experts, formal and informal groups, sometimes true
pressure groups concerned with various aspects of foreign relations, as well as the "politicians" and the leaders of business.
This "political class" in great democratic societies like the
United States and France is no social monolith, is indeed
variously divided in opinion. Still, it has a core that is best

described as a kind of team—and which therefore has the shared emotions we call team spirit. This fact needs to be registered firmly, because many, perhaps most Americans tend to believe that the behavior of these "professionals," if not always very noble, is basically rational, rational in the sense that the economist, for example, has to give the word. That sense in this case is the employing of suitable means for the ends of national interests, both ends and means having been arrived at without interference from any source of human emotions. On the contrary, of course, even foreign secretaries have strong and all too human emotions, never really held in abeyance in their professional activities.

The present struggle between the French team and the American team has roused in the members of each all sorts of emotions—pride, pooled self-esteem, crusading zeal, envy, annoyance, anger, outraged virtue, moral indignation. A brief review of the last decade of the struggle is in order. Relations between the political classes of the two countries were reasonably good until the early 1950's but the troubles of World War II—remember the "*so-called* Free French" of Secretary Hull—still rankled with many Frenchmen in high position; and their American opposites carried, beside their folk-inheritance of mingled distrust and contempt for the French, the special weight of disillusionment at the Fall of France and the subsequent difficulties with both Vichy and Free France. Moreover, American foreign policy had continued to emphasize the Rooseveltian condemnation of "imperialism" or "colonialism" around the globe. When in the early 1950's part of the former French Indo-China came with Ho Chi Minh under Communist control (and even somewhat earlier when such control was a mere threat), the United States reluctantly and certainly inconspicuously tried to help the French hold on, but such help was much too late. After their defeat at Dien Bien Phu in 1954, the French withdrew under the agreement drawn up that

summer at the Geneva Conference, a document the United
States did not sign. The loss of Indo-China further embittered
opinion against America among the French political class.

Early in the 1950's with the Cold War at its height we had
sought to add the potential military strength of West Germany
to our coalition against the Russian coalition, a policy in conflict with French fears of just that potential German strength.
After much negotiation the French, under Premier René
Pleven, proposed a European Defense Community (EDC)
with a common European army into which German units
would be merged—in fact, the French hoped, submerged. Yet,
although the United States backed the plan enthusiastically,
the French Assembly balked, and in the end the French in
August 1954 killed the plan by simply not voting at all on the
proposal in the Assembly.

All these accumulated Franco-American difficulties, be it
noted, came under the Fourth Republic, before de Gaulle came
to power and at a time when his actual influence, exerted from
the wings, was at a minimum. The most serious of the new
difficulties also came under the Fourth Republic, when in 1956
the Israelis, the British, and the French combined to attack
Egypt. Under Nasser the Egyptians had announced in mid-
summer that they were nationalizing the Suez Canal, hitherto
under British control through a private company internation-
ally financed and administered. Prolonged negotiations failing,
and with the Israelis chronically menaced by Nasser, the three
governments in old-fashioned secrecy and wickedness decided
to use force. The Israelis attacked first on October 29, 1956,
and when the Egyptians paid no attention to their joint ultimatum, Britain and France joined in. The attack at first went
well if not quite perfectly, but at once and in extraordinary
concert the United States and the Soviet Union by the channels
of the Assembly of the United Nations in emergency session
announced their firm and virtuous opposition. Moreover,

powerful liberal elements in both Britain and France were
horrified by the attack. There was nothing for the erring
governments to do but stop the invasion and allow the Egyptians to have the canal. This Suez crisis was for such leaders as
Anthony Eden in Britain and Guy Mollet and Pierre Mendès-
France in France no mere loss of face, but a trauma from which
none fully recovered; in France the failure of the Suez expedi-
tion was one of the more important influences to undermine the
Fourth Republic and set the stage for de Gaulle's skillful—and
lucky—play for power in 1958.

So all was by no means serene in Franco-American formal
relations even before the accession of de Gaulle in 1958. These
relations have certainly not improved since that date, though
at the outset of a rapid survey of the specific points at issue
between the two countries in the last decade I must note, first,
that on the whole relations have not really worsened and
deepened in their hold on the emotions of the two teams and,
more important, that even in 1967 France is officially neither
neutralist nor a member of the Russian coalition, but is still a
member, though by no means an enthusiastic member or from
the American point of view a satisfactory member, of what is
in fact still a loose "free world" and "free enterprise" coalition.

On the Algerian problem, it was quite clear that American
public opinion, when there was any real American concern,
and that mostly among "liberals," was firmly anti-French. Our
government did not actively support the native rebels or indeed
directly interfere at all. Of course we got no credit from either
French liberals or French conservatives for this policy. The
Right in particular circulated all sorts of rumors about American interference on the side of the rebels, and the name of
Robert Murphy, who had been active in North Africa at the
time of the Allied landings in 1942 and who was now supposed
to be up to all sorts of skullduggery, was freely bandied about.
The French press, which had heard about the American Cen-

tral Intelligence Agency, also accused it (the CIA) of working for the Algerian rebels of the National Liberation Front (FLN). Historians when they get access to the documents will probably find that the United States had little to do with the achievement of Algerian independence.

Among the number of specific cases in which official France has opposed official United States four major groups may stand as representative.

First, when in the Gaza strip, the former Belgian Congo, Cyprus, and other troubled areas, the United Nations, under American leadership or at least with strong American support, took the kind of direct action that the old League of Nations never dared take, de Gaulle's France increasingly disapproved and showed disapproval in the way calculated to annoy Americans most, that is, by refusing to pay assessments levied for such purposes. France in these years was prosperous, and her government could certainly have afforded to pay. The motives of de Gaulle and his team were not innocently economic, but complex and tied up with the widespread French feeling that the world is not ready for an international government armed with supranational instruments of direct action of a police or military nature. In de Gaulle's mind, a United Nations that could interfere directly with armed forces in the Congo might, under American pressure, so interfere in Europe and even in France.

Second, there is the whole story of French independent efforts to achieve membership in the "atomic club," which she finally attained in 1960 by exploding a nuclear bomb in the Sahara desert, then still formally part of France. But of course a bomb has to be capable of delivery on the enemy, and this de Gaulle's government has worked for steadily, first, through jet bombers, the well-known *force de frappe,* and, second, by developing a French medium-range missile. All this has cost money, but once more, not a sum that seems to have lessened

French economic growth, but has perhaps—disheartening thought for the pacifist—furthered that growth. In terms of injury to the sentiments, the pride, the attitudes of those who govern France, the response of American public opinion, clearly sustained by and sustaining American governmental attitudes, was important and very clear, perhaps as a case history more understandable than were to be the more complex climactic troubles of NATO. American editorials, American cartoons, American newspaper and newsweekly columns rubbed in mercilessly the piddling character of this French achievement, the futility of the tiny bomb—not even up to our Hiroshima standard—the ludicrous vanity displayed by that vain nation, the French, in the whole affair. Americans too were further annoyed by the surely quite natural position the French took in the circumstances against a treaty to ban nuclear testing.

Third, and of course central to the last decade of Franco-American relations, has been the gradual but fairly steady withdrawal of France from the North Atlantic Treaty Organization, which was a very tight coalition indeed, fully deserving the forceful word, "organization." It has never been as fully supranational as the European Defense Community was to have been. Still, with its interleaved staffs, its political and military governing and planning bodies, it was the firmest peacetime coalition yet achieved in the West. It was quite as strongly knit, and perhaps almost as much under the control of its dominant member, as was the rival Warsaw Pact coalition. The difficulties over the European Defense Community in the 1950's and its final rejection by the French were an indication that France, even without de Gaulle, was already restive and worried over the fullness of her commitment to the Atlantic Community. She was certainly worried over the American love affair with the late enemy Germany. De Gaulle himself had from the beginning in 1940 protested any measure that seemed to him an infringement of French "sovereignty," though in the course of the war he had to put up with many such. That a foreigner, even a staff in which French officers had a voice, should give orders to French forces seemed to him contrary to all the proprieties. That to Americans de Gaulle's behavior seemed unreasonable, not to say pathological, is certainly understandable. Our commanders have never, save for a few months under Foch in 1918, had to take orders from foreigners; and even then Pershing's position was always one of strength. Americans, again save for some of us in 1865, have never yet known what it means to be defeated in a war; and indeed our few lost battles tend, like Bunker Hill, to be moral victories. The French have had few such compensations: Waterloo, Sedan, the Battle of France in 1940, Dien Bien Phu could in no sense be made into moral victories.

De Gaulle's speeches and French policy in the United Nations and in NATO had given ample warning of what was to come. By the end of 1966 France had withdrawn from the North Atlantic Treaty Organization and had ordered the removal from French territory of all the military and research bodies of the organization, including SHAPE (Supreme Headquarters, Allied Powers, Europe)—and including naturally the SACEUR (Supreme Allied Commander, Europe), who has always been an American, and his deputy SACEUR who was then a British subject. This was not all. The French government also ordered the removal from French territory within a few months of all American installations, airfields, depots, and the rest of the complicated network that had been built up in France as rear-echelon support for the forces fronting the Iron Curtain further east in Germany. Because these installations gave employment to several thousand French citizens, and because the American personnel, in spite of the PX (Post Exchange) system which set up extraterritorial shopping centers for their use, spent a good deal of money in the neighborhood, there was a great outcry in parts of France against this wanton throwing away of jobs and money. Those Frenchmen directly injured by our withdrawal were, however, too few and too limited in geographic spread to put effective pressure on the government; moreover, the politically active groups which might really have made a national issue of this rejection of good American dollars, the Left and especially the Communists, were in full sympathy with the Gaullist policy of getting the American forces out of France. Yet it is not uninteresting or unimportant to note that for the most part the French people near the bases got on well with their American neighbors and were, in part, sorry for other than economic reasons to see them leave.

Still on this trouble over the alliance system, another important series of Gaullist measures in the 1960's, inspired and justified by sentiments of French sovereignty, was nevertheless not directly linked with the withdrawal from NATO and so far have not been carried to extremes. These measures culminated in de Gaulle's famous "veto" in 1963 on Britain's joining the Common Market (European Economic Community). It is quite clear that de Gaulle himself, however great his insistence on French sovereignty, did not wish to dissolve the Common Market, an institution which did permit non-Frenchmen under certain conditions to give orders to Frenchmen; or if his unconscious resented this subordination, his conscious mind, backed by advisers anxious rather to extend than to limit the powers of the Common Market, told him he must accept the institution. It is no doubt roughly true that French policy so far has been to accept the Common Market as an economic good, but to try to limit any development of it in the direction of a supranational institution that can take measures of clear political or military consequence and compel their acceptance by all member nations, a goal generally favored by American opinion. This line is hard to draw in real life. Certainly the push of

French policy as long as de Gaulle is president will be to hold back from any measures that seem likely to lead toward that United States of Western Europe which de Gaulle rejects as an ideal and for which he would substitute, in one of his favorite phrases, *"l'Europe des patries"*—Europe of the fatherlands— and, furthermore, not just a Western Europe, but a Europe "from the Atlantic to the Urals."

Our fourth major source of difficulty in Franco-American relations today goes back, like the others, well into the Fourth Republic and, indeed, back to Vichy. On colonialism or imperialism throughout the world American policymakers have been confronted with an insoluble problem, one that would have frustrated any of the great masters of foreign policy in the past, an Elizabeth I, a Richelieu, a Talleyrand, a Bismarck. American public opinion and, to be fair, the sentiments of most of our professional diplomatists and the rest of our political class, were strongly in favor of the liquidation of all empires, including our own. In the colonies of our allies, which we wished to see freed, however, the native ruling class, the *effendi* class, to generalize and widen a Middle Eastern term, though it might dislike its imperial masters and might well be nationalists desiring independence, was almost everywhere confronted with a native revolutionary movement on the part of the lower classes, usually supported by the intellectuals and what middle class there was. These rebels wanted not just freedom from foreign colonialist masters, but from upper-class native masters too; many wanted abolition of the whole "capitalist" system. These revolutionaries thought of themselves as Communists and welcomed aid from Russia. In the Cold War that developed after 1946 they were against us. In these countries, because there was no nice moderate democratic center, it seemed to American policymakers that we simply had to support the native masters; moreover, because the foreign masters and especially the British and the French were impor-

tant allies of ours in the Cold War, we could not go too far in
our obvious contributions to the liquidation of their empires.
When, as conspicuously in Viet Nam but in much of the Middle
East and other former dependencies also, it was clear that the
Communists would almost certainly overthrow the native ruling classes if left alone, we were faced with the need to intervene actively to support both kinds of masters, native and
foreign, where this was possible.

Intervene of course we did, directly or indirectly, but we
also continued to assert our unalterable opposition to colonialism, our sympathy for the oppressed natives, and our continued
devotion to the cause of democracy and self-determination of
peoples—though we did not use that Wilsonian phrase—all
over the world. Now, irrational though man, *homo sapiens,*
may be in some ineradicable aspects of his being, the spectacle
of someone asserting that he is doing one thing while he is
obviously doing exactly the opposite is one that most observers
find objectionable—and one, furthermore, that the doer himself
usually is quite aware of in the depth of his being, to the great
troubling of his conscience. It takes a really tough hypocrite
to be wholly undisturbed by an unconcealable gap between his
professions and his practice.

We have not directly aided in the liquidation of the French
colonial empire; and in Indo-China, though we now know that
Roosevelt himself thought the French should never be allowed
to go back in there, we put no serious obstacle in the way of
their return in 1946. After Dien Bien Phu in 1954 we actively
supported the very shaky "conservative" regimes in South Viet
Nam against what we have ever since called Communist
aggression. But words, and the sentiments they arouse, are
often quite as important as deeds. Our American hard-boiled
practice in these matters has no doubt contributed greatly to
our current difficulties with France. The French are especially
aware of and delighted to exploit the gap between our pro-

fessions and our actions. They blame us, in part, no doubt wholly unreasonably, for the loss of their Empire. They are angered by the frequent assertions in our press that we Americans are built of sterner stuff than French weaklings: *we* are not going to have a Dien Bien Phu. They resent the undeniable evidence events in Viet Nam afford of our much greater material and political strength that backs up our determination not to give up in that region.

On our side, it must be repeated that there exists among many Americans, not excepting members of the groups that make and carry out our foreign policies, an uneasy feeling that in Viet Nam at least we are not really quite living up to the principles of 1776 and 1789. Perhaps for the majority of Americans, however, the whole course of the last two decades in the former French Empire has reinforced their sentiments about French weakness and incompetence, and also cruelty and harshness toward their subjects in the Empire. Above all, the French are in this matter contrasted with ourselves, who readily granted independence to the Philippines with no fuss, or with the British who voluntarily granted independence to Burma, India, and other dependencies. The French did indeed try to hold on to their Empire too long and, in Indo-China and Algeria, gave up only after bitter fighting not always conducted in full accord with the Geneva Convention on the rules of civilized warfare. The historian can certainly find explanations and even excuses for this unwise French attempt to preserve their Empire. But at least they are now freed of its liabilities, while preserving to a surprising extent a cultural and economic influence within much of it. And when it comes to throwing stones, always a great sport in international affairs, the French can and do point out that in what are delicately called "outlying regions administered by the United States," we still have a largely "colonial" population of some 1,200,000 people not full citizens of the United States, to say nothing of our military bases abroad, and our present deployment in South Viet Nam. The Ryukyus, with some 932,000 inhabitants, make up most of this number. The French also do a little stone-throwing at our insistence that the Western Hemisphere in terms of international politics is not quite like the rest of the world. This hemisphere, they say, is an American "sphere of influence," a horrible survival of nineteenth-century ways.

2. It would be amazing if the withdrawal of France from NATO had not been taken in the United States, and especially in governing circles in this country, very badly indeed. Indignation, anger, regret, variously mingled and intense, are natural responses; surprise is not, and in reality such a reaction of surprise was probably limited to a few publicists in this country. The professionals certainly should have expected something of the sort. For though the cliché that all we learn from history is that we never learn from history has its grain of truth, it is surely not true that men never learn from experience of any sort. Within a system of international relations among "sovereign" states with a common culture of some sort, such as the European (now world) system that began among the Italian states and their neighbors five hundred years ago, men have had a long and well-known experience of what I have in this study quite deliberately called *coalitions,* though there are many partial synonyms—alliances, alignments, ententes, leagues, and such like, and in our own time even the somewhat ambitious and often misleading "organization" as in North Atlantic Treaty Organization, United Nations Organization, Organization of American States, and others.

Now one thing is certain from this five hundred years' experience of coalitions: they are very hard to hold together. A given coalition is usually put together under the leadership of one strong member for a quite specific purpose, opposition to the expansion of a rival member of the same state-system, itself generally the head of another and opposing coalition. The long tale since Florence and Naples combined in 1492 to despoil the Milan of Ludovico Sforza, who then called in Charles VIII of France for "protection," can have no place here. But I may take for illustration a particularly trying case of difficulties with coalition-making—and holding. In the great world war of 1792–1815 commonly listed as the "wars of the French Revolution and Napoleon," France, usually heading a form of coalition composed of a preponderant power and what are now called "satellites" or "puppets," fought wars against a varied series of coalitions—usually listed as four or five—all of which combined in population, total resources, and military capabilities, were usually stronger than France and its coalition. Only Great Britain was in that quarter of a century of fighting consistently at war against France. The other powers, big and little, were sometimes allied with France, sometimes neutral, sometimes allied against France. The final Grand Alliance was not formed until 1813 and included Britain, Russia, Austria, Prussia, and lesser states, in fact practically the whole of Europe. This coalition did hold together, even after the once beaten Napoleon returned from Elba in 1815 to take up arms again.

No master cause can be assigned for the failure of these coalitions of 1792–1813. French diplomatists in the first few wars did play successfully the old game of "divide and rule," now luring Prussia to make peace by promising her "compensations" at the expense of Austria, then promising Austria the same at the expense of Prussia, both of course in all secrecy. Napoleon in 1807 seems to have exercised his charisma on Emperor Alexander of Russia; at any rate, Alexander gave up fighting, leaving Britain in the lurch. What is much clearer, however, is that with the final successful coalition of powers long divided and almost as distrustful of their allies as of the enemy, a common interest and a common fear at last combined to give them military victory they ought, measured by material "capabilities," to have been able to win two decades earlier. Napoleon of course was a genius, but he was also a lucky man served by skillful diplomacy and by the failure of his enemies to unite solidly against him until the last moment.

Those were, you say, the days of kings, emperors, dynastic struggles, not today, when democratic states prevail in our West? Yet it seems quite clear that democratic states are ruled by the kind of people who are still moved by much of what moved the old dynasts. Our last two world wars were short in comparison with those of a century and a half ago, but the first saw Russia desert her allies as earlier Italy had deserted hers, and it also saw all sorts of combinations in the Balkans and in the Middle East. The second, it must be said, does afford an extraordinary example of determined leadership holding together after the Fall of France a most "unnatural" core coalition of the United States, Britain, and the Soviet Union—with what difficulties and at what cost is now well known.

What the historian Winston Churchill loved to call the "Grand Alliance" of World War II fell apart as soon as Germany and Japan were beaten. Its Western components, with a liberated France and a revived and forgiven West Germany added, kept and in some ways strengthened their coalition in the ensuing "Cold War" with Russia. The Cold War was a very real war. To many Americans and Russians at least, it continued as such in the 1960's. The West Europeans got great positive benefits from the working out of the Marshall Plan, and above all, they got some feeling of security against a Russia which seemed to threaten them at least as seriously as had Nazi Germany in the 1930's. Russia not only seemed to be an old-fashioned aggressive power bent on territorial expansion by the old method of adding "satellites"; she was also a new crusading power seeking to spread a new surrogate religion, one which had great attraction for many West Europeans and was an abomination to most Americans.

To simplify the lessons of experience in this matter: coalitions of "sovereign" states, more especially of great or near-great powers, are maintained by fear of aggression by a perturbing power and its allies, from which the coalition offers protection and, to a lesser but still important degree, by expectations of positive gains other than mere protection, economic aid, for example, and less materialistic gains in prestige and dignity. Cynically to deny to the men who manage the affairs of such coalitions any moral sentiments—willingness to keep one's promises, dislike of oppression, gratitude for aid, and much else—can be to carry cynicism to excess. Still, such sentiments are variables of much less importance in a crisis and in a long run than fear of defeat or hope of gain.

Almost no one in a responsible position in France today fears aggression from the Soviet Union, and not many more fear the spread of a really revolutionary Communism in France; in the prosperous France of 1967, though there are those who worry over the possibility of a serious economic recession, no one expects a renewal of Marshall Aid or any other direct economic assistance from the United States. In fact, there is a current of opinion, not so strong as some journalists in both countries maintain, that would stop or at least limit further direct American investment in France, a current that considers *"le gigantisme américain"* in terms of economic competition a far more dangerous thing in the world today than anything Russian. In short, and again simplifying, from de Gaulle on down a great many of the men who rule France today see little to gain and something to lose in continuing a relation with the United States which they no longer need for protection and which they find, to put it mildly, constraining.

This last *is* put mildly. There is no doubt that de Gaulle himself, in addition to the feelings aroused in him by American policy toward him during World War II, has come to feel that the United States, heir to the kind of ascendancy and leadership in the world that Britain, and before Britain France, had held, is in fact and in spite of its noble ideals, becoming a world tyrant instead of a world leader. This will appear a jaundiced view, and not only to Americans; and to a degree perhaps it is for de Gaulle himself a rationalization in defense of a parochial French patriotism. Nonetheless it is a real, indeed an honest, sentiment and opinion, by no means held solely by de Gaulle. It is at the moment a fact of international life, and we should at least make an effort to understand how it arose. Perhaps some of the things that we Americans, officially and unofficially, have said and done have had something to do with its arising?

3.   There is one basic fact that holds for both official and unofficial relations between France and the United States, for formal diplomatic relations and for those broader concerns that must be grouped as matters of "public opinion": the French are more concerned with and about us than we are about them. In international politics the French, having liquidated their Empire as far as formal sovereignty goes, no longer crop up as immediate concerns of ours outside Europe itself; but we, though de Gaulle has ejected us from our military bases in France—rather, in part *because* he has ejected us— bulk large in the concerns of the French government and the French people. In matters cultural—odd, shocking, though this must seem to Frenchmen over sixty-five years of age—the balance of trade has shifted remarkably in our favor. We Americans are certainly not cut off from French cultural influences in goods of luxury consumption, in the arts, and in literature; but France probably rates much higher with American middle-brows at all concerned with such matters than with American highbrows, who no longer flock to France as did our lost generation of the 1920's. But even as a love-hate relation, as it is with French intellectuals today, the influence or at least the

awareness of the United States in France is great; and with ordinary Frenchmen, and in matters of great range, from linguistic Americanisms (*Franglais*) through chewing gum and soft drinks to *les westerns* and *le jazz hot*, American imports are everywhere.

The much greater concern of the French with us than ours with them is commonplace; it is inferable a priori from the present position of the two countries and is confirmed readily enough by a cursory review of public opinion polls in the last few years. Such polls in the United States when they are at all concerned with international politics or foreign countries focus of recent years on Viet Nam, on President Johnson's other foreign policies, and occasionally on problems of the under-developed countries. They are rarely concerned directly with Franco-American relations, though the personality of de Gaulle figures now and then. But in polls taken in France, though there too the chief subjects are matters of domestic concern, the United States, American personalities, Americanization, figure conspicuously.*

The present trend in France is almost certainly slightly away from approval of de Gaulle's policy towards the United States. The following contrasts between opinion in January 1963 and March 1966 are good indicators. To the question, do you approve or disapprove of General de Gaulle's policy toward the United States, the following replies (in percentages)** were made:

	January 1963	March 1965
Approve	47	41
Disapprove	17	29
No opinion	36	30

* For France the quarterly *Sondages*, now in its twenty-eighth year, is a comprehensive source. A new quarterly, founded in 1965, *Polls* (Amsterdam) gives well-chosen summaries from polls all over the world.
  ** *Sondages*, no. 2 (1966), p. 31.

Because "no opinion" or "no answer" comes out quite a bit more frequently in French opinion polls than in such polls in other Western countries, the drop in percentage of "no opinion" is as important as the rise in "disapprove." If only because of the publicity given in the French press to the protests of French people thrown out of work by the banishment of American bases from France, an event that took place *after* this poll, it is almost certain that the number of disapprovals today is somewhat greater.

There is an ironic side to this current of approval-disapproval of de Gaulle's policy toward the United States. French Communists are understandably enough against de Gaulle and the Fifth Republic. He appears to them a Caesar, and they do not like Caesars in France; his Fifth Republic seems to them a shocking form of capitalist exploitation, the present increasing prosperity of French working classes partly a statistical lie of the Government's, partly a mere sop to protect the exploiting class, now richer than ever. They hate de Gaulle—and most of, but not all, his works. In the poll cited above 49 percent of those calling themselves Communists announced approval of de Gaulle's policy towards the United States. This is a normal attitude; the French Communist Party for years has been putting up graffitti like "Yankee, go home" or "Ridgway la peste" (this last an accusation of germ warfare on our part in Korea), and now de Gaulle was kicking the Yankees out. Of course they approved. For very many influential moderate conservatives or centrists there is also an ironic ambivalence. The followers of M. Lecanuet are for the most part strongly for "*l'Europe unie*" (EU is plastered often on the bumpers of their cars) and at least mildly pro-American in international politics. They therefore disapprove of de Gaulle's foreign policy at the moment; but they strongly approve of most of the rest of what he stands for.

These however are not unusual quandaries for the voters in a democracy; they are not unknown in the United States.

Usually, one suspects, the domestic side of the difficulty carries the day. Most of M. Lecanuet's followers in the run-off of 1965 voted for de Gaulle, though not in the duels of 1967 for the local Gaullist candidate; the Communists, in spite of the general position of the non-Communist Left mildly in favor of the North Atlantic Alliance and good relations—or at any rate, against bad relations—with the United States, voted for the non-Communist Leftist, Mitterand, and also, when they had to, voted in 1967 for the Federation of the Left.

There are times when attitudes toward one or more foreign powers seem to exercise the general public in a democracy, but this is usually only when, as in the United States in the 1790's when the Federalists were pro-British and the Antifederalists pro-French, the foreign countries symbolize a profound domestic difference of opinion. In spite of all the publicity given in the United States and in France to the necessity of being on the side of the angels in the Cold War, it is quite clear that there has been for some time among most Frenchmen no obsessive sense of the overriding necessity of choosing between the United States and the Soviet Union. Here too the polls are helpful. The question asked in May 1960 and again in May 1965 was: "Should France side with the USA, the USSR, or with neither?"*

	May 1960	May 1965
US	30	14
USSR	7	7
Neither	51	62
No answer	12	17

The constancy of the few choices for Russia is striking. The fall in the choices for the United States is about what, from the course of events in Viet Nam and in France itself, one would expect. No such poll of course can make the subtlest of distinctions. The 62 percent who chose "neither" in 1965 are cer-

* *Polls* (Amsterdam), Spring 1966, p. 25.

tainly no solid block of determined neutralists in the sense the term neutralist is commonly applied to the foreign policy of India; nor is this choice of "neither" necessarily a reflection of Mercutio's "a plague o' both your houses." A good many of that 62 percent are probably just satisfied with, or unexcited about, recent French foreign policy. This is confirmed by another poll, which asked: "Are you satisfied with the present role of France in international relations?"*

	February 1963	February 1965
Satisfied	36	44
Dissatisfied	17	16
No opinion	47	40

All these polls—and they are many—of which I have cited only a very small sample do set a problem of great importance in understanding the role of France in the world today. In comparison with other countries, and notably with the United States, the proportion of French people who give some form of the reply "no opinion" is strikingly greater. In an international poll, for instance, in answer to the question as to whether they were "satisfied with the position [a necessarily vague word] of their own country today," French and Americans divided as follows:

	France	USA
Satisfied	42	43
Dissatisfied	20	45
Don't know	38	12

There are no doubt differences caused by the use of not quite exactly synonymous terms like "don't know," "no answer," "no opinion" in these polls, but even so, no matter which phrasing is used, the French tend in greater numbers than other Western

* *Polls* (Amsterdam), Spring 1966, p. 21.

nationals to make a response that may be called simply "non-committal." Any explanation must content itself with suggesting a variety of factors producing this result. Some are hangovers from the old France of resentful individualism, a sense of privacy carried to extremes; "no opinion" really means a refusal to answer what it's no one's business to ask; some reflect an objection to opinion polls, market research, and the like as "Americanization," part of this bad new world to be rejected out of hand; something too of one of the oldest and most familiar clichés about the French national character is no doubt still at work—the Frenchman is too bright, too intellectual, too rational to accept, as the polls so often ask him to do, a choice between black and white; one may even admit, particularly if the poll goes into some isolated rural districts that some of the "don't knows" reflect the old marginal backwardness of France in comparison with her northern neighbors.

But there remains a residue of possibility that this "no opinion" reflects the new France of comparative calm and stability or at least a new France no longer torn by quite such deep-seated divisions on those ultimates which can be—must be—put in terms of black and white. That third of the body of French voters which the young men of SOFRES call the *marais* (see above, Chapter Five), part of which I have dared suggest may be more fairly labeled *independents,* or if you want a pejorative, *mugwumps,* can be pointed to as in part confirming this diagnosis. A certain amount of indifference to matters of politics may well be necessary in maintaining a stable society in equilibrium. This is a reflection that many good citizens will find both a platitude and an error. Perhaps something of the sort may be conveyed less offensively if it be suggested that in the case of France since 1789 there has been in politics, to use their own trite phrase, *trop de zèle*—and that there is every sign today that such zeal is diminishing.

The last of the polls to which I shall have recourse suggests that in this very important matter of the number of people who are dissatisfied with what they have and are, with what their country is, France no longer stands out as full of discontents, ripe for revolution and other indecencies. A Gallup international poll of the summer of 1963 asked a series of questions in the United States, Britain, France, West Germany, Norway, Denmark, and Switzerland, testing satisfaction or dissatisfaction of individuals with their work, their children's education, the prestige of their country in the world, future prospects for themselves and family, standards of living, leisure time, housing, family income, and "the honesty and standards of behavior of people in this country today." The diagram indicates the percentage in each country for each topic who were *dissatisfied.** The "don't knows" are not shown on the graph; France showed the greatest number of "don't knows" on six of the nine topics involved.

A glance at the graph confirms that in the smaller democracies of Norway, Denmark, and Switzerland, not tempted to greatness, satisfaction is greater, dissatisfaction less than in the four countries saddled with greatness and its burdens. De Gaulle's "Anglo-Saxons," the United Kingdom and the United States, are paired in dissatisfaction with the position of their country in the world today (Britain 48 percent, United States 45 percent, France a mere 20 percent), but otherwise the Big Four are not significantly far apart on any of the topics polled. It is perhaps a little surprising that Danes join Americans, Germans, and British in expressing a greater degree of dissatisfaction than do the French with the degree of honesty and good behavior achieved by their fellow countrymen. Still, this topic reflects quite strikingly the greatest degree of dissatisfaction in almost all countries, a result that should surprise only the most naive of moralists.

* *Polls* (Amsterdam), Spring 1965, pp. 62–64.

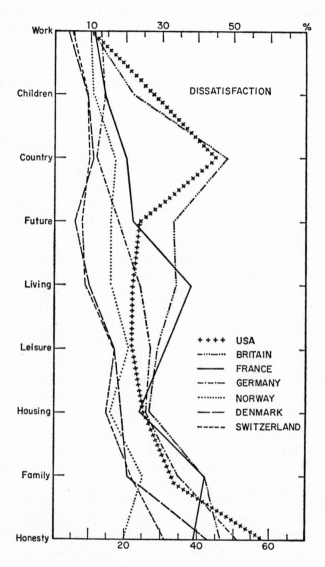

SOURCE: *Polls* (Amsterdam), Spring 1965, p. 63.

4.   On the American side not a great deal is new in the present
conjuncture of Franco-American relations. Among the
American professionals in foreign affairs and their following,
the people deeply concerned with international relations, de
Gaulle's final withdrawal from full participation in NATO and
the ejection of American forces from France had been so long
threatened that the final step itself had long been discounted.
Among many of them, the attitude was one rather of sorrow
than of anger; there was some hope that after de Gaulle France
would return to where she belonged. The American chauvinis-
tic press, the *Chicago Tribune* or the *New York Daily News*
for example, was nasty, indignant, and scornful as it had long
been toward those tenth-raters, the French, who were now
daring to assert themselves as something like our equals. There
was little new in this attitude either. Some of the great names
among American publicists, Lippmann, Sulzberger, Reston,
and a few others, did indeed come out firmly for moderation
and objectivity in trying to see what de Gaulle was about. And
among the very numerous worries that faced ordinary literate
and concerned Americans in these months, worry over the
behavior of France could not take a prominent place. But the
habit, the conditioned reflex, of tossing off smugly scornful
remarks about France continued. A reviewer in the *New York
Times* found the late Bernard Fall, a Frenchman, "defensive"
about the French in Viet Nam (and "waspish" about the Americans), but needless to say did not find such words to describe
the attitudes of other than French writers; John Gunther in a
book on South America, citing examples of how the United
States has displaced France among the upper classes there,
casually noted that only a few decades ago Latin Americans
studied medicine in France—which helped explain why their
medicine was so bad; and so on, in trivial instance after instance, all adding up to something far from trivial, a major

force for enmity among nations.* The mixture of attitudes of
our mythical friend, the average American, continued, one
guesses, much as it had for some time, with its inconsistencies
of admiration, dislike, distrust, envy, and somewhat contemptuous indifference toward France and French culture.

American liberal intellectuals, however, have been confronted, as de Gaulle's power and policies unfolded, with some
of the same difficulties confronting their parallels in France.
Like the old French Left, always Jacobin, or at any rate
Girondin, at heart they had long ago (even in the war years
when he first came to their attention) ticketed this man de
Gaulle, royalist, Catholic, military man, A Bad Thing. Many,
though of course not all, American liberals were confirmed in
this judgment when in 1958 de Gaulle came back into power
and in their view began a career just like other Bad Things in
the modern history of France—the two Napoleons, Boulanger,
Pétain. Nothing de Gaulle could do, not his breaking of the
terrorist OAS (Organization of the Secret Army), not his
solution of the Algerian problem, not his condemnation of
American policy in Viet Nam, could overcome this basic simplification: de Gaulle is black, all black. American liberals on this
matter often take without examination, even though they have
traveled and lived in France since 1958, the judgments of their
French fellow Leftist intellectuals at face value and really seem
to believe that Gaullist France in 1967 was a one-party totalitarian state, with none of the democratic freedoms of speech,
association, or the press—a society in which all dissent was
simply smothered. For the French Leftists, all this is good, or at
any rate conventional, propaganda, in which somehow or other
they seem able to indulge themselves quite publicly and profit-
ably in the midst of this repressive totalitarian society. But for

* *New York Times Book Review*, June 4, 1967, p. 3; John Gunther,
Inside South America (New York: Harper and Row, 1967), p. 119.

Americans such judgments are just natural laziness, natural dogmatism of the liberal mind at its most unrealistic. It is particularly unfortunate that so many Americans who do know enough about contemporary France to qualify a little these grave oversimplifications have continued to make them as they long have. For some incurably acid-minded American intellectuals, the world, including both France and the United States, seems to be as bad as the Sartres, the Beauvoirs, and the rest hold it to be. But most of us would resent being so ticketed. We shall not, however, get much further in any effort to find some accommodation with the France of the Fifth Republic if we continue to refuse to acknowledge the complexity of its chief founder's personality and the even greater complexities of the fundamentally democratic society over which he presides. If only because of these manifold complexities, there are a number of possible futures in Franco-American relations.

Chapter Nine

The United States and France:

The Possible Future

1. For a few years after the end of the fighting in 1945 the international power system was almost as simple as the publicists then liked to make it out to be. The United States and the Soviet Union were the two overwhelmingly powerful "superpowers" contending in a rapidly intensifying "Cold War" in a world in which the other old "great powers" seemed no longer to deserve the name. The two superpowers each had its own coalition and, once the Soviet Union produced its own atomic bomb in 1949, seemed to be in a rough balance of power. The neutrals were few and weak and hardly counted in the equations of power. Though the peoples under Communist domination presumably followed their leaders and their persistent propaganda in holding the United States to be the perturber, in most of the rest of the world the balance of opinion was pretty clearly in favor of the United States as a defender and preserver of peace.

Those were the days when some wise and experienced publicists and scholars were regretting the self-destruction of old Europe, once in the forefront of civilization but now finished, forever relegated to the back benches of history. China, only just taken over by the Communists, seemed a powerless giant, likely to remain a simple, loyal member of the Russian system. The old Western empires of Britain, France, the Netherlands were clearly disintegrating, but the chief importance of this fact seemed to be that it signalized further the impotence of the mother countries, not the rise of new nations which might seriously affect the simple balance of power between the two superpowers. Finally, those were the days when France and the other members of NATO were only slowly—in the eyes of many important Americans, almost invisibly—recovering from the disasters of the war, the days when Berlin was the most conspicuous trouble spot on earth, when, to repeat, the notion that only the United States and the Soviet Union counted seemed not implausible.

It was never a realistic notion. However impressive statistically the industrial and military capabilities of the two superpowers in the late forties and early fifties in contrast with those of the rest of the world, their bases in territory and population, in potential capabilities, even taken together, were by no means equal to that of the rest of the world—and, of course, they could never be "taken together" in the real world. Both the United States and Russia showed by their actions that they were fully aware of the importance of lesser powers; both worked hard at building and maintaining alliance systems, at gaining influence and prestige all over the world. For neither was the task an easy one. It has now become for both increasingly difficult to hold their systems together tightly and neatly.

The world of international politics in the 1960's once more took on a clearly pluralistic form. The Communist system, once centered in Moscow, was divided between Moscow and Peking, with stragglers elsewhere. The Russians in particular found their Warsaw Pact partners in eastern and central Europe restive, hard to control. Yugoslavia became almost independent in the old-fashioned sense. It would be absurd to compare at all closely the difficulties that the United States has long had with France and those the Soviet Union has had with China. Dimensions and intensities are vastly different. Nevertheless, the prosperous Western Europe of the 1960's was feeling its oats, was increasingly, with France in the lead, confident that the Soviet Union would not seek to expand westward, and restive under what seemed to many Europeans American tutelage, American bossing, American failure to recognize that this was no longer the world of 1947.

Moreover, the trouble spots no longer centered so clearly in Europe. There was indeed one world in terms of travel and communication, and the 120-odd member-states of the United Nations covered the globe. But there was no real unity, nor even duality; instead, a series of subsystems of states with complex rivalries among their members had varying relations with the two old superpowers. Both the United States and the Soviet Union had interests and agents of all sorts pretty well everywhere; but China and those two once-dead great powers, Britain and France, were perversely active in many parts of the world. Africa was certainly no preserve of the two old superpowers, though they were rivals there as everywhere. The Middle East, as the events of the summer of 1967 showed, was not to be wholly controlled even by the current duumvirs, successors of Roosevelt and Stalin. So too for other subsystems in international politics, South Asia, Southeast Asia, even Latin America: glib American dismissals of the major European powers—definitely including West Germany—as no longer counting was denial of the simple facts. There was no longer the old simple Cold War out of which NATO and other alliance systems headed by the United States had been born, but a complicated and shifting series of rivalries, tribal, national, regional, very hard to sort out into neat categories.

Some order can be achieved by considering the historical background of modern general wars with a simple question in mind: what power or groups of powers has been judged the aggressor? World War II is a clear-cut example of a great degree of unanimity on this point: Germany and Japan were very generally ticketed, and not only by their immediate enemies, as the aggressors, the powers who disturbed the balance of power. This verdict has managed to withstand even the attacks of professional historians, who make a living by revising history. At the time and since the verdict on the war of 1914–1918 has been contested; still, the balance of blame has gone to the Central powers (one hopes not solely because they lost the war). Further back, Napoleon I, Louis XIV, Phillip II of Spain are pretty firmly ticketed as the disturbers, the aggressors—and as failures in the end. In the confusing complexity of world politics in the 1960's there was no firm verdict as to who was the potential aggressor. Indeed the distinction between aggressive and defensive war and diplomacy, so necessary if we are to show a decent respect to the opinions of mankind, is not one that can be established in and for a present with even the rough agreement historians manage to arrive at for a past. The aggressor in the modern Christian world has never publicly admitted his aggression, although Hitler did so firmly and unmistakably in private. More, in the democratic world today the aggressor has to accuse the defensive side of aggression. All this suggests that moral ideas play a part in international relations, if only in the sense of La Rochefoucauld's epigram, "Hypocrisy is the tribute vice pays to virtue."

It would be too much to expect that any great number of people in any part of the world would continue to feel toward the United States as they felt at the end of World War II. We are clearly top dog, ahead in all the statistics, the wealthiest nation in the world. Nations in this position are envied rather than loved or even respected. We are also the strongest nation, and since 1945 we have increasingly displayed that power in all parts of this earth. We are as ubiquitous as the British used to be as diplomatists, military men, travelers, entrepreneurs, students, agents open and secret. Indeed, the historian willing to risk himself in the dangerous field of comparative history is bound to conclude that we have taken over, in a very different world and on an even greater scale, that hegemony exercised by Britain in Victorian times—and once, only two long lifetimes ago, by France.

Those who make our foreign policy would find public admission that we are now trying to run the world unwise, and perhaps untrue. And phrased in just that way the statement is not quite fair. There is a sense, granted we are placed in a position of world leadership that we did not seek out, granted even, as has been said of both imperial Rome and imperial Britain, that we have blundered into our present position— there is a sense in which we should really like to do a better job than our predecessors did. Americans for the most part do believe in their democratic ideals, do want a world of live and let live, do not deserve the perpetual reproach that we are imperialists.

Nevertheless, a very great many people all over the world, and particularly in Western Europe, have in the last two decades come to doubt whether we are using wisely the power we have acquired—or that has been thrust upon us. And of course the millions who have come under the influence of our enemies would state the case even more strongly. To be brief: we see ourselves as basically on the defensive since the Cold War began; by the late 1960's it was almost certainly true that even in countries like France, Britain, and West Germany, a majority of educated people held that we are conducting a worldwide offensive against any form of what we call Communism. A decent respect to the opinions of mankind, to which Jefferson once so eloquently appealed in a most famous document, demands that we face up to the problem of what our reputation in the rest of the world really is. It may well be that our position is misunderstood; but the misunderstanding is there and is quite as effective in this harsh world as understanding.

The basic reason why our relations with France at this juncture are so critical and so important, far beyond any question of how "strong" or how "great" a power France may be in reality, is that these relations are a test case for our reputation in the world, a test case of the degree to which we have done better or worse than our predecessors as top dogs. They are a test of our ability to maintain a leadership largely acceptable to the rest of the world. If we cannot get on with France and the French, we shall indeed find hard going ahead.

But are not the French, or at least de Gaulle and his followers, really to blame? Why should we try to get on with people who do not want to get on with us? Certainly French policy since de Gaulle's accession to power, and indeed before that—recall Suez in 1956—has not been in accord with the Golden Rule. But one thing is quite clear: France cannot possibly take on again the role of aggressor, cannot even be a serious perturber in international politics. It is worthwhile trying to go further into the realities that lie behind French (Gaullist, if you want to oversimplify) policies. De Gaulle certainly wants an important role for France in Europe, and a respectable role in the world. He bridles when he hears, as he has often had to in the last three decades, that France is finished, a minor power, not even in the league. He cannot help having nostalgic feelings for the days not so long ago when no "Anglo-Saxon" historian would think of tossing off a phrase like "the *pretensions* of France to the status of a great power."*

---

* Italics mine. The quotation is from A. J. P. Taylor, "Munich Twenty Years After," *Manchester Guardian Weekly*, September 30, 1958. Taylor adds to the insult, at least for a Frenchman, by coupling France with Italy in having these unfounded "pretensions." But the British as world leaders were perhaps even more tactless than we Americans have been, and Taylor has shown other signs of cultural lag.

But just as the evidence contradicts the myth that de Gaulle, however arrogantly undemocratic he is by nature, must be ranked with the dictators, the men on horseback, the would-be Caesars in domestic politics, so the evidence contradicts the myth that he hopes, that he seriously attempts, to restore France to the kind of material as well as cultural predominance she enjoyed in Europe and the world until 1870. He may wish France were a nation of 180,000,000, but he knows very well that she is not and cannot be in any sensible future.

On the other hand, neither in de Gaulle himself, nor in his followers, nor for that matter in most of his opponents is there nowadays much trace of that other emotional push for greater French greatness which springs from fear of Germany in particular and which came out so clearly in 1918–1919 in the attempt to detach the Rhineland from Germany. Note that even in 1918 the Anglo-Saxons misunderstood this French drive as a sign that once more a Napoleon, even if only a little one, was in the saddle. Fear, in the masculine world of international politics most emphatically, often takes the form of aggression. Desire for more territory no longer seems to influence those who rule France. In 1945 they made no effort to expand at the expense of Italy, though there are several thousand French-speaking Savoyards in the Val d'Aosta just over the Alpine border. The French have given up trying to add to the hexagon.

Why then all this bother by de Gaulle and other important Frenchmen about the grandeur, the prestige, of France? What they mean by the greatness of France is not purely a material preponderance, not one measured by the usual statistics. They do not, on the other hand, mean a kind of wholly spiritual, cultural, artistic distinction, something nobly other-worldly, something not measured in any kind of quantitative rank-order. Some of their publicists have indeed consoled themselves and their readers by something as simple—and as little consoling for the average man—as this: let the Americans and the Rus-

sians boast of material *gigantisme;* France will still be the most
civilized, most artistic, most cultured of nations, *aere peren-
nius.* But this is wounded vanity, not wounded pride. The
French rather more than other Western nations, none of which
come very near seeking a collective transcendence of this
world, seem willing to accept the world almost as it is. Right
now they want, and are getting, material prosperity. What they
want in addition to this is perhaps better put as *prestige* than
as *grandeur.*

That powerful little word is in French nearer its Latin
origin than it is in English. *Praestigia* in Latin was no more
than a juggler's trick, a prestidigitation, and in French it still
carries a hint, if not quite of deception, at least of the marvelous, the out-of-the-ordinary, of something not crudely and
obviously measured in statistics. In fact, the current Larousse,
best known of popular French dictionaries, cites as an example
of its proper use *"le prestige de la France a l'étranger"*—the
prestige of France among foreign nations. And the present
government awards to the liner *France,* which well deserves it,
a formal *diplôme du prestige de la France.* And then, recall
those champions, some of them world champions, of sport to
whom de Gaulle himself presented the medal and ribbon of the
Legion of Honor. But prestige, though for the pure moralist
deceptive, is something that cannot be wholly or for long faked.
It has to rest on some acknowledged achievement; it has to be,
if not statistically measurable, at least capable of measurement
in this-worldly, commonsense terms. De Gaulle would probably
settle, has so far settled, for a France whose *total* prestige,
material *and* spiritual or cultural, would be measured against
that of her old neighbors and foes, Britain, Germany, Italy,
and not in purely material terms against the United States or
even Russia.

Another phase of these nation-centered emotions that Americans usually find it hard to understand, or merely to allow for

in others, centers on the word "independence." We got our independence so long ago and for many reasons so comparatively easily and completely that we cannot really see why France or any other nation should be irked by dependence on an American Supreme Commander and a British Deputy Supreme Commander in NATO. De Gaulle himself, it has to be admitted, is no doubt unduly sensitive in such matters. Still, this is the way he is, and he is not going to change—he is much too old. The French want, then, prestige and independence. These things are really things, just as much as material wealth and power. Without them, even material wealth and power are not enough.

At bottom, then, the French "team" headed by de Gaulle wants nothing like world conquest, nothing like the burden of such leadership as the United States now has, but wants to be in Europe in some respects *primus inter pares,* though willing to settle in some fields for the status of less than first, always among equals. They want to be in the major league. They are fully aware that such a status requires the maintenance of recent French economic growth and that this in turn is related to the continuing development and extension of the European Economic Community. All the possible futures for France depend on this one; this one alone, however, in itself, it must be insisted, is just not enough.

The economists believe that they now know enough to prevent any such disastrous depression as that of the 1930's. The government of the Fifth Republic is staffed with well-trained and confident experts, who in the centralized French state have a favorable field of action. They are, if not precisely popular with the general public, at least not generally subject to the distrust and abuse their American counterparts often undergo. But, as the more modest economists themselves admit, the science of economics does not encompass all the variables that determine the material condition of a given society. The generation that made the new France may not be followed by another so energetic, so imaginative, so prolific. The old France of *mesure*—too much *mesure*—the France of the rentier mentality, the France of the old men, the France of all the worn-out phrases, may once more take over, for like all pasts, it still exists.

It is fairly certain, again in terms of simple economics, that for an economy maintaining modern large-scale production and distribution, for a society at all resembling in its economic standards those achieved in the United States, a base larger than any single Western European state is necessary. Complete autarky is impossible, or at any rate does not exist in this world; but presumably the United States, the USSR, and potentially other really big territorial units like Brazil, some possible Latin American combinations of now sovereign states, and China have the land, the extensive free market, the population, the demand, that permits full "modernization" if other conditions, political, social, psychological are right. France, West Germany (even with East Germany added), Italy, Spain, Britain (as she now is taken separately) are just not *big* enough. Europe this side of the Iron Curtain—I can almost write, the former Iron Curtain—if it really existed as a political, social, and economic entity (it is clearly a cultural entity), would be big enough not only for full economic modernization, but big enough to rate that fine word, superpower. What a world of four superpowers, the United States of America, the Soviet Union, the United States of Europe, and China would be like in terms of alliances and alignments is an interesting but unprofitable subject for speculation; a true United States of Europe, a *Bundestaat* not a *Staatenbund*, is extremely unlikely in our time or in our children's.

An extension of the free or nearly free market to include both the present Inner Six (West Germany, France, Italy, the three countries of Benelux) and the Outer Seven (Austria, Britain, Denmark, Norway, Portugal, Sweden, and Switzerland) plus Finland and probably also Spain is by no means altogether unlikely in some measurable future. At any rate the Common Market of the Six seems to be a going concern and unlikely to run into difficulties worse than those over agricultural tariffs already surmounted. De Gaulle is often said by his enemies to be both uninterested in and stupid about matters of economics. Even if this is so, he is surrounded by men who are neither and who seem to influence French policy. De Gaulle's government has proved to be a hard bargainer in the necessary give and take of the administration of the Common Market, but ever since its inception as the Coal and Steel Community in 1950 (under the Schuman Plan, better called from its real father the Monnet Plan) the Common Market has had the support of French governments and French public opinion.

It looks as though for the near future Western Europe would be economically united enough for the French and the other national economies to continue to flourish. No doubt complete mergers, not just cartels or similar "arrangements," made and maintained with no regard for national boundaries would be necessary to achieve many large-scale industries on the American scale, and such may not prove to be impossible. For the most elaborate computers, for space exploration, for some other phases of the latest and necessarily most gigantic industrial efforts of the latest of industrial revolutions, no single Western European country, not even a reunited Germany, is in itself big enough. But something less than the scale of, say, General Motors will still permit effective competition in the automobile industry in the European market and in parts of the world market. There may well be some limits still to the all-embracing efficiencies of the largest-scale industry. At any rate, for the present, the problem of the market would not seem to be an insoluble one for the French, always assuming they can keep up their present *élan*.

The most serious danger to French economic growth is political. The "mix" of the French mixed economy is perhaps a rather more delicate one than in countries like Sweden or even Britain and certainly more so than in the United States. A complete victory of a Left with a firm "anticapitalist" or Communist mission would certainly create difficulties. No such victory seems likely and now is almost impossible before 1972. The Left will come into power eventually, or the Fifth Republic really will be no democracy; but in the new France one can hazard the guess that a victorious Left would be a moderate one that would not attempt to revolutionize the basic structure of the French economy any more than the victorious British Labour Party did in 1945, or if this seems a comparison of evil omen, a not great deal more relatively than did the New Deal here in the United States in 1933. Right now such organs of the new Left as Servan-Schreiber's *L'Express* sound very New Dealish; they want a more effective income tax, with some soaking of the rich but also a tightening up on the farmers and the small businessmen, energetic backing for the Common Market and other forms of united European effort, encouragement of and also regulation of investment in modern industry, a lifting of the bottom layers of the working population— in short, though the word is avoided, Americanization. The threat from the opposite direction, embodied under the Fourth Republic by the Poujadistes, that *rentiers*, small farmers, small businessmen for whom the "government" is the great enemy might combine to try to destroy the mixed economy and return to a past of laissez faire that never existed—this threat has pretty well disappeared in the Fifth Republic today. By and large, it looks as though the economic future of France is fairly bright.

2.   The France of de Gaulle and, one guesses, his successors is then no direct menace to the United States and seems unlikely, short of terrifying world depression, to indulge herself in another of those revolutions that shock us so. Such a revolu-

tion would be a Communist revolution and therefore inevitably a menace to us. As a member of the Common Market, however, France is already committed to a measure of abandonment of her sovereignty, to participation in a supernational organization. Is the Europe of the future likely to menace us, perhaps with France as one of its leaders?

American opinion even (or perhaps above all) among those who concern themselves most directly with our foreign policy has for some time been strongly in favor of a united Europe, a free Europe west of the Russian state system. Such a Europe, a true United States of Europe, would be what no single state of old Europe can be, a full equal in population, material strength, and military capabilities of the United States or the Soviet Union, would be in short a superpower. The frequent American denigrations of such potential European strength are not very valid. Lack of certain raw materials is in a world of rapid transportation like ours—always assuming some degree of peace—not a major weakness; phrases like "old," "worn-out," "exhausted" are bad journalistic rhetoric. The Machiavellian, the realist, perhaps also the historian would have to note that such a superpower would by no means necessarily prove to be a friendly and peaceful collaborator of ours or of Russia's. But this need not directly concern us or perhaps the next generation.

A Europe reverting, in spite of the presence of the Soviet Union, to the old permutations and combinations of the European balance of power is surely almost as unlikely—though not quite so much so in the eyes of the realist—as a United States of Europe. In case of a reversion to the kind of European alignments that existed on the eve of war in 1914 and 1939, say a Franco-Russian system against a Germano-British one, it would surely be impossible for the United States to avoid taking sides. Nothing in our recent history suggests that we could keep our hands off Europe. Realists and military experts

have long urged that we concentrate on the Pacific, not the
Atlantic. But vague, unreal, immeasurable though the pull of
tradition, the past, the culture may seem to the naive, the fact
remains that even in California, minds and even dollars, travelers' dollars, move toward Europe and not nearly to the same
extent toward Asia or toward Latin America.

The dilemma of choosing sides in Europe may not, however,
face us. The most likely prediction for Europe in the near
future would be for a middle way between the extreme of a
United States of Europe and a Europe of old-fashioned alliances and ententes. Such a modestly improved Europe would
perhaps include Russia and would have something like a
common market, the kind of successful functional international
bodies that already make travel, communication, pursuit of
criminals, some forms of scientific research (as in Euratom),
and much else so much easier in spite of national borders than
they were only thirty years ago. There will be as well, perhaps,
strengthened formal consultative bodies like those now centered in Strasbourg. Within such a system, national rivalries,
indeed strong national dislikes, would certainly exist and
would, working along with genuine (that is, in the American
world view, economic) conflicts of interests, put severe strains
on the relatively weak union and might well break it up. Still
the chances in the long run for an informal organization of
European states, including Russia, are reasonably good. Such
an organization would be independent of the United States in
the way NATO is not, but would not necessarily be hostile to
the United States. Into such an organization the France of the
Fifth Republic ought to be able to fit well enough, even under
another de Gaulle. Certainly the bulk of her new class of
scientists, technologists, industrialists, social scientists, and
civil servants want to do so, and it is fairly clear from the polls
that a very important part of the French nation shares this
desire. It is always conceivable, especially while de Gaulle

lives, but hardly possible, that France will be on the limited European scene now and in the near future a real perturber, prickly, vain, seeking once more, as under the Sun King, to dominate in art, fashion, taste, war, and peace. But such a France in 1967 is in fact the invention of some American publicists, backed by French intellectuals hostile to the Fifth Republic and not very friendly to the whole human race. It is not the real France, the new France.

3. In conclusion, the possibilities of Franco-American relations may be reviewed under three quite obvious headings: they remain about the same, they get worse, they improve.

It is possible that for the next few years anyway these relations may continue in something like their present status. With American installations and American personnel removed from French territory, NATO may still go along as usual, the Cold War persisting at about the same temperature. We may still carry on all sorts of relations with France, from tourism and student exchanges to conventional diplomatic pursuits. Each nation might continue its cultural attachés, its propaganda and promotional literature, all the many kinds of informal interchanges that go on within our common culture. The balance of ambivalences in public opinion in both countries might be maintained for years.

In these days, however, change is more conspicuous than permanence. The possibilities of deterioration in Franco-American relations are great. Without any diabolic intent, indeed with the best of intentions, our policymakers may continue to try to strengthen the "North Atlantic Community" against an isolated France. They would have hard sledding, but they might have partial success. Such success would almost certainly bring France and the Soviet Union, with some at least of its satellites, together in a renewal of something like the old

Franco-Russian alliance of 1894 that contributed so much to
the bringing on of World War I. This is a nightmare prospect,
and not only for historians. Short of such horrid consequences,
an increased tension between the United States and France
would at the very least postpone the organization of Europe on
any sort of stable basis.

There is always the prospect that, in spite of all our assets,
wealth, power, and prestige, we might fail to organize Europe
in our train, might have to face a dissolution of NATO against
our will. This is in some ways an even more dismal prospect
than some of the preceding possibilities, if only because we are
not used to defeat, even in diplomacy, we take it very hard,
and we are likely to keep on trying to do what cannot be done.

The prospects for immediate and considerable betterment in
Franco-American relations are slim indeed. At the level of
diplomacy sudden and drastic shifts are not uncommon in the
modern state system. There was the famous "diplomatic revolution" of 1756 when Austria and Prussia switched sides in
between two wars; in our own time there was the bombshell
of the agreement between Stalin and Hitler in 1939, not to
speak of the comparative brevity of the interval that saw
Japanese-American relations shift from enmity to friendship.
No such rapid change seems in the offing for Franco-American
relations. The tensions of the modern world are great, but in
Europe itself not quite at the hair-line point at which diplomatic revolutions are likely.

Not even the disappearance of de Gaulle from the scene
(though it might in later perspective be seen as a turning point
towards improvement) would be likely to have an immediate
effect. If the de Gaulle government were succeeded by a
government of the Left, even of what looks like the tamed Left
of today, tensions between the two countries might well increase. For the Left, though it damns de Gaulle's foreign policy
as a whole, though it has less professed concern than he for

French *grandeur* and independence of the Anglo-Saxons, none-theless fundamentally distrusts the United States as a reactionary power, with a Metternich-like policy of resistance to social change everywhere. On the other hand, were de Gaulle to be succeeded as president by someone like Valéry Giscard d'Estaing or Georges Pompidou, there would be a lessening in some of the economic difficulties and minor improvements in other respects. But it is hard to imagine a French Rightist-Centrist government returning meekly to the fold of NATO.

De Gaulle himself is certainly a block to major improvements in Franco-American relations at the formal level. There are a number of other blocks, difficulties, problems, all contributing to the total situation, no one in itself crucial, all in the long run and with patience on both sides capable of compromises. The problems of direct American investments in French industries, the domination of the dollar in international monetary transactions, American economic "imperialism" in general are real, but like most problems where no more than rational human interests are involved, not insoluble, always given patience. Where human ideas, ideals, and sentiments are involved—and do not forget that diplomatists, policymakers, and experts all have such—solutions are more difficult. There is a fine syndrome of interests, ideas, and sentiments already well developed in France—that is, in Frenchmen, important Frenchmen—over the situation in Viet Nam and, beyond that, over the American policy of containment of Communism all over the globe. It is hardly necessary to expatiate at this point. There are ungenerous sentiments involved in French attitudes —envy of our superior strength and determination in continuing a struggle where the French failed, fear that we may succeed after all and become even more enviable, as well as more generous ones of sympathy for the sufferings the struggle has brought to the people of Viet Nam. As long as this grave trouble spot remains, it will be idle to hope for much bettering of French opinion, especially among the intellectuals, toward the present American government.

On the other hand, if the situation in Southeast Asia can be cleared up, at least in a kind of stand-off of the kind achieved in Korea, French policy makers are unlikely to nurse serious permanent grudges over our position in the world outside Europe. France, the "France" of the diplomatic historian, is going to have to accept our position as top dog unless we abuse that position in Europe beyond their endurance. Contrary to the expressed opinion of some American journalists, the men in charge of formulating and carrying out French foreign policy are realists, well trained, beneficiaries of a long professional tradition, and fully aware of the facts of international life. They no doubt feel superior (though not more so than their British opposite numbers) to us simple and untrained Americans, and this is hard for our diplomatists and other experts to bear. But they ought to be able to put up with it.

Any great and rapid improvement of popular attitudes, popular understanding, on both sides of the Atlantic is not to be looked for. In such matters, change is usually slow, for the conditions that almost overnight changed the Japanese in American eyes from dirty yellow sons of bitches to kindly friends and allies are just not present in Franco-American relations. The process of modernization or "Americanization" of France might seem at first glance a condition favorable to improved attitudes between the two peoples even at the top. If, however, any neat simple aphoristic statement about relations between the peoples of modern nation-states can be made, it is that similarity does not breed affection. We and the French have long shared the "principles of 1776 and 1779"; we are both children of the eighteenth-century Enlightenment; we have long had a great deal in common. Yet over two centuries the record shows that in formal relations we have often been at odds and that on both sides popular as well as educated opinion has been full of ambivalences. "Franco-American friendship," even as a myth, has by no means been a fruitful Sorelian myth.

Yet on both sides there exists even in these bad days a tremendous fund of good will. The young of both peoples, though their behavior shocks their elders, though some of their brightest and best are in what seems to their elders pointless and endless revolt, are trying to break through to a better society. Both peoples have their full share of energy, inventiveness, and even a chastened optimism; both are pluralistic societies, full of conflicts but not incapable of compromise, immensely varied in their range of beliefs, tastes, interests, habits, but not incapable of toleration. Their falling out is a diminishing of the human condition.

Still on the level of relations between peoples, there *are* bright spots. The increased exchange of persons through travel and study and, in particular on the French side, their new mobility, their new interest in the world outside France, are surely in the balance a good omen. In the high culture there is always the possibility that out of the apparent chaos of "modernism" there will appear a new shared art and literature, capable of being understood by the many. Both countries are likely to share in any such achievement, which though no sure formula for peace on earth, should nonetheless be counted a good omen. At this particular moment, neither French nor American artistic, literary, or scholarly intellectuals are likely to be factors in improving relations between the two peoples. On the other hand, social scientists in both countries, relatively free of existentialist moral despair, often actually hopeful about their work and its effects on human relations, may increasingly influence these relations for good. It would be most helpful if there were a few more highbrow publicists in both countries who might turn their attention a bit more away from the immediate newsworthy problems of current events to what journalists like to call "background," in fact, to precisely the work of these enterprizing new social scientists in Europe and America.

This study of the Americans and the French has no doubt leaned too much toward blaming, or at least explaining, current Franco-American difficulties in terms of American sins of omission and commission. A wholly detached analyst would no doubt find the French, *le peuple* and the ruling class alike, at least as much at fault, as much responsible by moral and amoral standards, as the Americans. The French since 1939 have certainly been prickly and oversensitive, their leaders too disposed to nurse past wounds, real wounds though they were. Yet when all qualifications are made, there is growing evidence, clear to all but the blindest believers in the tradition of an American mission of peace and good will, a *pax Americana,* John Foster Dulles style, that we are losing ground, not only in French, but in world opinion. It ought not to be impossible for us to regain some of this ground, and that without appeasing anyone who ought not by our standards of right and wrong to be so appeased. One of the bits of land—a good big bit in all but square miles—where such regaining of ground should be possible is France. No doubt the French will have to do their share of the regaining. Still, in the balance we have what ought to be psychologically the easier task. *Puissance,* in the absence of *noblesse, oblige.* We are strong enough to be magnanimous or, at the very least, realistically aware that in this world diplomacy involves some compromise with, some glossing over, the facts of life, and most emphatically, the facts of the pecking order among the 120-odd sovereign nations of this world. In fact, we are strong enough to treat France as a great power, as, it is just possible, she is and will long be.

Appendix

Facts about France

A statistical measure of what I have in this book called the "high culture" is impossible, and the mere suggestion that it might be attempted is offensive to many. It would be easy, and not very meaningful, for example, to work out for each country since the Nobel Prizes were first awarded in 1901 a numerical ratio of awards in all fields to the total population. France, in spite of its long years without a prize in the three scientific fields, would probably come out rather well in Nobel Prizes per capita of population.

On the other hand, a series of statistical indices of a kind could easily be devised to measure in other than absolute quantities what I have occasionally in this book called "Americanization." No doubt "modernization" would be a better term, or even, though the word "mass" has in this use unavoidably pejorative overtones, "contemporary mass culture." In an interesting and long forgotten series of articles in the *American Mercury* for September, October, and November 1931, H. L. Mencken and Charles Angoff used for comparison among American states some ninety tables dealing with such matters as tangible property per capita through illiteracy and hospital beds to listings in *Who's Who* and in *American Men of Science* and subscribers to the *Nation.* They announce at the beginning that they are trying to measure "progressiveness" or "civilization"; but their semantic worries in this respect do not seriously disturb them.

There can be no doubt that in a similar comparison among the hundred and more "sovereign" states of the world today France would rank in the first dozen, though no doubt preceded by most of the small democracies of northern and western Europe and such members of the old British Commonwealth as New Zealand. West Germany and the United Kingdom would almost certainly come out somewhat ahead of France, but it is not clear that either the Soviet Union or the United States would do so. The following tables make no attempt at any such ambitious comparative rankings. They do, however, aim to give the reader the kind of statistical information that will enable him to make his own comparisons if he so desires.

The most complete single source for statistics about France is the *Annuaire statistique de la France,* a yearly government publication distributed by the Presses Universitaires de la France, 108 Boulevard St. Germain, Paris 6me. For purposes of comparison with other countries the *United Nations Statistical Yearbook,* published annually by the United Nations Publishing Service in New York City, should be consulted. The British *Statesman's Yearbook* gives far more current information on France than any of its American counterparts like the *World Almanac.*

Table 1. Area and Population

Region	Area (sq. mi.)	Population (estimated)
Metropolitan France (including Corsica)	212,659[a]	46,520,300 (1962)[b]
France overseas[c]		
Departments		
French Guiana	35,135	35,000 (1963)
Guadeloupe	687	306,000 (1963)
Martinique	425	303,000 (1963)
Reunion	969	382,000 (1964)
Territories		
French Somaliland[d]	8,880	86,000 (1963)
Comoro Islands	863	207,000 (1964)
St. Pierre and Miquelon	93	5,025 (1963)
French Polynesia[e]	ca. 1,544	90,000 (1966)
New Caledonia and dependencies	7,335	86,500 (1966)
Wallis and Futuna Islands[f]	106	11,000 (1963)
French Antarctica[g]	—	—
Condominium (with Great Britain) New Hebrides	ca. 5,700	70,000 (1963)

[a] Texas: 262,840 sq. mi.

[b] 1967 estimate: 50 million.

[c] Of the old Empire, there was left in 1967 four Overseas Departments, with full membership in the National Assembly, seven Overseas Territories, and one Condominium. Six African republics, technically independent and with membership in the United Nations, nonetheless are formally members of the French Community. These are Central African Republic, Chad, Congo (Brazzaville), Gabon, Malagasy Republic, Senegal. The rest of the Empire is now totally free of formal links to France, though the actual economic and cultural relations of these lands with France varies greatly.

[d] In a much criticized plebiscite in 1967, this territory voted to remain part of France. There is, however, a strong movement for independence.

[e] Includes Society Islands, Marquesas Islands, Tuamoto Archipelago, Gambier Islands, and Austral Islands. Administrative center is in Tahiti.

[f] An Overseas Territory since 1961.

[g] Research stations only.

Table 2. Cities with a Population over 100,000
    (*1962 Census, revised*)

City	City proper[a]	Urban agglomeration
Paris[b]	2,790,091	7,369,387
Marseille	778,071	807,499
Lyon	528,535	885,944[c]
Toulouse	323,724	329,044
Nice	292,958	310,063
Bordeaux	249,688	462,171
Nantes	240,028	327,636
Strasbourg	228,971	302,303
Saint-Etienne	201,242	289,958
Lille	193,096	431,148

[a] Data for city proper refer to communes which are the centers of urban agglomerations.

[b] Data refer to the "agglomération étendue" comprising the city of Paris, its urban surroundings, and suburban surroundings.

[c] Includes Villeurbanne.

NOTE. The Paris population increased by over 1,000,000 during 1954–62. However, the medium-sized towns are the great beneficiaries of the rural exodus. Of 12 urban agglomerations of over 250,000 inhabitants, only Toulouse, Nantes, Rouen, and Roubaix have increased appreciably. On the other hand, the 350 agglomerations of over 10,000 inhabitants increased their respective populations an average of 30% in the period 1936–62. And out of 812 towns having 3,000–10,000 inhabitants, 721 have increased about 20%. Almost all of the weight of population decrease has fallen on villages of fewer than 500 inhabitants. They have lost more than 20% of their population.

The accompanying diagram shows clearly the swing to the Left opposition in the election of 1967. Note the position of the P.C. (Parti Communist) on the extreme left of the amphitheatre facing the presiding officer. The split indicated in 1967 in the old Gaullist party (colored black in both years) takes account of "dissident Gaullists," mostly followers of Valery Giscard d'Estaing.

The core of Gaullists is now formally the "Democratic Union for the Fifth Republic," essentially moderate to strong conservatives. The Center is now christened the party of "Progress and Modern Democracy." Its core is still Catholic and centrist.

1962

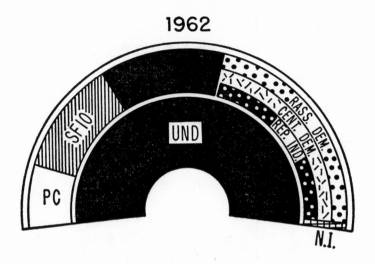

1967

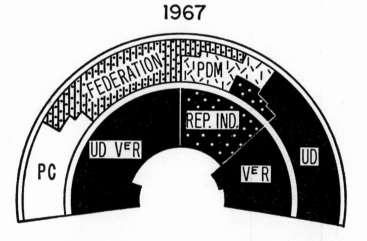

Seating of the Parliamentary Groups on the Floor of the Palais
Bourbon: PC—Communist Party; SFIO—Socialist Party; UNR-
UDT—Union for the New Republic and Democratic Workers Union
coalition; Rass. Dem.—Democratic Rally; Cent. Dem.—Demo-
cratic Center; Rep. Ind.—Independent Republicans; Federation—
Federation of the Democratic & Socialist Left; PDM—Progress &
Modern Democracy; UD VeR.—Democratic Union for the Fifth
Republic; N.I.—nonaligned.

Table 3. Anticipated variation in the population of French regions, 1963–1978[a] (in thousands)

Region[b]	Population 1963	Natural Increase (excess of births over deaths)	Migrations	Population 1978	Increase of Population, 1963–1978 (percent)
Paris Region[c]	8,710	690	1,980	11,380	30.7
Rhone-Alps[c]	4,140	410	420	4,970	20.0
North[d]	3,710	680	—10	4,380	18.0
Provence-Côte D'Azur[c]	3,000	170	460	3,630	21.1
Lorraine[d]	2,240	440	110	2,790	24.7
Loire Country[d]	2,500	430	—150	2,780	11.2
Aquitaine[e]	2,370	170	20	2,560	8.0
Brittany[f]	2,420	290	—270	2,440	0.9
Pyrenees-South	2,150	120	—30	2,240	4.5
Center	1,890	190	40	2,120	12.3
Picardy	1,510	260	—30	1,740	15.5
Languedoc	1,630	90	—20	1,700	4.3
Upper Normandy	1,420	260	—20	1,660	16.7
Burgundy	1,460	140	10	1,610	10.4
Poitou-Charentes	1,470	200	—100	1,570	6.7

Alsace	1,340	150	70	1,560	16.6
Champagne	1,230	220	—40	1,410	14.6
Auvergne	1,290	80	—20	1,350	4.9
Lower Normandy	1,220	210	—140	1,290	5.6
Franche-Comte	950	140	40	1,130	19.2
Limousin^g	740	10	—50	700	—5.0
ALL OF FRANCE	47,570	5,380	2,250	55,200	16.0

SOURCE: Secretariat Général du Gouvernement, Direction de la Documentation, Documents d'Actualité—No. 60, November–December 1965, pp. i–iv.

a The hypothesis employed is that future migrations will be analogous, in direction and numbers, to the migrations that took place during the period 1954–1962. These figures were prepared by the National Institute for Statistics and Economic Studies (INSEE) for the Commissariat for Planning.

b French territory is divided into 21 territorial units for regional development.

c Paris Region, Rhone-Alps, Provence-Côte D'Azur. Here the large increase is due to both a high rate of migration and a high rate of natural increase. Even if migrations prove to be less than predicted, a high rate of population growth is inevitable.

d North, Lorraine, Loire Country, Upper Normandy, Picardy, Champagne. Here the increase, large or medium, is due essentially to the natural increase of population.

e Center, Alsace, Aquitaine, Franche-Comte, Burgundy. Here the moderate increase is due principally to natural increase, plus some migration. Any eventual modification in migrations will barely alter the moderate character of the population increase.

f Poitou-Charentes, Lower Normandy, Brittany. Here the large natural increase is balanced by a large emigration.

g Pyrenees-South, Languedoc, Auvergne, Limousin. Here population is stationary or on the decrease because of a low rate of natural increase and a traditional pattern of emigration out of these regions.

Table 4. Political Affiliation in the National Assembly, 1967[a]

Political group	Chairman	Number of members	Number of affiliates
Communist Group (PC)	Robert Ballanger	71	2
Democratic Union for the Fifth Republic (UD)	Henri Rey	180	20
Federation of the Democratic & Socialist Left (FDG)	Gaston Deferre	116	5
Independent Republicans (RI)	Raymond Mondon	39	3
Progress and Modern Democracy (PDM)	Jacques Duhamel	38	3
Nonaligned		9	

[a] SOURCE: *Journal Officiel,* April 4, 1967

Table 5. Gross National Product 1949, 1955, 1959, and 1964

	1949	1955	1959	1964
Volume index, preceding year $= 100$[a]	—[b]	105.1	102.7	105.4
Volume index, base year $1949 = 100$	100.0	132.6	155.5	206.5
Volume index, base year $1959 = 100$	64.3	85.2	100.0	132.8

SOURCE: Institut National de la Statistique et des Études Économiques, *Annuaire Statistique de la France, 1965,* p. 545.

[a] Preceding year refers to year immediately preceding, and not to preceding year shown on table.

[b] — = no figure possible because of nature of table.

Table 6. *Utilization of Gross National Product, at Constant Prices, 1949, 1955, 1959, and 1964 (Unit: thousand million francs at 1959 prices)*

	1949	1955	1959	1964
Private consumption	111,30	150,98	173,599	230,422
Public consumption	24,28	30,46	37,314	43,641
Gross capital formation	36,15	41,61	52,643	83,101
GROSS NATIONAL EXPENDITURE	171,73	223,05	263,556	357,164
Exports of goods and services and factor income from abroad	21,58	35,06	39,444	58,660
less: Imports of goods and services and factor income to abroad	−21,39	−30,23	−35,623	−60,828
GROSS NATIONAL PRODUCT AT MARKET PRICES	171,92	227,88	267,377	354,996

SOURCE: Institut National de la Statistique et des Études Économiques, *Annuaire statistique de la France, 1965*, p. 546.

Table 7. Annual Rates of Growth (in volume)

	From Base Year 1961		Achieved in			Requisite Rates of Growth in 1965 to realize the forecasts of the Plan
	4th Plan 1962-65	Achieved 1962-64	1962	1963	1964	
Gross Domestic Product	5.5	6.0	6.8	5.5	5.7	−17.9
Imports	5.3	14.3	11.1	17.1	13.4	4.0
Total resources	5.5	6.8	7.3	6.7	6.5	1.1
Consumption:						
Households	5.2	6.0	7.0	6.8	4.1	3.0
Government	5.1	8.4	10.6	8.3	6.2	−4.1
Investments:	6.8	7.8	7.9	6.9	8.5	4.0
of which: Non-Residential	6.4	6.1	7.7	5.1	5.4	7.4
Residential	5.7	10.4	6.0	10.0	15.5	−7.3
Government	10.7	10.7	12.9	9.7	9.4	10.8
Exports	4.7	6.1	1.9	8.9	7.5	0.7

Table 8. National Budget, 1965 (Unit: million francs)

Revenue		Expenditure	
Direct taxes	34,628	Ordinary civil	64,751
Turnover taxes[a]	33,937	Military	19,535
Fees, stamps	5,816	Capital ⎫	
Other indirect taxes	7,512	War Damage ⎭	13,923
Customs	11,685	Total	98,209
Government property, etc.	8,229		
Total	101,807		

SOURCE: *The Europa Year Book, 1967* (London: Europa Publications Limited), pp. 546–547.

[a] This is essentially a form of what in the United States is called a sales tax; it is paid by the businessman, but of course passes on to the buyers of what he sells.

Table 9. National Accounts (Unit: thousand million francs)

	1962	1965
Net national income	272,400	346,773
Gross national expenditure	353,260	457,007
Gross National Product (GNP)	356,294	461,437

SOURCE: *The Europa Year Book, 1967* (London: Europa Publications Limited), pp. 546–547.

Table 10. Agricultural Production (thousand metric tons)

	1948–52	1955	1959	1962	1963[a]
Wheat	7,791	10,365	11,544	14,054	10,152
Rye	573	440	470	356	347
Maize (corn)	452	1,107	1,865	1,867	3,715
Barley	1,534	2,671	4,931	6,003	7,384
Oats	3,393	3,640	2,851	2,628	2,876
Rice (rough or paddy)	46	81	132	130	114
Linseed (flaxseed)	15	23	27	51	—[b]
Potatoes (including garden crop)	13,734	15,052	13,264	13,389	15,631
Tobacco	49.1	56.3	52.0	39.4	46.2
Milk[c]	14,817	19,903[d]	20,607	24,739	—

SOURCE: *U.N. Statistical Yearbook,* 1964, pp. 127–160.
[a] Provisional, preliminary, or estimated figure.
[b] Data not available.
[c] Total production of milk for consumption fresh or for conversion into products such as butter, cheese, condensed milk, etc.
[d] 1956 figure.

Table 11. Livestock Population (thousand head)

		1947/48–1951/52	1959/60	1962/63
Cattle	1 Oct.	15,605	18,735	20,265
Pigs	1 Oct.	6,582	8,357	9,080
Sheep	1 Oct.	7,498	8,942	8,945
Horses	1 Oct.	2,403	1,825	1,526
Mules	1 Oct.	89	71	56
Asses	1 Oct.	145	82	64

SOURCE: *U. N. Statistical Yearbook,* 1964, pp. 127–160.

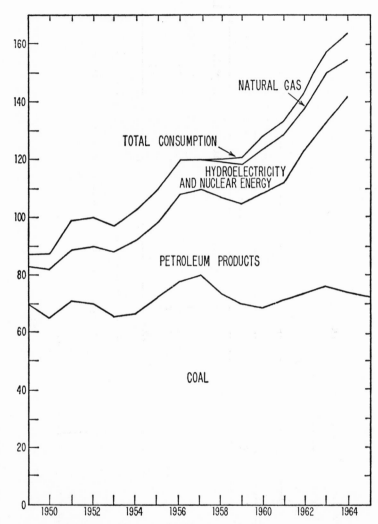

Total consumption of Primary Energy, 1949–1965. (Unit: millions of tons, coal equivalent).

Table 12. *External Trade of France—Monetary Value, and Price and Volume Indices, 1950, 1955, 1959, 1964*
Monetary value: million francs[a]
Indices: Base year 1958 = 100

Year	Monetary value Merchandise		Index numbers Quantum[b]		Unit value[c]	
	Imports	Exports	Imports	Exports	Imports	Exports
1950	10,604	10,630	60	69	74	73
1955	16,587	17,191	82	97	83	82
1959	25,102	27,674	98	120	109	109
1964	49,700	44,386	187	174	113	119

SOURCE: Statistical Office of the United Nations, Department of Economic and Social Affairs, *Yearbook of International Trade Statistics, 1964* (New York, 1966), p. 262.
[a] Although the new franc, with a value of 100 old francs, was introduced in 1960, all data are shown in terms of the new franc for the sake of comparison.
[b] Volume of aggregate merchandise trade.
[c] Average price of aggregate merchandise trade.

Table 13. French Trade with The United States, 1964
  (*Unit: thousand francs*)

Category of commodities	Imports	Exports
Food and live animals	602,341	86,259
Beverages and tobacco	46,611	188,995
Crude materials, inedible, excluding fuels	723,355	139,850
Mineral fuels, lubricants	285,667	4,977
Animal and vegetable oils and fats	15,678	683
Chemicals	620,192	267,509
Manufactured articles, classified by material	703,832	694,816
Machinery and transport equipment	2,241,555	435,592
Miscellaneous manufactured articles	361,619	506,036
Commodities and transactions not elsewhere specified	1,967	9,733
TOTAL	5,611,817	2,334,450

SOURCE: Direction Générale des Douanes et Droits Indirect. *Statistiques du commerce de la France avec les pays hors Zone Franc et la Zone Franc, 1964*, pp. 3, 5.

Table 14. Rate of School Enrollment by Sex, Age, and Level of School, Public and Private Education, Academic Year 1963–64 (Unit: percentage, rounded out to nearest 5)

Age on 1 January 1964	Of all males	Of all females
Preschool		
3	40	40
4	70	70
Preschool and elementary		
5	95	95
6	100	100
Elementary and secondary		
7–12	100	100
13	95	95
14	70	75
15	55	60
Elementary, secondary, and teacher's colleges		
16	45	50
Secondary, teacher's colleges, and university		
17	35	35
18	25	25
19	20	15
20	10	10
21	10	8
22 and over	less than 5	less than 5

SOURCE: Institut National de la Statistique et des Études Économiques, *Annuaire statistique de la France, 1965,* between pp. 104 and 105.

Table 15. Number of Students in Secondary School

School	Academic Year 1937–38	Academic Year 1951–52	Academic Year 1964–65
Public	269,152	456,290	2,552,000
Private	241,566	340,733	772,000
TOTAL	510,718	797,023	3,324,000

SOURCES: Institut National de la Statistique et des Études Économiques, *Annuaire statistique de la France, 1946,* pp. 36–38; Institut National de la Statistique et des Études Économiques, *Annuaire statistique de la France, 1952,* p. 56; Ambassade de France, Service de Presse et d'Information, *France and the Rising Generation* (New York, 1965), p. 6.

Table 16. Trends In Higher Education—Public Universities 1930–1964

Academic year(s)	Average total annual enrollment[a]
1930–34	83,000
1935–39	71,000
1940–44	92,000
1945–49	129,000
1950–54	147,000
1955–59	180,000
1959–60	194,763
1960–61	203,375
1961–62	232,610
1962–63	270,788
1963–64	308,189

SOURCES: United Nations Educational, Scientific and Cultural Organization, *World Survey of Education,* vol. IV (New York, 1966), p. 479; Institut National de la Statistique et des Études Économiques, *Annuaire Statistique de la France, 1965,* p. 110.

[a] Figures for 1930–1959 have been rounded to the nearest thousand.

*Table 17. Number of Students Enrolled in the Faculties of Public
Universities (Academic Years 1951–52 and 1962–63)*

University	Date of founding	1951–52	1962–63
Aix	1409	7,836	21,129
Besançon	1485	942	3,312
Bordeaux	1441	8,367	15,743
Caen	1432	3,218	8,426
Clermont-Ferrand	1808	2,079	6,025
Dijon	1722	1,904	5,124
Grenoble	1339	3,993	11,854
Lille	1530	6,355	13,754
Lyon	1808	8,286	15,931
Montpelier	1289	6,295	15,458
Nancy	1572	4,731	9,591
Nantes	1961	—	4,542
Orleans	1961	—	2,464
Paris	1150	59,609	89,936
Poitiers	1431	4,244	7,312
Reims	1961	—	1,489
Rennes	1735	6,517	9,720
Strasbourg	1567	5,073	12,288
Toulouse	1230	7,460	16,690
Algiers		5,154	—
TOTAL		142,063	270,788

SOURCES: Institut National de la Statistique et des Études Économiques, *Annuaire Statistique de la France, 1952,* p. 58; Institut National de la Statistique et des Études Économiques, *Annuaire Statistique de la France, 1965,* p. 110; S. H. Steinberg, ed., *The Statesman's Year-Book 1965–66* (London, 1965), p. 984.

Elements of Modern Mass Culture

  a. The love affair with the automobile

	Cars	Trucks, trailers, and buses	Tractors	Motorcycles	Totals
1955	2,677,000	1,136,500	257,500	not given	4,171,000
1964	7,800,000	2,135,900	949,100	4,900,000	15,785,900

There were probably some four million motorcycles in 1955, making the true total over eight million. But from the point of view of traffic density, even these figures are misleading. There were in 1964 over five million other two-wheeled vehicles equipped with some kind of engine, not to mention a good many plain bicycles. Moreover the above figures do not include cars under foreign registry, which are numerous in these days of the Common Market and easy passage of frontiers for motorists. By 1967 the total number of French-registered four-wheeled motor vehicles was between fourteen and fifteen millions; there has been an actual decrease in the number of motorcycles.

  b. Communications

	Telephones	Radios	Television Sets
1957	3,412,000	10,199,000	683,200
1965	6,014,000	8,937,000	6,989,000

  c. Movie production, number of films

	Solely French	Collaborative with other countries	Average cost per film (in new francs)
1957	81	61	1,150,000
1965	34	108	2,120,000

d. Book production, number of titles

	France	United States	Great Britain
1964	13,479	28,451	25,079

e. Paid entrances, selected monuments and museums

	1962	1964
Eiffel Tower	1,735,800	2,143,200
Louvre	801,700	1,012,100
Chateau of Versailles	878,200	1,076,100
Abbey of Mont-St. Michel	350,800	402,000
Chateau of Chenonceaux	260,000	320,000
Guided tours and terraces, two Paris airports	3,752,000	3,956,300

It should be noted that there are many free admissions on certain days to the museum of the Louvre, very few to the Eiffel Tower or the Orly and Le Bourget airports guided tours and terraces.

SOURCE for this section, *Annuaire Statistique de la France,* 1966

Reading Suggestions

The reader who wishes a somewhat fuller bibliography of books dealing with France published before 1951 is referred to the excellent annotated list appended to an earlier volume of the American Foreign Policy Library, Donald C. McKay, *The United States and France* (Cambridge, Mass.: Harvard University Press, 1951), pp. 310–319. There is a useful selective bibliography on modern French history covering publications up to 1960 in G. F. Howe and others, *The American Historical Association's Guide to Historical Literature* (New York: Macmillan, 1961), pp. 464–502. The following reading suggestions will be heavily weighted toward books published since 1950.

1. The Land and the People

The French are excellent geographers, particularly good at what they call *la géographie humaine*. Jean Brunhès, *Géographie humaine de la France,* 2 vols. (Paris: Plon-Nourret, 1920–1929) is an admirable example. The older Vidal de la Blache, *La France: Tableau géographique* (Paris: Hachette, 1908) deals more at length with physical and economic geography. Both are well illustrated. There is an extraordinary series of some seventy volumes,

Ardouin-Dumazet, *Voyage en France* (Paris: Berger-Levrault) in various editions, the latest mostly in the first two decades of the twentieth century. This series deals in detail with the geography, history and "look of the land" for all the little *pays* of France. The *Atlas historique de la France Contemporaine, 1800–1965* (Paris: Armand Colin, 1966) is a most useful set of maps on demography, industry, agriculture, indeed all sorts of important matters. No one ever travels seriously in France without the latest annual number of the *Guide Michelin*, which lists—and grades—hotels and restaurants according to high standards and with, to an American, surprising independence of commercial pressures.

On the French national character there is a great deal of writing. At the lowest level of ethnic insults and popular aphorisms about nationality there is A. A. Roback, *A Dictionary of International Slurs (Ethnophaulisms)* (Cambridge, Mass.: Sci-Art Publishers, 1944) a fascinating collection arranged by country for most of Europe, including France. At the highest level there is the work of the German scholar E. R. Curtius, *The Civilization of France,* English translation (New York: Macmillan, 1932). Curtius was interested rather in literature and the arts of living than in politics, and he was clearly a Francophile, but this is the best of many such books. Most commentators on the French cannot resist the temptation to show them the error of their ways. The Anglo-Saxons are nowadays not so much shocked by French *amour* as they were a few generations ago, but they continue to feel that the French are politically indecent and industrially backward. The Germans usually display a tinge of envy in dealing with French culture, but they too find the French not quite up to date. Still, the following all have something to contribute: Friedrich Sieburg, *Who Are These French?* English translation (New York: Macmillan, 1932) which in the original German was entitled, after a well-known German folk-saying, *Wie Gott in Frankreich* (Like God in France); Paul Cohen-Portheim, *The Spirit of France,* English translation (New York: E. P. Dutton, 1933); Donald C. McKay, *The United States and France* (Cambridge, Mass.: Harvard University Press, 1951); H. Luethy, *France against Herself,* English translation (New York: Praeger, 1955); Salvador de Madariaga, *Englishmen, Frenchmen, Spaniards*

(London: Oxford University Press, 1929); André Siegfried, *France: A Study in Nationality* (New Haven: Yale University Press, 1930); David Schoenbrunn, *As France Goes* (New York: Harper, 1957); Raymond Aron, *France: Steadfast and Changing* (Cambridge, Mass.: Harvard University Press, 1960); Patrick E. Charvet, *France* (New York: Praeger, 1955); Edgar S. Furniss, Jr., *France, Troubled Ally* (New York: Praeger, 1960); Edward R. Tannenbaum, *The New France* (Chicago: University of Chicago Press, 1961). Most of these books are concerned with a general account of what contemporary France is like, with no more than occasional references to the French national character.

2. History

There is an admirable general history of France from its beginnings, Georges Duby and Robert Mandrou, *A History of French Civilization,* translated from the French (New York: Random House, 1964). The authors emphasize social and cultural history, but not to the neglect of other aspects of history. For a more conventional political narrative, there is Charles Seignobos, *A History of the French Nation,* translated from the French (London: Jonathan Cape, 1933), the work of a distinguished academic historian of the last generation, and André Maurois, *A History of France* (New York: Farrar, Straus and Cudahy, 1957), by a well-known literary figure. Albert Léon Guerard, *France, a Modern History* (Ann Arbor: University of Michigan Press, 1959), is somewhat misleadingly titled, in fact goes back to pre-Roman Gaul. This readable general history is the final work of a distinguished French historian and man of letters who made his career in the United States. For modern France there is a lively and allusive work, D. W. Brogan, *The French Nation from Napoleon to Pétain* (New York: Harper, 1957) and by the same author with the editors of *Life, France* (New York: Time Inc., 1966), which is well illustrated, and two good American textbooks, Gordon Wright, *France in Modern Times* (Chicago: Rand, McNally, 1960) and Paul A. Gagnon, *France since 1789* (New York: Harper and Row, 1964).

For those who want a very detailed professional history in many volumes, there is as yet no real substitute for Ernest Lavisse, ed., *Histoire de France depuis les origines jusqu'à la Révolution*, 18 vols. (Paris: Hachette, 1900–1911) and by the same editor, *Histoire de France contemporaine, depuis la Révolution jusqu'à la paix de 1919*, 10 vols. (Paris: Hachette, 1920–1922). These are collaborative works, somewhat out of date now. For the French Empire there is Stephen Roberts, *History of French Colonial Policy, 1870–1925*, 2 vols. (London: P. S. King & Son, 1929) and H. Brunschwig, *Mythes et réalités de l'impérialisme colonial français, 1871–1914* (Paris: Colin, 1960). There is a great deal to be learned about the break-up of the formal French colonial structure—and the survival of much French influence in her former colonies—in Jean Lacouture, *Cinq hommes et la France* (Paris: Editions du Seuil, 1961). The five men are Ho Chi Minh, Bourguiba, Mohammed V of Morocco, Ferhat Abbas, and Sékou Touré.

3. Government

For a full understanding of the structure of government of the Fifth Republic some knowledge of the way France has been governed at least for the last half-century is necessary. Three books will cover this ground: Walter R. Sharp, *The Government of the French* [Third] *Republic* (New York: Van Nostrand, 1938); Dorothy Pickles, *France between the Republics* (London: Contact Publications, 1946), which deals with Vichy France; and O. R. Taylor, *The Fourth Republic of France: Constitution and Political Parties* (London: Royal Institute of International Affairs, 1951). For the Fifth Republic, the best short analysis is Dorothy Pickles, *The Fifth French Republic*, 3rd ed. (New York: Praeger, 1966), which contains an English translation of the constitution of the Fifth Republic. Roy C. Macridis and Bernard Brown, *The De Gaulle Republic* (Homewood, Ill.: Dorsey Press, 1960) is a good contemporaneous study of the Fifth Republic in its beginning. The French text of the constitution of the Fifth Republic will be found in the early pages (p. 7 of the 1965 edition) of the annual publication known as the *Bottin administratif et documentaire.* This is a very complete official directory of French government and administration in all fields of activity. Its text of the constitution of the Fifth Republic is preceded by a very succinct tabular analysis of all the French constitutions since 1789. Another useful annual publication is the *Political Handbook and Atlas of the World: Parliaments, Press, Parties,* published by Harper and Row for the Council of Foreign Relations in New York City and edited by Walter H. Mallory. Under the heading "France" will be founded the latest information on the topics indicated in the subtitle.

4. *Franco-American Relations*

Especially in these days, Franco-American relations are thoroughly tied in with world affairs. The publications of the Council on Foreign Relations in New York afford the student an essential tool for work in almost any phase of such relations. Of particular importance are the four volumes entitled *Foreign Affairs Bibliography,* under various editors covering the decades 1919–1932, 1932–1942, 1942–1952, 1952–1962 and the annual *The United States in World Affairs* begun in 1932 under the editorship of Walter Lippmann and continuing under various editors to the present. Libraries usually list these under "Council on Foreign Relations."

Diplomatic history in the usual sense can be studied in two American textbooks, Thomas A. Bailey, *A Diplomatic History of the American People,* 7th ed. (New York: Appleton-Century-Crofts, 1964) and Samuel Flagg Bemis, *A Diplomatic History of the United States,* 5th ed. (New York: Holt, Rinehart & Winston, 1965) and from the French side in the old classic, Emile Bourgeois, *Manuel historique de politique étrangère,* 4 vols. (Paris: Belin frères, 1893–1926). The immediate background for current difficulties is well covered in Robert Strausz-Hupé and S. F. Possony, *International Relations in the Age of Conflict between Democracy and Dictatorship* (New York: McGraw-Hill, 1954). Current Franco-American diplomatic relations are of course touched on in many of the books listed above, and especially in Edgar Furniss, *France: Troubled Ally* (New York: Praeger, 1960), a work commissioned by the Council on Foreign Relations of New York.

On cultural or "informal relations" there is Howard Mumford Jones, *America and French Culture, 1750–1848* (Chapel Hill: University of North Carolina Press, 1927); Elizabeth Brett White, *American Opinion of France: From Lafayette to Poincaré* (New York: Knopf, 1927); Raymond Aron and August Hecksher, *A Diversity of Worlds* (New York: Reynal, 1957). André Tardieu, *Devant l'Obstacle: L'Amérique et nous* (Paris: Emile-Paul, 1927) is by a major political figure of his time, sympathetic toward the United States. Léonie Villard, *La France et les Etats-Unis: Echanges et rencontres, 1524–1800* (Lyon: Editions I A C, 1952) is a pleasant miscellany.

5. Vichy, Resistance, Liberation

On the "collapse" of France in 1940 there is a very large amount of writing, of which the following can serve as a sample: Marc Bloch, *Strange Defeat* (New York: Oxford University Press, 1949), a translation of a posthumously published book by a most distinguished medieval historian, victim of the Gestapo; René de Chambrun, *I Saw France Fall* (New York: Morrow, 1940), by a Rightist son-in-law of Laval, incidentally, a descendant of Lafayette; André Géraud (Pertinax), *The Grave Diggers of France* (Garden City: Doubleday, Doran, 1944), by a most pessimistic contemporary journalist; Colonel Adolphe Goutard, *The Battle of France, 1940* (New York: Washburn, 1959), a more recent and more detached military analysis.

On the years of Pétain's rule the best by all odds is Robert Aron and Georgette Elgey, *Histoire de Vichy, édition illustrée* (Paris: Les productions de Paris, 1960), still of course lacking the full detachment time may provide. On our American policy toward Vichy there is a very fair treatment by a distinguished historian, W. L. Langer, *Our Vichy Gamble* (New York: Knopf, 1947). Langer's book, up to a point a defense of our policy, aroused much opposition in the United States, well represented by L. R. Gottschalk, "Our Vichy Fumble," *Journal of Modern History*, 20 (March 1948), 47–56. For American attitudes to both Vichy and de Gaulle in those years the reader had best go to accounts of contemporaries, notably Cordell Hull, *Memoirs*, 2 vols. (New York: Macmillan, 1948); Dwight D. Eisenhower, *Crusade in Europe* (New York: Doubleday, 1948); Admiral W. D. Leahy, *I Was There* (New York: McGraw-Hill, 1950); Henry L. Stimson and McGeorge Bundy, *On Active Service in Peace and War* (New York: Harper, 1947); Robert L. Sherwood, *Roosevelt and Hopkins* (New York: Harper, 1948).

The French are naturally proud of their Resistance and Liberation, and detachment is difficult for them. Yet such historians as Henri Michel and Robert Aron have written good sound history— contemporary history inevitably, without the full documentation and the detachment only time can bring. Henri Michel, *Bibliographie critique de la Résistance* (Paris: Institut Pédagogique National, 1964) is an essential start for serious work in the subject. The same author's *Histoire de la Résistance*, 2nd ed. (Paris: Presses universitaires, 1958) in the series "Que sais-je?" is an admirable brief account. Henri Michel and Boris Mirkine-Guétzévitch, *Les idées politiques et sociales de la Résistance* (Paris: Presses universitaires, 1954) is a fascinating later collection of contemporary documents published during the occupation. Robert Aron, *France Reborn* (New York: Scribner's, 1964) is good history. This English translation is slightly shortened from the French original, *Histoire de la Libération de la France* (Paris: Fayard, 1959). Janet Teissier du Cros, *Divided Loyalties* (New York: Knopf, 1964), is a fascinating book, perhaps the best "document" on life in occupied France. Larry Collins and Dominique Lapierre, *Is Paris Burning?* (New York: Simon and Schuster, 1965) is readable, but, perhaps for American consumption, it exaggerates the danger of a Communist take-over in Paris in August–September 1944.

On de Gaulle, the Free or Fighting French, the Committee of National Liberation, there is first of all de Gaulle's own memoirs, published in English in three volumes plus two volumes of documents, *The War Memoirs of Charles de Gaulle* (New York: Simon and Schuster, 1960–1964). These memoirs are certainly major ones, as French as Churchill's are British. De Gaulle's controversial *Au fil de l'épée* is available in English as *Edge of the Sword* (New York: Criterion, 1960). By now there are many books about de Gaulle. One of the best brief ones, somewhat allusive for an American reader, is Jean Lacouture, *De Gaulle,* English translation (New York: New American Library, 1966). Alexander Werth's *De Gaulle* (Harmondsworth, England: Penguin Books, 1965) is for a brilliant journalist with Leftist sympathies a surprisingly objective book; it has a most useful brief bibliographical note, pp. 379–382. Jean-Raymond Tournoux, *Sons of France: Pétain and de Gaulle* (New York: Viking, 1966), an English translation of *Pétain et de Gaulle* (Paris: Plon, 1964), and Edward Ashcroft, *De Gaulle* (London: Oldhams Press, 1962), have many interesting personal details on his life. Primarily focused on the Gaullist "movement," though with much on de Gaulle himself, is Henri Michel, *Histoire de la France libre* (Paris: Presses universitaires, 1963).

6. The New France

The following books of the 1950's give some indication of the social and political changes stirring in the old and still very real France of tradition: E. M. Earle, ed., *Modern France* (Princeton: Princeton University Press, 1951); H. W. Ehrmann, *Organized Business in France* (Princeton: Princeton University Press, 1957); Crane Brinton, *The Temper of Western Europe* (Cambridge, Mass.: Harvard University Press, 1953); W. C. Baum, *The French Economy and the State* (Princeton: Princeton University Press: 1958); André Maurois, *La France change de visage* (Paris: Gallimard, 1956); Alexander Werth, *France, 1940–1955* (New York: Holt, 1956). Edward Tannenbaum's *The New France* (1961), already listed, is perhaps the first to use that title and remains a perceptive study, with much attention to literature and the arts.

Stanley Hoffman and others, *In Search of France* (Cambridge, Mass.: Harvard University Press, 1963) is no mere record of a symposium but a good unified study of the new France by a number of specialists; in it Jesse Pitts, "Change in Bourgeois France," pp. 235–304, is central to a study of the New France, but all the contributions in this book are important. Stephen R. Graubard, ed., *A New Europe?* (Boston: Houghton Mifflin, 1964), a volume in the excellent *Daedalus* series sponsored by the American Academy of Arts and Sciences, though it is organized topically in essays covering Europe outside the old Iron Curtain, has a great deal to interest the student of contemporary France. Michel Crozier's "The Cultural Revolution: Notes on the Changes in the Intellectual Climate of France" (pp. 602–630) is especially notable. Lawrence Wylie, *Village in the Vaucluse*, 2nd ed. enlarged (Cambridge, Mass.: Harvard University Press, 1961) and Lawrence Wylie, ed., *Chanzeau: A Village in Anjou* (Cambridge, Mass.: Harvard University Press, 1966) are two well-known studies of French small-town life, the first set in a Provençal village, radical-socialist in politics and pretty indifferent in religion, the second in Anjou, relatively Rightist in politics and Catholic. Both are admirable examples of this kind of "grass roots" study and are mutually complementary.

Charles P. Kindleberger, *Economic Growth in France and Britain* (Cambridge, Mass.: Harvard University Press, 1964), together with his chapter on "The Postwar Resurgence of the French Economy" in the above listed *In Search of France* (1963) make up the best account of the subject, clearly written by a specialist. On the modernization of agriculture there is an excellent recent study, Gordon Wright, *Rural Revolution in France: The Peasantry in the Twentieth Century* (Stanford: Stanford University Press, 1964).

John and Anne-Marie Hackett, *Economic Planning in France* (London: George Allen & Unwin, 1963) deals very completely and competently with the subject. Michel Crozier, *The Bureaucratic Phenomenon*, English translation (Chicago: University of Chicago Press, 1964) is the work of one of the ablest of the new generation that has raised the reputation of French social science very considerably. Jacques Soustelle, *A New Road for France*, English translation (New York: Robert Speller, 1963) is the indignant apologia of a former colleague of de Gaulle's who split with him over the freeing of Algeria. It does give a point of view with which most Americans are not familiar.

James S. Meisel, *The Fall of the Republic* (Ann Arbor: University of Michigan Press, 1962) is much more than an historic account of the fall of the Fourth Republic. It is a sociological analysis by an experienced political scientist. On pp. 300–304 there is a very full bibliography of various phases of the crisis centered on the Algerian problem, but extending throughout French society. Etiemble, *Parlez-vous Franglais?* (Paris: Gallimard, 1964) is a remarkable collection of Anglicisms, better, Americanisms, dug up by a conservative professor from various sources, mostly the mass media. The book is invaluable contemporary social history, though its author, a crusading devotee of the old France of *mesure* and good taste, hardly meant it to be anything less than a declaration of war. Françoise Giroud, *La Nouvelle Vague* (Paris: Gallimard, 1958) is another very useful sociological study of a phase of the New France, meant as such. It is a series of answers from the new generation, those of both sexes between 18 and 30 years of age in the late fifties, to a written questionnaire covering all sorts of concerns from art to international relations. The February 1960 number of *Réalités* (English language edition) under the title "What Are They Thinking?" provides another study of French contemporary youth.

The use of literary and artistic materials to arrive at an understanding of how any such collectivity as a modern Western nation-state behaves in international relations is extremely difficult, largely though not wholly because of the gap common to all Western nations between the high culture of the intellectuals and their admirers and the popular culture of the many. Yet not to have some experience of contemporary French high culture would seriously diminish one's understanding of France and Franco-American relations. H. Stuart Hughes, *The Obstructed Path* (New York: Harper and Row, 1968) is an admirable critical study of serious (*sérieux*) French moral, political, and social thought in the last three decades. The reader of Sartre, Camus, and others in the following brief sampling should, however, most certainly read as an antidote at least Raymond Aron, *The Opium of the Intellectuals*, English translation (Garden City: Doubleday, 1957) and the article by Michel Crozier, "The Cultural Revolution: Notes on the Changes in the Intellectual Climate of France," in S. R. Graubard, ed., *A New Europe?* (1964), listed above. He should also, even if he cannot read French, look over a few current numbers of *Paris-Match,* and *Elle,* illustrated magazines with very large circulations, from which some notion of what many Frenchmen and women, middlebrows for the most part, with a scattering of lowbrows, have or hope to have in this world.

Henri Peyre, *Contemporary French Literature* (New York: Harper and Row, 1964) is an excellent anthology, with somewhat brief excerpts, chosen, however, from a wide range. The book is designed for French language classes, and the texts excerpted are in French; but Professor Peyre supplies in English admirable brief explanatory prefaces for each author, and good reading suggestions, some in English. Another anthology, also with excellent notes and on a European scale, is Eugen Weber, *Paths to the Present: Aspects of European Thought from Romanticism to Existentialism* (New York: Dodd, Mead, 1960). In this book the writings excerpted are translated. Germaine Brée and Margaret Guiton, *An Age of Fiction: The French Novel from Gide to Camus* (New Brunswick: Rutgers University Press, 1957) is a sympathetic critical essay. Much more specialized and addressed to an audience already familiar with things French is W. M. Frohock, *Style and Temper: Studies in French Fiction, 1925–1960* (Oxford: Blackwell, 1967).

Here is a sampling, no more, all available in English translation. My classification, it must be admitted, is somewhat arbitrary. First, the old guard, not so much conventional writers as older men formed in the days of French clarity and *mesure:* André Maurois, *Proust: A Biography* (a Meridian paperback), by a prolific and surely not atypical French writer of many books, biographies, criticism, history; André Malraux, *Man's Fate* (a Modern Library paperback) a novel of his days as at least a Communist sympathizer, laid in the then French Indo-China; François Mauriac, *Viper's Tangle* (an Image paperback), one of the best-known novels of this sensitive Catholic writer; Jacques Maritain, *God and the Permission of Evil* (Milwaukee: Bruce Publishing Company, 1966) a controversial essay by a

Catholic intellectual; Julien Green, *Diary, 1928–1957* (New York: Harcourt, Brace & World, 1964), by a subtle French psychological writer of American antecedents.

Next the existentialists, beginning with one who never called himself an existentialist, Albert Camus, *The Plague* (a Modern Library paperback), perhaps his masterpiece. The grand priest of existentialism of the non-, if not anti-, Christian kind is Jean-Paul Sartre. A good piece of his mind can be made out from his best known novel, *Nausea* (a New Directions paperback) and from a collection of his plays, *No Exit and Three Others* (*The Flies, Dirty Hands, The Respectful Prostitute*) (a Vintage paperback). His companion in life, Simone de Beauvoir, is almost as prolific. Her novel, *The Mandarins* (a Meridian paperback), is an analysis from within of French intellectuals of the postwar years; even more revealing is her three-volume autobiography, of which the first volume, *Memoirs of a Dutiful Daughter* is not indeed conformist, but at times almost gentle in tone; the second, *Prime of Life,* shows her fighting the good vain existentialist fight (both these are available in Meridian paperbacks); in the third, *Force of Circumstance* (New York: Putnam's, 1965), she is still fighting frantically and, for most readers, predictably, the same fight, to the point of boredom for us and probably for herself.

Two good specimens of a kind of writing no doubt still offensive to a great many all over the Western world, the literature of despair, violence, sex, four-letter words, all unrelieved, are Louis-Ferdinand Céline, *Journey to the End of the Night* (New York: New Directions, 1959) and Jean Genet, *The Maids and Deathwatch,* two plays, with an introduction by Jean-Paul Sartre (an Evergreen paperback); Genet's *The Screens* (New York: Grove Press, 1962) —this is the play bitterly attacking the French record in Algeria which against vigorous protests was maintained on the stage of the state-supported theater of the Odéon; and an extraordinary piece of autobiographical writing, his *The Thief's Journal* (New York: Grove Press, 1964).

The critical and expository literature on formal philosophical existentialism and on French writings on man's fate in general is enormous. Ralph Harper, *Nostalgia: An Existentialist Exploration*

of Longing and Fulfillment in the Modern Age (Cleveland: Press
of Western Reserve University, 1966) is exceedingly sympathetic;
J. D. Collins, *The Existentialists: A Critical Study* (Chicago: Reg-
nery, 1952) is a good study from a Catholic position. Then there
are the works of the French existentialists themselves: J. P. Sartre,
Being and Nothingness: An Essay in Phenomenological Analysis
(New York: Citadel, 1956) a somewhat abridged translation from
the French of a very heavy treatise, and M. Merleau-Ponty, *Phe-
nomenology of Perception,* English translation (New York: Humanities Press, 1962); and as an example of Christian existentialism,
Gabriel Marcel, *Philosophy of Existentialism,* English translation
(a Citadel paperback). Two other philosophical men of letters must
not be omitted, though they are hard to classify, save perhaps as
"humanists" in contrast to "positivists" or "scientists": Antoine de St.
Exupéry, *Night Flight* (New York: Century, 1932) and P. Teilhard
de Chardin, *The Future of Man* (New York: Harper and Row,
1964).

It is true that France has not contributed greatly to "logical
positivism" or whatever label one gives to the twentieth-century
current of thought and feeling descending directly from the eighteenth-century Enlightenment to which France contributed so
much. But this older current of "rationalism" still flows strongly in
France and especially on the political Left, old or new. On the
whole, it is strongest among the social scientists, the new bureaucrats and planners, the "technocrats." Four quite different writers,
all major figures, may be sampled in any of their works; Bertrand de
Jouvenel, Michel Crozier, Raymond Aron, Claude Lévi-Strauss.

7. Keeping Up with Things French

The historian at least must be convinced that the last quarter of a
century has made the ordinarily difficult task of attaining some kind
of objectivity in studying Franco-American relations much more
difficult. There is no need to bring up the first stone-throwing:
Americans are biased about matters French, and the French are
biased about matters American. The American who cannot read

French can help himself toward a degree of objectivity in these matters if he will frankly discount a certain set of biases inevitably present in the best current reporting on France. This best is to be found in the services of the *New York Times* and those of the *Washington Post–Los Angeles Times*. The major American news-weeklies are generally hostile to and distrustful of France, inclined to denigrate its contemporary culture, and smug about our own. The highbrow weeklies in the United States, inclined toward the Left in politics, cannot forgive France de Gaulle. Their writers, and indeed many correspondents and other staff men of the mass media in America, tend to rely too much on information from their friends and associates in the French opposition press and from French intellectual circles generally. Yet a discerning reader of the best of the American press will at least find plenty of information about what is going on in France. The quarterly *Foreign Affairs,* oriented toward American participation in international politics in what may perhaps misleadingly be called the tradition of high-minded universalism, is admirably edited in a scholarly tradition and makes a point of publishing articles with biases other than its own; it has much material on French affairs.

The French point of view is readily available in the English language through the services of the *Service de Presse et d'Information* of the French Embassy, located at 972 Fifth Avenue, New York, N.Y. 10021. This branch of the Embassy will gladly furnish on request English translations of all sorts of official materials, speeches of leading French political figures, notes on many phases of French life, and other information. The Comité France Actuelle, a "private association of French business men" but perhaps at least semiofficial, publishes in English an illustrated semimonthly periodical, *France Actuelle,* oriented toward business and technology, but with some attempt to cover the whole range of contemporary French culture (published at 221 Southern Building, Washington, D.C. 20005). It is well done in the style of similar American publicity. See also *Today in France* (published monthly at 38 West 53 Street, New York, N.Y. 10019).

For the reader of French there is a vast current output of the printed word. Walter H. Mallory, ed., *Political Handbook and Atlas of the World,* published annually by Harper and Row for the Council on Foreign Relations of New York, prints under the rubric "France" a brief representative listing of Parisian and provincial dailies and of the periodical press, together with an indication of political affiliation and, for the newspapers, circulation.

The following Parisian newspapers, though far from fully covering the spectrums of politics and of cultural levels, will at least give the reader a not unrepresentative survey; they are likely to be available in major American libraries: *Le Monde,* much admired by newspaper men, formally independent of any political party, but tending toward an intellectualist moderate Left, and critical of American policies; *Le Figaro,* also independent of direct political control, but basically conservative, well edited, and, for a French newspaper, often even friendly toward the United States; *L'Humanité,* the Communist organ. For the best representative of the old French moderate left one has to go to the provincial *La Dépêche du Midi* of Toulouse.

Of the periodical press, there is again a very considerable quantity, short of Anglo-Saxon abundance, but with an equal range. *Paris-Match,* an illustrated weekly, is comparable to American magazines like *Life* or *Look* and appeals to a large audience; somewhat more select an audience, though by no means a wholly highbrow one, reads the well-illustrated and well-edited *Réalités,* which publishes longish articles and attempts to show various points of view. The only major French newsweekly to adopt the format of *Time* magazine (for which some of its old readers among French intellectuals have never forgiven it) is *L'Express,* edited by the *Mendèsiste* Jean-Jacques Servan-Schreiber; it is definitely non-Communist Left in position, hostile to de Gaulle and de Gaullism, but by no means bitterly hostile to the United States. *Les Temps Modernes,* directed by Sartre, is pro-Communist and anti-American; *France Nouvelle* is formally affiliated with the Communist party. *Rivarol* proves that the Far Right is not extinct and is still abusive; *Le Nouvel Observateur* is a good average Leftist weekly, comparable in many ways, though not in format, to such American publications as the *New Republic* or the *Nation. Le Canard Enchaîné,* an old protesting journal with a newspaper format is *très français* indeed, in the critical tradition of French caricature; most Americans will need a dictionary of modern French slang to make much out of it. There are many quarterly learned, literary, political, or professional publications, of which the somewhat old fashioned conservative *Revue des Deux Mondes,* now well into its second century, must be mentioned. *Esprit,* Leftist and liberal Catholic in orientation, is an admirable review, which usually concentrates a given number on a single major topic. *La Nouvelle Revue Française,* at its height in the era of Proust and Gide, still holds interest for those concerned with literature and the arts. A special form of *Figaro,* the *Figaro Littéraire,* is perhaps the best single publication for those who wish to keep up with current French publications and corresponds roughly to the *London Times Literary Supplement* and the book review section of the *New York Times.*

Index

Action Française, 164, 208
Adams, John, 51, 55
Africa: colonial Empire in, 59, 85, 100, 138; Liberia, 60; Dakar, 84, 85; North, 85–86, 92; West, 85; Morocco, 86, 137; immigration from, 104, 105. *See* Algeria
Agriculture: wheat, 3, 6; vegetables, 7–8; grapes, 7, 22; rice, 8, 118; evaluated, 118–121; statistics on, 272
Algeria: Free French in, 83; Gaullist government, 86–89, 123, 139–140; revolt in (1954), 100, 136–140, 145, 218; *colons*, 105, 137–138, 140, 145, 195; *Treize Mai* (1958), 137, 139–140; OAS, 145–146; FLN, 145, 219; Rightists, 218
Alsatians. *See* Ethnic groups
American Mercury, 261
AMGOT (Allied Military Government in Occupied Territory), 88, 89, 94, 97
Anglo-American relations: Jay's Treaty, 55; War of 1812, 56; Liberia, 60; World War II, 82, 86, 88–90, 91, 228
Anglo-French relations, 62, 78, 83–86, 88–90, 91, 217–218, 227

Angoff, Charles, 261–262
Annuaire statistique de la France, 262
Anticlericalism: in education, 16; present status, 23, 148; Third Republic, 101, 159–160; Enlightened Church, 160, 184–186; origin of, 185; defined, 185; Leftists, 187, 199; Communists, 189
Anti-intellectuals: popular culture (*le peuple*), 191, 199, 204–207, 209; *vs* intellectuals, 206; in press, 208–209
Anti-Semitism, 23, 186
Ardouin-Dumazet (author), 19
Arnold, Matthew, 30, 32
Aron, Raymond, 204
Aron, Robert, 89
Aulard, Professor, 175

Bagehot, Walter, 40, 70
Basques. *See* Ethnic groups
Beauvoir, Simone de, 72, 155, 203
Benda, Julien, 183
Blum, Léon, 63
Boorstin, Daniel, 103
Bourbon Restoration, 40, 186
Bretons. *See* Ethnic groups
Britain, 115–117 *passim*, 124, 131, 193, 243, 245, 248, 250

Brittany, 3, 6, 9, 11, 13, 17, 19, 118
Burgundy, 4, 7, 12, 15, 17, 18, 20, 22

Cadres, 123, 124, 159, 160
Camelots du Roi, 164, 196
Camus, Albert, 202
Canada, 52, 55, 67, 82, 150
Canard enchaîné, 142, 209
Candide, 210
Carlyle, Thomas, 114
Catholics: French Revolution, 9; strongholds of, 23; Socialism, 102; Fifth Republic politics, 148–149, 165, 188, 264; Fourth republic politics, 150–151; schools, 16, 174, 189; Concordate (1801), 185–186; Restoration (1815–1830), 186; de Gaulle, 188
Centre Democratic (CD). See Parties, political
Centre de Recherches et de Documentation sur la Consummation (CREDOC), 113
Centre des Jeunes Patrons, 123
Chamber of Deputies, 58, 133, 160
Chanzeaux, 119–121
Characteristics, national: rationality, le génie Latin, 10, 12, 33, 45, mesure, 10, 32, 65, 72, 117, 132, 181, 250, anticlericalism, 23, love of Reason, 31–32; immediacy, 33–34; conservatism, 34, 35, 45; sensory pleasures, 35–36, 45; esprit, 38, 65, 204
Chicago Tribune, 238
China (Communist), 36, 132, 241–242, 243, 250
Christian Democrats, 198
Churchill, Sir Winston, 84, 85, 88, 94, 96, 142
Civil Service, 69, 134
Clemenceau, Georges, 62, 141, 186
Clercs. See Intellectuals
Climate, 8–9
"Clubistes." See Leftists
Clutton-Brock, Arthur, 44

Cocteau, Jean, 35
Cohen-Portheim, Paul, 33
Coleridge, Samuel, 31–32
Collège. See Education
Colons. See Algeria
Comté Nationale de libération (CNL), 87–89, 94, 97
Common Market, 102, 222, 249–253 passim
Communard Revolt (1871), 24
Communists: "Red Belt," 25, 157; intellectuals, 72, 101, 154–155, 198, 200; Resistance, 81, 91, 158; Liberation, 91, 203; political parties, 99, 148, 149, 151, 159, 160, 167–168; coal production, 123; nationalization, 129; ideology, 157–159; anticlericalism, 189; present status, 199; Indo-China, 216; on de Gaulle, 222, 232; in 1967 elections, 233
Concordate (1801), 185–186
Confédération National de Patrons Français, 123
Conseil National du Patronat Français (C.N.P.F.), 128, 129
Consulate, Republic of, 40
Coolidge, Calvin, 64
Cooper, James Fenimore, 57
Cot, Pierre, 160
Cousin, Victor, 33
Crèvecoeur, St. John de, 103
Crozier, Michel, 200
Curtius, Ernst Robert, 30, 31, 35, 48, 115

Dakar. See Africa
Darlan, Admiral Jean, 86
D-Day. See World War II
Debré, Michel, 166
Deferre, Gaston, 148, 166, 268
Democratic Revue, 57
Departments. See Unification
Deutsch, E., 153
Dien Bien Phu (1954), 100, 136, 216, 221, 224
Directory, Republic of, 40, 55
Dreyfus affair, 23, 159, 174, 186

Eboué, Felix, 85
Echo de Paris, L', 208
Ecole: Normale Supérieure, 16,
177; Polytechnique, 16, 177; de
Guerre, 143; de Paris, 203
Economic growth: "regions," 15;
Marshall Plan, 99, 122; Common Market, 102, 119, 122, 131,
161, 165; effect on population,
106; before 1914, 115; evaluated, 115–124, 132, 211; Schuman Plan, 122, 251; "mixed
economies," 122–125, 130, 212,
251–252; nationalization, 125–
126, 129; planning, 126–128,
129; "private sector," 127–128;
inflation, 130–131, 211; Fourth
Republic, 136–137; effect on
culture, 206; statistics on, 268–
270
Eden, Anthony, 218
Education: national system of, 15–
16, 156; special schools, 16, 177;
Church schools, 16; *loi Barangé*,
174, 189; private schools, 16;
science, 115, 183; defined, 173–
174; in Fifth Republic, 174–175;
ministry of, 174; primary, 175;
coeducation, 175–176; secondary (*lycée*), 176–182; *collège*,
176–177; baccalaureate, 177–
178; higher education, 177–182;
University of Paris, 180; professional schools, 180; present
status, 183–184; statistics on,
276–278. *See also* Ecole
Eisenhower, Dwight D., 92
Elle, 204, 209
Emerson, Ralph Waldo, 43
Empire, colonial: Guadaloupe, 12,
82; Martinique, 12, 82; Tahiti,
60, 263nd; French Guiana, 12;
Réunion, 12; St. Pierre, 82, 138;
Miquelon, 82, 138; North Africa
(Algeria), 83, 85, 100, 137–140,
225; West Africa, 84, 85; mandates (Syria, Lebanon), 84;
Indo-China, 100, 136, 216, 221,
224–225; decline of, 100; loss

of, 116; Tunisia, 137; Morocco,
137; present status, 263nc
Empire, Republic of, 40
Enlightened Church. *See* Anti-
clericalism
Enlightenment (18th century), 13,
31, 39, 45, 51, 66, 202, 258
Espérey, Marshal Franchet, 186
Ethnic groups: Basques, 19–21,
194; Flemings, 19, 194; Alsa-
tians, 19, 20, 194; Bretons, 19,
194; status of, 21
Etiemble, Professor, 210
European Defense Community
(EDC), 217, 220
European Economic Community.
See Common Market
Express, L', 209, 252

Federation of the Left. *See* Leftists
Fifth Republic: Basques in, 20–21;
stability of, 69, 205; Franco-
American relations, 99–100; economic growth, 122, 251–252,
statistics of, 268–275; Algeria,
145–146; constitution of, 146–
147, 169–171; 1965 election,
148; 1967 election, 149–152,
159, 264; political parties, 150–
154, 159, 164, 167; party system
evaluated, 156–157, 168–169;
"Clubistes," 161; educational
system, 174–175, statistics of,
276–278; Catholicism, 174, 188–
189; attitude toward intellectuals, 206; Common Market,
222, 249–253 *passim;* officials of,
249, 251, 258; mass culture,
279–280
Figaro, 208, 210
Flaubert, Gustave, 187, 199
Flemings. *See* Ethnic groups
Font Romeu, 46, 118
Forces Française de l'Intérieure
(F.F.I.), 91
Fortune, 129
Fourth Republic: instability, 40,
69, 133–136; *vs* Third, 94; political parties, 98, 134–136, 144,

150–151, 165, 206, 252; de Gaulle, 98–99; Franco-American relations, 99–101 *passim;* Socialists, 102; Common Market, 102; economic growth, 122; fall of (1958), 136; attitude toward intellectuals, 206; Indo-China, 217; Egypt, 217–218; colonialism, 223

France Actuelle, 112n

France, Anatole, 187

France Nouvelle, 209

France-Soir, 208

Franco, Francisco, 20, 42, 63

Franco-American relations: alliance (1778): 50–53; Monroe Doctrine, 53, 56–59 *passim;* privateering (1792–1815): 54–55; "Citizen" Genet, 54; XYZ affair, 55, 59; Louisiana Purchase, 55–56; Thomas Jefferson, 56; James Monroe, 56; Andrew Jackson, 57; spoilation claims, 58, 59; Mexico, 58–59; Revolution of 1848, 58; Liberia, 60; Panama Canal, 60–61; World War I, 61–63; present attitudes, 64–75, 76, 79, 154–156, 203, 210, 215–217 *passim,* 229, 230–240 *passim,* 246; World War II, 76–80, 94–96; Vichy, 80–81; Resistance, 80–83, 101–102; colonial Empire, 84–85, 100, 216–217, 223–225; North Africa, 85–86, 218; de Gaulle, 87–88, 99–100, 140; Occupation, 88–90; Gaullists, 88, 97; Communists, 91; Franklin Roosevelt, 96–97; Liberation, 98–99, 101–102, 203; Marshall Plan, 99; Fourth Republic, 99–102 *passim;* Cold War, 101; Suez crisis, 218; UN conflicts, 219; nuclear bombing, 219–220; NATO, 220, 221, 226; SHAPE and SACEUR, 221; future of, 255–260

Franco-German relations, 62, 68, 92, 95

Franco-Russian relations, 91, 100, 227, 229, 233, 256

Franco-Spanish relations, 57, 58

Francstireurs et Partisans (F.T.P.), 91

Franklin, Benjamin, 71, 184

Free French (Resistance; Gaullists): stronghold of, 22; growth of, 77–79, 84–85; relations with America, 79, 80–83, 87–91, 101; relations with Britain, 80, 83–84; North Africa, 86–87; unification of, 87, 89; *maquis,* 91; Communist support, 91, 158; liberation of Paris, 93; effect on Church, 165, 188

French Guiana. *See* Empire, colonial

Freud, Sigmund, 29

Gaulle, Charles de: Franco-American relations, 2, 47–48, 79–80, 82–83, 87–88, 102, 132, 229–230, 257; Resistance, 10, 77–79, 83, 143–144; conflict with Roosevelt, 62, 83, 93–94, 96–97; relations with army, 81; Anglo-French relations, 84; North Africa, 86–87, 139–140; Operation Overlord, 88; on AMGOT, 89, 97–98; on Communists, 91; on Pétain, 92; Liberation, 92–93; Churchill on, 96; French support of, 97; political retirement (1946), 98–99; return to power (1958), 99, 102; foreign policy, 99–100, 162, 246–247, 249; nationalization, 125; price stabilization (1963), 130; Common Market, 131, 222; on political parties, 136, 144; fall of Fourth Republic, 136–140 *passim;* early years, 141; army career, 141–143; as intellectual, 142–144; RPF, 144; in exile, 144; evaluated, 144–145, 171–172; President, Fifth Republic, 146–148; UNR, 148; intellectuals on, 154–156; domestic policy, 162, 247–249; Catholicism, 188; *colons* on, 195; on UN, 219, 221; NATO, 221; SHAPE and SACEUR, 221; Viet Nam, 239

Gaullists: American opinion of, 80, 88–89, 97, 123; in North Africa, 85–87, 140; Liberation, 89–91; public support of, 90, 156; UNR, 148–151, 161–166; Democratic Union, 264. *See also* Free French

General Planning Commissariat, 126

Genet, "Citizen," 54, 72

Genet (author), 197

Geneva Convention, 217, 225

Germany: Third Reich (Nazism), 41, 45, 228; Weimar Republic, 41, 61, 169; West German Federal Republic, 41, 61, 217, 242, 245, 250; Wilhemine Empire, 41–42; East German Democratic Republic, 41; Axis, 63; French armistice, 77–78; occupation of France, 87, 92; economy, 117; Common Market, 119

Génie Latin. See Characteristics, national

Giraud, General Henri, 85, 86

Girondins, 23, 53–54

Giscard-d'Estaing, Valéry, 151, 257, 264

Greece, 109

Guadaloupe. *See* Empire, colonial

Gunther, John, 238–239

Hackett, Anne-Marie, 126–127, 129

Hackett, John, 126–127, 129

Hayes, Carlton, 44

Hitler, Adolf, 76, 78, 81, 93, 163, 244, 256

Ho Chi Minh, 216

Holland, 115, 117

Hughes, H. Stuart, 202n

Hull, Cordell, 82–83, 216

Humanité, L', 157–158, 208

Indo-China. *See* Empire, colonial

Industry, Ministry of, 126

Inflation. *See* Economic growth

Ingersol, Robert, 184

Instability, political, 40–41, 42, 45, 47, 69, 133–136

Institut Scientifique d'Economie Appliquée, 123

Intellectuals: Communists groups, 101, 198–199; present attitude, 154–156; Sartre, 155; Beauvoir, 155; religious revival, 188; high culture, 198, 201–203; *clercs*, 141, 198; Leftists, 154–155, 200; *philosophes*, 201–202; literature, 202–204; sciences, 202–204; existentialism, 202; music, 203; painting, 203–204; *vs* anti-intellectuals, 205–206, 213; anti-Americanization, 206, 230, 258; *école de Paris*, 203; press, 208–209

Italy, 63, 88, 104, 109, 117, 118, 247, 248, 250

Jackson, Andrew, 57

Jacobins, 23, 148, 175, 200

James, William, 163

Japan, 61, 63, 80, 115, 228, 244, 256

Jay's Treaty. *See* Anglo-American relations

Jefferson, Thomas, 51, 56, 184, 245

Jews, 22–23, 185–186

Johnson, Andrew, 171

Johnson, Lyndon, 154

Jones, Howard Mumford, 67

Journal, Le, 208

Jours de France, 209

Keynes, John, 62

Kindleberger, Charles P., 105n, 121, 123

Labor, Ministry of, 123

Lacouture, Jean, 140, 143

Lafayette, Marquis de, 39, 52

Langer, W. L., 79

Language: Madariaga on, 29–30, 37; definition of, 31; Americanization of, 210
La Rochefoucauld, François, 38, 39, 244
Laval, Pierre, 92, 97
League of Nations, 62, 84
Lecanuet, Jean, 148–149, 165, 166, 232, 233
Leclerc, General Pierre, 92, 93
Leftists: *vs* Communists, 66; ideology of, 135–136; in Fifth Republic, 147–152, 222, 239; Federation of the Left, 149, 150, 159–161 *passim*, 233; Radical-Socialists, 151, 159; political parties, 151; in Convention (1792), 53; intellectuals, 154–155, 200; Socialists, 159; present status, 160–161, 168–169, 172; "Clubistes," 161; 1967 election, 165, 167; anticlericalism, 174, 187, 199; Dreyfus affair, 186
Lesseps, Ferdinand, 60
Liberation: Gaullists, 89–91; Communists, 91; punishments, 91–92; importance of, 92; Paris, 92–93; American opinion of, 101, 203; nationalization, 125–126; economic planning, 126; effect on Church, 165, 188; intellectuals on, 200; effect on newspapers, 207–208
Liberia. *See* Africa
Lindon, D., 153
Lippmann, Walter, 238
Loi Barangé. See Education
Louis XI, 12
Louis XIV, 52, 77, 95, 172, 244
Louisiana Purchase (1803), 55, 56
Louis Philippe, 40, 57
Lowell, James Russell, 68, 70
Lycée. See Education

Madariaga, Salvador de, 29–30, 31, 37
Madison, James, 56
Maghreb, Arab, 137, 138
Malaux, André, 206

Maquis. See Resistance
Marais. See Parties, political
Marcel, Gabriel, 202
Marshall Plan (1947), 62, 80, 99, 122, 228, 229
Martinique. *See* Empire, colonial
Matin, Le, 208
Maurras, Charles, 17, 44, 141, 165, 200
Maximilian, Emperor of Mexico, 58–59
McKay, Donald, 34, 41
Mencken, H. L., 261–262
Mendès-France, Pierre, 111, 166, 218
Meredith, George, 96
Mesure. See Characteristics, national
Mexico, 58, 59
Miquelon. *See* Empire, colonial
Mistral, Frédéric, 24
Mitterand, François, 148, 166, 233
Molière, Jean, 190
Mollet, Guy, 159, 166, 218
Molotov-Ribbentrop agreement, 76, 81
Monarchies: Capetian, 10–12 *passim;* Constitutional, 40; Louis Philippe, 40
Monde, Le, 179, 208
Monnet, Jean, 123
Monroe Doctrine. *See* Franco-American relations
Morocco. *See* Africa
Mosca, Gaetano, 215
Mouvement Republican Populaire (MRP). *See* Parties, political
Murphy, Robert, 218
Muselier, Admiral Émile, 82–83
Mussolini, Benito, 63, 163

Napoleon I: national education, 15–16, 174, 183; effect on patriotism, 44, 45; Napoleonic Wars, 52, 59, 227–228; Louisiana Purchase, 55; Concordate of 1801, 185
Napoleon III: Mexican crisis, 58–59; imperialism, 147

Nation, The, 73
National Assembly: government units (1791), 12–13; present operation, 169–170
Nationalism: Hayes on, 44; Clutton-Brock on, 44; French *vs* American, 45; after Liberation, 125–126; Rightists, 162
Nation-state concept, 10, 12, 44, 77
Nazism. *See Germany*
Negroes, 195, 197
New Republic, 73
Newsweek, 209
New York Daily News, 238
New York Times, 109, 238
Nicolson, Harold, 62
Niebuhr, Reinhold, 71
Normandy, 6, 7, 11, 17, 78, 88, 95, 118
North Atlantic Treaty Organization (NATO), 99, 165, 220, 221, 226, 238, 242, 243, 249, 254, 255–257 *passim,* 264
Norton, Charles Eliot, 68
Nouvel Observateur, 209

Operations Anvil and Overlord. *See* World War II
Organisation de l'armée secrète (OAS), 145–146, 239

Panama Canal, 60
Paris: metropolitan district, 15; *vs* provinces, 23, 24; Communard Revolt, 24; importance of, 24–25; liberation of, 92–93; World War II, 95; Ministry of Education, 174; University of, 180
Paris-Match, 113, 204, 207, 209, 210
Parti Communiste Français (PCF). *See* Parties, political
Parti Socialiste Unifié (PSU). *See* Parties, political
Parties, political: splinter groups, 40–41, 98, in Third and Fourth Republics, 133, 135–136, *giscardiens,* 151, 152, PSU, 151,

159, 167, 168; Popular Front, 63, 149, 159, 160, 168; *vs.* American, 135; de Gaulle on, 144; in Fourth Republic (RPF), 144; in Fifth Republic, 147–151; UNR, 148–152 *passim,* 155, 161–165; MRP, 149, 150–151, 164–165, 188; Poujadists, 149, 206, 252; Federation of the Left, 149, 159; CD, 151, 164, 165; UD VᵉR, 151; SFIO, 151, 159; PDM, 151, 165, 264; PCF, 151, 159, 167, 264; *marais,* 152–154, 157, 166, 235; "Clubistes," 161; 1967 chairmen, 268. *See also* Communists, Leftists, Radical-Socialists, Rightists, Socialists
Pays (land units), 17–19
Pétain, Marshal Philippe, 40, 77, 80, 81, 87, 92, 97, 142
Peuple, Le. See Anti-intellectuals
Philosophes. See Intellectuals
Pleven, René, 217
Poincaré, Raymond, 44
Poland, 104
Pompidou, Georges, 166, 257
Popular Front. *See* Parties, political
Population: shift in, 14; in 1939, 104; in 1949, 104–105, 106; in 1963, 105n; in 1967, 105, 211; government family allowance, 106; effect on economy, 106, 117, 122, 211; in 18th century, 114–115; statistics on, 263–264, 266–267
Potsdam Conference (1945), 79, 94
Poujadists. *See* Parties, political
Press (daily and periodical): after Liberation, 207–208; present day, 208–209; on Algerian revolt, 218–219
Productivity Commissariat, 126
Progrès et Democratie Moderne (PDM). *See* Parties, political
Protestants: stronghold of, 5–6; present status, 22–23; Concordate of 1801, 185

Provinces: in tourist industry, 18; *vs* Paris, 23
Public Works and Transports, Ministry of, 126

Racine, Jean, 39
Racism, 69, 70, 89
Radicals (Leftists): in Fifth Republic, 148–149, 151, 161; *vs* Communists, 160
Radical-Socialists (Leftists): in Fifth Republic, 148; SFIO, 151; ideology of, 159–160
Ralliement du Peuple Française (RPF), 144
Rentiers, 42, 46, 101, 116, 149, 193, 250
Republic of 1792, 40, 53
Resistance. *See* Free French
Reston, James, 238
Revolution, American, 50–51, 101
Revolution, French: unifying factor, 11–12, 20, 44; Jacobins, 23, 148, 161, 175; Girondins, 23, 54; Reign of Terror, 54, 92, 152, 185; conflict with Church, 185–186
Revolution of 1830, 57, 104
Revolution of 1848, 58, 147
Revolution, Social, 189–196
Revue des Deux Mondes, 204
Rightists: goals of, 135; in Algiers, 137, 140, 145, 218; on Fifth Republic, 147; 1965 election, 149; 1967 election, 151–152, 165; political parties, 151, 164–166; ideology of, 153, 162; in Convention (1792), 153
Rivarol, 209
Robespierre, Maximilien, 70
Rolland, Romain, 33
Roosevelt, Franklin Delano: conflict with de Gaulle, 62, 82–83, 85, 94, 96–97; anti-imperialist policy, 84, 216, 224; Occupation of France, 88–89, 94
Roosevelt, Theodore, 60, 70
Rosseau, Jean Jacques, 97
Rostow, Walt W., 114

St. Joan of Arc, 12, 45, 77, 85, 97
St. Pierre. *See* Empire, colonial
San Francisco Conference (1944), 94
Sartre, Jean-Paul, 72, 155, 188, 199, 200, 202
Schlichter, Sumner, 131
Schuman Plan. *See* Economic growth
Second Empire, 40, 69
Second Republic, 40, 147
Section Française de l'Internationale Ouvière (S.F.I.O.), 151, 159
Sieburg, Friedrich, 30, 35, 46
Socialists (Leftists): Fourth Republic, 101–102; Fifth Republic, 148–149, 151, 159, 161; political parties, 151, 159; *vs* Communists, 159; ideology of, 159
SOFRES, 152 and n, 154, 166, 235
Soviet Union: Molotov-Ribbentrop agreement, 76; support of Resistance, 18, 91; Marshall Plan, 91; Moscow, 91, 157; status in France, 101, 155, 229, 243; Cold War, 101, 217, 223–224, 228, 233, 241, 243, 245, 255; Indo-China, 216–217; Viet Nam, 224; Warsaw Pact, 242
Spain, 56–57, 104, 109, 244, 250
Spanish-American relations, 56–57
Spiegel, Der, 209
Stael, Madame Anne de, 33
Stalin, Joseph, 142, 157, 166, 256
Suez crisis, 217–218, 246
Sulzberger, Arthur, 109
Supreme Allied Command, Europe (SACEUR), 221
Supreme Headquarters, Allied Powers, Europe (SHAPE), 221
Système D, 44

Taft, William Howard, 60
Taine, Hippolyte, 35
Talleyrand, Charles Maurice de, 55
Taylor, A. J. P., 246n
Temps, Le, 208
Third Republic: Royalists on, 17; Basque problem, 20; political

instability, 40, 69, 133–136 *passim*, 144; relations with America, 59; military failure, 79; anticlericalism, 101–102, 148, 186–187; population problem, 106; Radical-Socialists, 159; economy of, 195

Thorez, Maurice, 91

Time, 203, 209

Tixier-Vigancour, Jean-Louis, 148, 149, 165

Tocqueville, Alexis, 12, 46

Topography, 3–8

Toynbee, Arnold, 45

Tourism, 18, 107–110

Treize Mai. See Algeria

Unification: difficulties of, 10–11, 19; departments, 12–13, 15; subdivisions, 13–14; ethnic groups, 19–21

Union Démocratique pour la Cinquième République (UD VᵉR). *See* Parties, political

Union pour la Nouvelle République (UNR). *See* Parties, political

United Socialist Party (PSU). *See* Parties, political

United Nations (UN): Security Council, 94; Relief and Rehabilitation, 98; French crises, 217, 219, 221

Vallon amendment, 162

Verona, Congress of, 57

Versailles, 62

Vichy government: department consolidation, 15; support of, 77–78; foreign relations, 79–87, 223

Vie Parisienne, 209

Viet Nam, 224, 225, 226, 257–258

Washington, George, 51–54 *passim*, 143–144

WASPS, 68–69

Weill, P., 153

Wilde, Oscar, 28

William, Duke of Normandy, 12

Wilson, Woodrow, 61, 62, 170

World War I, 7, 61, 74, 84, 186, 201, 244, 256

World War II: Battle of the Bulge, 5; Allied invasion, 6; French defeat, 76; Operation Overlord, 88; D-day, 88–89, 96; Operation Anvil, 93, 95; postwar years, 211, 216; Resistance, *see* Free French

Wylie, Laurence, 119–121

XYZ affair. *See* Franco-American relations

Youth and Sports, Ministry of, 179

Zola, Émile, 121

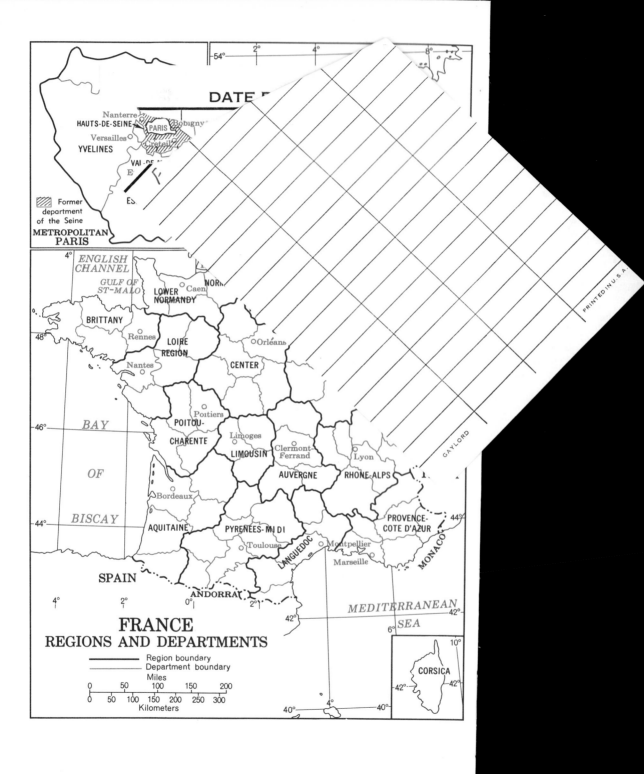

FRANCE
REGIONS AND DEPARTMENTS

—— Region boundary
—— Department boundary

Miles
0   50   100   150   200
0 50 100 150 200 250 300
Kilometers